Change Detection and Image Time Series Analysis 2

SCIENCES

Image, Field Director – Laure Blanc-Feraud

Remote Sensing Imagery, Subject Heads –
Emmanuel Trouvé and Avik Bhattacharya

Change Detection and Image Time Series Analysis 2

Supervised Methods

Coordinated by
Abdourrahmane M. Atto
Francesca Bovolo
Lorenzo Bruzzone

WILEY

First published 2021 in Great Britain and the United States by ISTE Ltd and John Wiley & Sons, Inc.

ISTE Ltd
27-37 St George's Road
London SW19 4EU
UK

www.iste.co.uk

John Wiley & Sons, Inc.
111 River Street
Hoboken, NJ 07030
USA

www.wiley.com

Library of Congress Control Number: 2021941720

British Library Cataloguing-in-Publication Data
A CIP record for this book is available from the British Library
ISBN 978-1-78945-057-6

ERC code:
PE1 Mathematics
   PE1_18 Scientific computing and data processing
PE10 Earth System Science
   PE10_3 Climatology and climate change
   PE10_4 Terrestrial ecology, land cover change
   PE10_14 Earth observations from space/remote sensing

Contents

Chapter 2. Pixel-based Classification Techniques for Satellite Image Time Series   33
Charlotte PELLETIER and Silvia VALERO

Chapter 3. Semantic Analysis of Satellite Image Time Series   85
Corneliu Octavian DUMITRU and Mihai DATCU

Chapter 4. Optical Satellite Image Time Series Analysis for Environment Applications: From Classical Methods to Deep Learning and Beyond 109

Matthieu MOLINIER, Jukka MIETTINEN, Dino IENCO, Shi QIU and Zhe ZHU

Chapter 5. A Review on Multi-temporal Earthquake Damage Assessment Using Satellite Images 155

Gülşen TAŞKIN, Esra ERTEN and Enes Oğuzhan ALATAŞ

Preface

**Abdourrahmane M. Atto[1], Francesca Bovolo[2]
and Lorenzo Bruzzone[3]**

[1] University Savoie Mont Blanc, Annecy, France
[2] Fondazione Bruno Kessler, Trento, Italy
[3] University of Trento, Italy

This book is part of the ISTE-Wiley *"SCIENCES"* Encyclopedia and belongs to the *Image* field of the *Engineering and Systems* department. The *Image* field covers the entire processing chain from acquisition to interpretation by analyzing the data provided by various imaging systems. This field is split into seven subjects, including *Remote Sensing Imagery* (RSI). The heads of this subject are Emmanuel Trouvé and Avik Bhattacharya. In this subject, we propose a series of books that portray diverse and comprehensive topics in advanced remote-sensing images and their application for *Earth Observation* (EO). There has been an increasing demand for monitoring and predicting our planet's evolution on a local, regional and global scale. Hence, over the past few decades, airborne, space-borne and ground-based platforms with active and passive sensors acquire images that measure several features at various spatial and temporal resolutions.

RSI has become a broad multidisciplinary domain attracting scientists across the diverse fields of science and engineering. The aim of the books proposed in this RSI series is to present the state-of-the-art and available scientific knowledge about the primary sources of images acquired by optical and radar sensors. The books cover the processing methods developed by the signal and image processing community to extract useful information for end-users for an extensive range of EO applications in natural resources.

In this project, each RSI book focuses on general topics such as change detection, surface displacement measurement, target detection, model inversion and data assimilation. This first book of the RSI series is dedicated to *Change Detection and Image Time Series Analysis*. It presents methods developed to detect changes and analyze their temporal evolutions using optical and/or synthetic aperture radar (SAR) images in diverse settings (e.g. image pairs, image time series). According to the numerous works and applications in this domain, this book is divided into two volumes, dedicated to *unsupervised* and *supervised* approaches, respectively. Unsupervised methods require little to no expert-based information to resolve a problem, whereas the contrary holds true, especially for methods that are supervised in the sense of providing a wide amount of labeled training data to the method, before testing this method.

Volume 1: Unsupervised methods

A significant part of this book is dedicated to a wide range of unsupervised methods. The first chapter provides an insight into the motivations of this behavior and introduces two unsupervised approaches to multiple-change detection in bitemporal multispectral images. Chapters 2 and 3 introduce the concept of change detection in time series and postulate it in the context of statistical analysis of covariance matrices. The former chapter focuses on a directional analysis for multiple-change detection and exercises on a time series of SAR polarimetric data. The latter focuses on local analysis for binary change detection and proposes several covariance matrix estimators and their corresponding information-theoretic measures for multivariate SAR data. The last four chapters focus more on applications. Chapter 4 addresses functional representations (wavelets and convolutional neural network filters) for feature extraction in an unsupervised approach. It proposes anomaly detection and functional evolution clustering from this framework by using relative entropy information extracted from SAR data decomposition. Chapter 5 deals with the selection of metrics that are sensitive to snow state variation in the context of the cryosphere, with a focus on mountain areas. Metrics such as cross-correlation ratios and Hausdorff distance are analyzed with respect to optimal reference images to identify optimal thresholding strategies for the detection of wet snow by using Sentinel-1 image time series. Chapter 6 presents time series analysis in the context of spatio-temporal forecasting and monitoring fast-moving meteorological events such as cyclones. The application benefits from the fusion of remote sensing data under the fractional dynamic field assumption on the cyclone behavior. Chapter 7 proposes an analysis based on characteristic points for texture modeling with graph theory. Such an approach overcomes issues arising from large-size dense neighborhoods that affect spatial context-based approaches. The application proposed in this chapter concerns glacier flow measurement in bitemporal images. Chapter 8 focuses on detecting new land-cover types by classification-based change detection or feature/pixel-based change detection. Monitoring the construction of new buildings in urban and suburban scenarios at a large regional scale by means of Sentinel-1 and -2 images is considered as an application. Chapter 9 focuses on the statistical modeling of classes in the difference image and derives from scratch a multiclass model for it in the context of change vector analysis.

Volume 2: Supervised methods

The second volume of this book is dedicated to supervised methods. Chapter 1 of this volume addresses the fusion of multisensor, multiresolution and multitemporal data. This chapter reviews recent advances in the literature and proposes two supervised Markov random field-based solutions: one relies on a quadtree and the second one is specifically designed to deal with multimission, multifrequency and multiresolution time series. Chapter 2 provides an overview of pixel-based methods for time series classification from the earliest shallow-learning methods to the most recent deep learning-based approaches. This chapter also includes best practices for reference data preparation and management, which are crucial tasks in supervised methods. Chapter 3 focuses on very high spatial resolution data time series and the use of semantic information for modeling spatio-temporal evolution patterns. Chapter 4 focuses on the challenges of dense time series analysis, including pre-processing aspects and a taxonomy of existing methodologies. Finally, since the evaluation of a learning system can be subject to multiple considerations, Chapters 5 and 6 propose extensive evaluations of the methodologies used to produce earthquake-induced change maps, with an emphasis on their strengths and shortcomings (Chapter 5) and the deep learning systems in the context of multiclass multilabel change-of-state classification on glacier observations (Chapter 6).

This book covers both methodological and application topics. From the methodological viewpoint, contributions are provided with respect to feature extraction and a large number of evaluation metrics for change detection, classification and forecasting issues. Analysis has been performed in both bitemporal images and time series, illustrating both unsupervised and supervised methods and considering both binary- and multiclass outputs. Several applications are mentioned in the chapters, including agriculture, urban areas and cryosphere analysis, among others. This book provides a deep insight into the evolution of change detection and time series analysis in the state-of-the-art, as well as an overview of the most recent developments.

July 2021

List of Notations

$\mathcal{I} = (\mathcal{I}_k(p, q))_{k,p,q}$ — Image Time Series: time index k and pixel position (p, q)

$\mathcal{I} = (\mathcal{I}_k^c(p, q))_{k,p,q,c}$ — Vector Image Time Series: band/spectral index c

$\mathcal{I} = \left(\mathcal{I}_k^{(u,v)}(p, q)\right)_{k,p,q,u,v}$ — Matrix Image Time Series: (polarimetric indices (u, v))

$\mathbb{N}, \mathbb{Z}, \mathbb{R}, \mathbb{C}$ — Sets of Natural Numbers, Integers, Real and Complex Numbers

$\mu, \boldsymbol{\mu}$ — Means of Random Variables and Random Vectors

$\mathbf{C}, \boldsymbol{\Sigma}$ — Physical and Statistical Variance–Covariance Matrices

pdf — Probability Density Function

Change Detection and Image Time Series Analysis 2,
coordinated by Abdourrahmane M. ATTO, Francesca BOVOLO and Lorenzo BRUZZONE.
© ISTE Ltd 2021.

1

Hierarchical Markov Random Fields for High Resolution Land Cover Classification of Multisensor and Multiresolution Image Time Series

Ihsen HEDHLI[1], Gabriele MOSER[2], Sebastiano B. SERPICO[2]
and Josiane ZERUBIA[3]

[1]*Institute Intelligence and Data, Université Laval, Quebec City, Canada*
[2]*University of Genoa, Italy*
[3]*INRIA, Université Cote d'Azur, Nice, France*

1.1. Introduction

1.1.1. *The role of multisensor data in time series classification*

Accurate and time-efficient classification methods for multitemporal imagery and satellite image time series are important tools required to support the rapid and reliable extraction of information on a monitored region, especially when an extensive area is considered. Given the substantial amount and variety of data currently available from last-generation, very-high spatial resolution satellite missions, the main difficulty is developing a classifier that uses the benefits of input time series that are possibly composed of multimission, multisensor, multiresolution and multifrequency

Change Detection and Image Time Series Analysis 2,
coordinated by Abdourrahmane M. ATTO, Francesca BOVOLO and Lorenzo BRUZZONE.
© ISTE Ltd 2021.

imagery (Gómez-Chova *et al.* 2015). From an application-oriented viewpoint, the goal is to take advantage of this variety of input sources, in order to maximize the accuracy and effectiveness of the resulting thematic mapping products. From a methodological viewpoint, this goal aims for the development of novel data fusion techniques. These techniques should be flexible enough to support the joint classification of a time series of images collected in the same area, by different sensors, at different times, and associated with multiple spatial resolutions and wavelength ranges.

In this chapter, this joint fusion problem is addressed. First, an overview of the major concepts and of the recent literature in the area of remote sensing data fusion is presented (see section 1.1.3). Then, two advanced methods for the joint supervised classification of multimission image time series, including multisensor optical and Synthetic Aperture Radar (SAR) components acquired at multiple spatial resolutions, are described (see section 1.2). The two techniques address different problems of supervised classification of satellite image time series and share a common methodological formulation based on hierarchical Markov random field (MRF) models. Examples of the experimental results obtained by the proposed approaches in the application to very-high-resolution time series are also presented and discussed (see section 1.3).

On the one hand, the use of multiresolution and multiband imagery has been previously shown to optimize the classification results in terms of accuracy and computation time. On the other hand, the integration of the temporal dimension into a classification scheme can both enhance the results in terms of reliability and capture the evolution in time of the monitored area. However, the joint problem of the fusion of several distinct data modalities (e.g. multitemporal, multiresolution and multisensor) has been much more scarcely addressed in the remote sensing literature so far.

1.1.2. *Multisensor and multiresolution classification*

The availability of different kinds of sensors is very advantageous for land cover mapping applications. It allows us to capture a wide variety of properties of the objects contained in a scene, as measured by each sensor at each acquisition time. These properties can be exploited to extract richer information about the imaged area. In particular, the opportunity of joint availability of SAR and optical images within a time series can possibly offer high-resolution, all-weather, day/night, short revisit time data with polarimetric, multifrequency and multispectral acquisition capabilities. This potential is especially emphasized by current satellite missions for Earth Observation (EO), for example, Sentinel-1 and -2, Pléiades, TerraSAR-X, COSMO-SkyMed and COSMO-SkyMed Second Generation, RADARSAT-2 and RADARSAT Constellation, GeoEye-1, WorldView-1, -2, -3, and WorldView Legion, or PRISMA, which convey a huge potential for multisensor optical and SAR observations. They allow a spatially distributed and temporally repetitive view of the monitored area at multiple spatial scales. However, the use of multisource image analysis for land cover classification purposes has been mostly addressed so far by focusing on single-resolution multisensor optical–SAR imagery, whereas the joint use of multisensor and multiresolution capabilities within a time series of images of the same scene has been more scarcely investigated. This approach bears the obvious advantage of simplicity but is, in general, suboptimal. From a methodological viewpoint, when multisensor (optical and SAR) or multiresolution images of a given scene are available, using them separately discards part of the correlations among these multiple data sources and, most importantly, their complementarity.

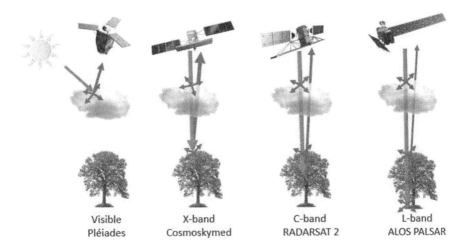

Visible	X-band	C-band	L-band
Pléiades	Cosmoskymed	RADARSAT 2	ALOS PALSAR

Figure 1.1. *Sensitivity to cloud cover and object size using different wavelength ranges. For a color version of this figure, see www.iste.co.uk/atto/change2.zip*

As illustrated in Figure 1.1, SAR and multispectral images exhibit complementary properties in terms of wavelength range (active microwave vs. passive visible and infrared), noisy behavior (often strong in SAR due to speckle, usually less critical in optical imagery), feasibility of photo-interpretation (usually easier with optical than with SAR data), impact of atmospheric conditions and cloud cover (strong for optical acquisitions and almost negligible for SAR) and sensitivity to sun-illumination (strong for optical imagery and negligible for SAR) (Landgrebe 2003; Ulaby and Long 2015). This makes the joint use of high-resolution optical and SAR imagery particularly interesting for many applications related to environmental monitoring and risk management (Serpico *et al.* 2012).

Within this framework, there is a definite need for classification methods that automatically correlate different sets of images taken at different times, in the same area, from different sensors and at different resolutions. One way to address this problem is to resort to an explicit statistical modeling by finding a joint probability distribution, given the class-conditional marginal probability density function (PDF) of the data collected by each sensor (see Figure 1.2). The joint statistics can be designed by resorting to meta-Gaussian distributions (Storvik *et al.* 2009), multivariate statistics such as multivariate copulas (Voisin *et al.* 2014) or non-parametric density estimators (Fukunaga 2013). However, employing heterogeneous data (SAR–optical in our case) makes the task of finding an appropriate multivariate statistical model complex, time demanding and possibly prone to overfitting.

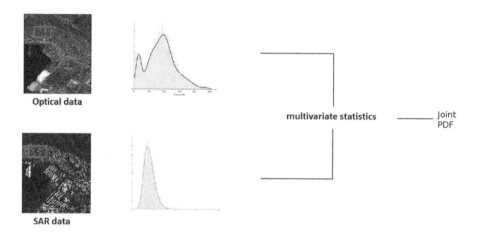

Optical data

SAR data

multivariate statistics   Joint
                               PDF

Figure 1.2. *Multivariate statistical modeling for optical–SAR data fusion. For a color version of this figure, see www.iste.co.uk/atto/change2.zip*

In this context, the rationale of both approaches described in section 1.2 is to benefit from the data fusion capabilities of hierarchical MRFs and avoid the computation of joint statistics. An approach based on multiple quad-trees in cascade and applied to multisensor and multiresolution fusion is described. In the first proposed method, for each sensor, the input images of the series are associated with separate quad-tree structures according to their resolutions. The goal is to generate a classification map based on a series of SAR and optical images acquired over the same area. The proposed approach formalizes, within this multiple quad-tree topology, a supervised Bayesian classifier that combines a class-conditional statistical model for pixelwise information and a hierarchical MRF for multisensor and multiresolution contextual information. The second proposed method regards the case of the multimission fusion of multifrequency SAR data collected by the COSMO-SkyMed and RADARSAT-2 sensors, together with optical Pléiades data. A multiple quad-tree structure is used again, but optical and SAR images are both included in all cascaded quad-trees to take into account the specifics of the spatial resolutions of the considered satellite instruments. Compared to the first method, which considers the fusion of data from generally arbitrary SAR and optical sensors, this second method focuses on a specific combination of spaceborne SAR and optical sensors, in order to investigate the synergy among the multifrequency and multiresolution information they provide.

1.1.3. *Previous work*

The literature in remote sensing data fusion is extensive, indicating intense interest in this topic, as highlighted by the recent sharp increase in the number of papers published in the major remote sensing journals, and the increasing number of related sessions in international conferences. Indeed, data fusion has given rise to a continuing tradition in remote sensing, since EO is by definition dynamic (thus implying the multitemporal capability of remote sensing instruments), multiresolution (multiple spatial and spectral resolutions) and related to different physical quantities (thus requiring multiview/multisensor capability) (Waltz and Llinas 1990).

Data fusion is defined differently depending on the final goal of the user. Indeed, (Li *et al.* 1995; Pohl and van Genderen 2014) considered data fusion in remote sensing as the combination of two or more algorithms. This may include, but is not restricted to *multiresolution fusion and pansharpening techniques*, whose aim is to obtain multispectral images of increased spatial resolution (Vivone *et al.* 2015), *resolution blending* that consists of providing time series of data at their maximum spatial and spectral resolutions (referred to as parallel pansharpening in the multitemporal domain) (Huang and Song 2012), and *data fusion for missing information reconstruction*, by using complementary data (Wang and Liang 2014).

An alternative perspective is to define data fusion in remote sensing as a decision fusion process that combines the information that is obtained from different data sets and provides sufficient generalization capability (Wald 1999). According to this definition, any type of image processing that combines two or more data sets, for example, for land cover classification, atmospheric correction or application of vegetation indices, could be considered as data fusion.

Within the former definition, various families of data fusion techniques have been proposed in the literature. On the one hand, these methods may generally differ in their *application requirements*, such as the availability of ground reference data, the collected prior information and/or some ancillary data that can be used in the development of the system according to a multisource processing architecture. On the other hand, it is important to properly understand the *user needs* with respect to economic costs and processing time and performance. Figure 1.3 summarizes the general architecture of a data fusion technique.

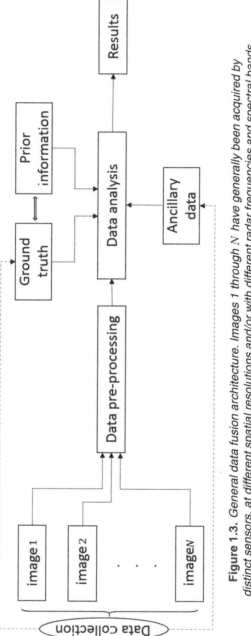

Figure 1.3. *General data fusion architecture. Images 1 through N have generally been acquired by distinct sensors, at different spatial resolutions and/or with different radar frequencies and spectral bands*

As discussed previously, the availability of remote sensing imagery at varying resolutions has increased. Merging images of different spatial resolutions has become a significant operation in the field of digital remote sensing. A variety of different multiscale fusion approaches have been developed since the late 1980s. In the following, we give an overview of the most common approaches found in the literature. We can broadly divide them into two groups: (i) transformation techniques and (ii) modeling techniques.

Methods in (i) consist of replacing the entire set of multiscale images by a single composite representation that incorporates all relevant data. The multiscale transformations usually employ pyramid transforms (Burt 1984), the discrete wavelet transform (Piella 2003; Forster *et al.* 2004; Zhang and Hong 2005), the undecimated wavelet transform (Rockinger 1996; Chibani and Houacine 2003), the dual-tree complex wavelet transform (Demirel and Anbarjafari 2010; Iqbal *et al.* 2013; Zhang and Kingsbury 2015; Nelson *et al.* 2018), the curvelet transform (Choi *et al.* 2005; Nencini *et al.* 2007), the contourlet transform (ALEjaily *et al.* 2008; Shah *et al.* 2008) and the nonsubsampled contourlet transform (Yang *et al.* 2007).

Techniques in (ii) include multiscale approaches with a focus on the use of the coarser resolutions in the data set, in order to obtain fast computational algorithms. In the seminal papers (Basseville *et al.* 1992a, 1992b), the basis for multiscale autoregressive modeling in dyadic trees was introduced. Since then, straightforward approaches were performed to deal with multiresolution images using trees (Pérez 1993; Chardin 2000; Laferté *et al.* 2000; Kato and Zerubia 2012; Voisin 2012; Hedhli *et al.* 2014). A detailed review of some of these methods can be found in Graffigne *et al.* (1995) and Willsky (2002).

In broader terms, multisensor analysis encompasses all processes dealing with data and information from multiple sensors to achieve refined/improved information, compared to the result that could be obtained by using data from only one individual source (Waltz and Llinas 1990; Pohl and van Genderen 1998; Hall and Llinas 2001). The accuracy of the classification of remote sensing images, for instance, is generally improved when multiple source image data are introduced in the processing chain in a suitable manner (e.g. (Dousset and Gourmelon 2003; Nguyen *et al.* 2011; Gamba *et al.* 2011; Hedhli *et al.* 2015)). As mentioned above, images from microwave and optical sensors provide complementary information that helps in discriminating the different classes. Several procedures have been introduced in the literature including, on the one hand, post-classification techniques in which, first, the two data sets are separately segmented, and then the joint classification is produced by using, for example, random forest (e.g. Waske and van der Linden 2008), support vector machines with *ad hoc* kernels (Muñoz-Marí *et al.* 2010) and artificial neural networks (Mas and Flores 2008). On the other hand, other methods directly classify the combined multisensor data by using, for instance, statistical mixture models (e.g. (Dousset and Gourmelon 2003; Voisin *et al.* 2012; Prendes 2015)), entropy-based techniques (e.g. Roberts *et al.* 2008) and fuzzy analysis (e.g. Benz 1999; Stroppiana *et al.* 2015). Furthermore, for complex data, especially when dealing with urban areas, radar images can contribute to the differentiation between different land covers, owing to the differences in surface roughness, shape, and moisture content of the observed ground surface (e.g. Brunner *et al.* 2010). The use of multisensor data in image classification has become increasingly popular with the increased availability of sophisticated software and hardware facilities to handle the increasing volumes of data. The decision on which of these techniques is the most suitable is very much driven by the applications and the typology of input remote sensing data.

Recently, with the exposure of neural networks, several multisensor data fusion techniques have been proposed based on feed-forward multilayer perceptron and convolutional neural network (CNN) architectures. Indeed, the huge amount of data makes the use of deep neural network (DNN) models possible. Many effective multi-task approaches have been developed recently to train DNN models on some large-scale remote sensing benchmarks (e.g. Chen *et al.* 2017; Carvalho *et al.* 2019; Cheng *et al.* 2020). The aim of these multi-task methods is to learn an embedding space from different sensors (i.e. task). This could be done by first learning the embedding of each modality separately and then combining all of the learned features as a joint representation. Then, this representation is used as an input for the last layers of different high level visual applications, for example, remote sensing classification, monitoring or change detection. Alternatively, DNN models could be used as an heterogeneous data fusion framework, learning the related parameters from all of the input sources (e.g. Ghamisi *et al.* 2016; Benedetti *et al.* 2018; Minh *et al.* 2018). Despite the regularization techniques used to mitigate the high computational complexity of DNN methods (Pan *et al.* 2015), the training of these techniques is still greedy and hard to converge, especially with remote sensing data sets.

In the next section, we will describe two advanced methods for the supervised classification of multisource satellite image time series. These methods have the advantage of being applicable to series of two or more images taken by single or multiple sensors, operating at the same or different spatial resolutions, and with the same or different radar frequencies and spectral bands. In general, the available images in the series are temporally and spatially correlated. Indeed, temporal and spatial contextual constraints are unavoidable in multitemporal data interpretation. Within this framework, Markov models provide a convenient and consistent way of modeling context-dependent spatio-temporal entities originated from multiple information sources, such as images in a multitemporal, multisensor, multiresolution and multimission context.

1.2. Methodology

1.2.1. *Overview of the proposed approaches*

Let us consider a time series $(\mathcal{I}_k(p, q))_{k,p,q}$ composed of K images, acquired over the same area on K acquisition dates, by up to K optical and SAR different sensors. Each image in the series is generally composed of multiple features (i.e. it is vector-valued), possibly corresponding to distinct spectral bands or radar polarizations. Specifically, $\mathcal{I}_k(p, q)$ indicates the feature vector of pixel (p, q) in the k-th image in the series ($k = 1, 2, \ldots, K$). In general, each sensor may operate at a distinct spatial resolution; hence, a multisensor and multiresolution time series is being considered.

The acquisition times of the images in the series are assumed to be close enough so that no significant changes occur in the land cover of the observed area. In particular, we assume that no abrupt changes (e.g. due to natural disasters such as floods or earthquakes) occur within the overall time span of the series. This assumption makes it possible to use the whole time series to classify the land cover in the scene, by using the benefit of the complementary properties of the images acquired by different sensors and at different spatial resolutions. Furthermore, this assumption may be especially relevant when the temporal dynamic of the ground scene *per se* is an indicator of land cover membership, such as in the case of forested (e.g. deciduous vs. evergreen) or agricultural areas. We denote as $\omega_1, \omega_2, \ldots, \omega_M$ the land cover classes in the scene and as $\Omega = \{\omega_1, \omega_2, \ldots, \omega_M\}$ their set. We operate in a supervised framework; hence, we assume that training samples are available for all of these classes.

The overall formulation introduced in Hedhli *et al.* (2016) to address multitemporal fusion in the case of single-sensor imagery, and based on multiple quad-trees in cascade, is generalized here to take benefit from the images acquired by different sensors and from their mutual synergy. The multiscale topology of the quad-trees and of hierarchical MRFs defined on quad-trees intrinsically allows multiresolution and multisensor data to be naturally fused in the land cover mapping process.

In this framework, two specific algorithms are defined. In the first one, the k-th image in the series is assigned to a separate quad-tree based on its own spatial resolution. A hierarchical MRF is defined on this quad-tree topology, and inference on the resulting probabilistic graphical model is addressed using the Bayesian marginal posterior mode (MPM) criterion (Kato and Zerubia 2012). In the second proposed algorithm, the focus is on a specific case of multimission, multifrequency and multiresolution time series: multifrequency X-band COSMO-SkyMed and C-band RADARSAT-2 SAR images are used alongside optical visible and near-infrared

(VNIR) Pléiades data. This scenario is of special current interest, both because of the potential of exploiting the synergy among these missions and especially in view of the recent COSMO-SkyMed Second Generation and RADARSAT Constellation programs. In the case of the second method, different quad-trees are also used, but both optical and SAR data are associated with each quad-tree in order to benefit from the finest resolution available from the considered sensors. Both approaches exploit the potential of hierarchical probabilistic graphical models (Kato and Zerubia 2012) to address challenging problems of multimodal classification of an image time series.

1.2.2. *Hierarchical model associated with the first proposed method*

Let us first define the multiple quad-tree structure associated with the first proposed method. The K images $\mathcal{I}_1, \mathcal{I}_2, \ldots, \mathcal{I}_K$ in the series are included in the finest-scale layers (i.e. the leaves) of K distinct quad-trees. The coarser-scale layers of each quad-tree are filled in by applying wavelet transforms to the image on the finest-scale layer (Mallat 2008). The roots of the K quad-trees are assumed to correspond to the same spatial resolution. The rationale of this hierarchical structure is that each image in the input series originates from a separate multiscale quad-tree, generally with a different number of layers and the input image on the leaves, and that the roots of these quad-trees share a common spatial resolution (see Figure 1.4). This graph topology implicitly means that the spatial resolutions of the input images in the series are in a power-of-2 mutual relation. In general terms, this is a restriction but when concerning current high-resolution satellite missions, this condition is easily met up to possible minor resampling.

Let $\mathcal{I}_{k\ell}$ be the image associated with the ℓ-th layer of the k-th quad-tree in the series. We will index the common root with $\ell = 0$ and the leaves of the k-th quad-tree with $\ell = L_k$, i.e. $\mathcal{I}_{k,L_k}$ coincides with the original input image $\mathcal{I}_k$ ($k = 1, 2, \ldots, K$). The images $\mathcal{I}_{k\ell}$ in the other layers ($\ell = 0, 1, \ldots, L_k - 1$) have been obtained through wavelets from $\mathcal{I}_{k,L_k} = \mathcal{I}_k$. The whole time series of multiscale images, either acquired by the considered sensors or obtained through wavelets, will be denoted as $\mathcal{I} = (\mathcal{I}_{k\ell}(p, q))_{k,\ell,p,q}$.

We will also indicate as $\mathcal{S}_{k\ell}$ the pixel lattice of the ℓ-th layer of the k-th quadtree ($\ell = 0, 1, \ldots, L_k; k = 1, 2, \ldots, K$). We will denote as $s = (p, q)$ the coordinate pair of a generic pixel in one of these layers ($s \in \mathcal{S}_{k\ell}$). Following the literature of hierarchical MRFs, the site will be named s in the following. Sites in the described quad-tree structure are linked by parent–child relations – within each quad-tree and across consecutive quad-trees – as a function of their spatial scale. Specifically, if $s \in \mathcal{S}_{k\ell}$ is a site in the ℓ-th layer of the k-th quadtree and $\ell \in \{1, 2, \ldots, L_k\}$, i.e. s is not on the root layer, then $s^- \in \mathcal{S}_{k,\ell-1}$ indicates its parent node in the same quad-tree

($k = 1, 2, \ldots, K$). Similarly, if $s \in \mathcal{S}_{k\ell}$ with $\ell \in \{0, 1, \ldots, L_k - 1\}$, i.e. s is not on the leaves layer, then $s^+ \subset \mathcal{S}_{k,\ell+1}$ denotes the set of its four children nodes in the same quad-tree. Finally, if $s \in \mathcal{S}_{k\ell}$ with $\ell \in \{1, 2, \ldots, L_k\}$ and $k \in \{2, 3, \ldots, K\}$, i.e. if s is neither in the first quad-tree of the series nor in the root of the other quad-trees, then $s^= \in \mathcal{S}_{k-1,\ell-1}$ indicates its parent node in the $(k - 1)$-th quad-tree, i.e. in the quad-tree associated with the previous image of the series (see Figure 1.4). From a graph-theoretic perspective, if the sites in the quad-trees are meant as nodes in a graph, then the pairs $(s, s^-), (s, s^=)$ and (s, r) with $r \in s^+$ define the corresponding edges.

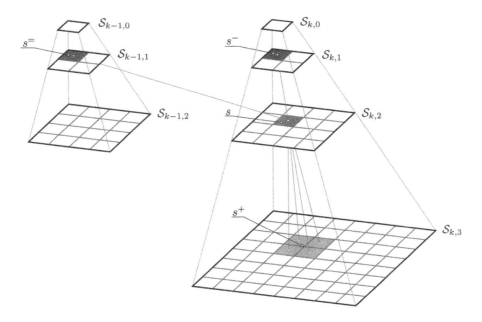

Figure 1.4. *Quad-trees associated with the input multisensor and multiresolution time series and related notations. For a color version of this figure, see www.iste.co.uk/atto/change2.zip*

   Given this multiple quad-tree topology, a probabilistic graphical model based on a hierarchical MRF is defined. It is made of a series of random fields associated with the various scales and connected by transition relations associated with the links $s \mapsto s^-, s \mapsto s^=$ and $s \mapsto s^+$ among the sites. In particular, the quad-trees are meant to be in cascade, consistently with the input time series. Let $\mathcal{M}_{k\ell}(s) \in \Omega$ be the class label of site $s \in \mathcal{S}_{k\ell}$ ($\ell = 0, 1, \ldots, L_k; k = 1, 2, \ldots, K$), and let $\mathcal{M} = (\mathcal{M}_{k\ell}(s))_{k,\ell,s}$ be the corresponding time series of random fields associated with all multiscale layers. Each realization of $\mathcal{M}$ corresponds to a set of classification maps for all images in the series and all scales in the corresponding quad-trees.

The key assumption in the hierarchical MRF model is that the random fields $\mathcal{M}$ are Markovian, both across scales and time ($\ell = 1, 2, \ldots, L_k; k = 2, 3, \ldots, K$) (Kato and Zerubia 2012):

$$P(\mathcal{M}_{k\ell}|\mathcal{M}_{hm}, h \leqslant k, m \leqslant \ell, (h,m) \neq (k,\ell)) \tag{1.1}$$
$$= P(\mathcal{M}_{k\ell}|\mathcal{M}_{k,\ell-1}, \mathcal{M}_{k-1,\ell-1}),$$

where $P(\cdot)$ indicates the probability mass function (pmf) of discrete random variables and fields. Equation [1.1] implies that the distribution of the labels in each layer of each quad-tree, conditioned on the labels in all above layers of the same quad-tree and of the previous quad-trees in the series, can only be restricted to the distribution conditioned on the labels of the upper layers in the same and previous quad-trees. Furthermore, this distribution factorizes in a conditionally independent fashion – a common assumption in the area of latent Markov models ($\ell = 1, 2, \ldots, L_k$; $k = 2, 3, \ldots, K$) (Li 2009; Kato and Zerubia 2012):

$$P(\mathcal{M}_{k\ell}|\mathcal{M}_{k,\ell-1}, \mathcal{M}_{k-1,\ell-1})$$
$$= \prod_{s \in \mathcal{S}_{k\ell}} P(\mathcal{M}_{k\ell}(s)|\mathcal{M}_{k,\ell-1}(s^-), \mathcal{M}_{k-1,\ell-1}(s^=)). \tag{1.2}$$

In the case of the first quad-tree in the series, these Markovianity and conditional independence assumptions are naturally adapted as follows ($\ell = 1, 2, \ldots, L_0$):

$$P(\mathcal{M}_{1,\ell}|\mathcal{M}_{1,m}, m < \ell) = P(\mathcal{M}_{1,\ell}|\mathcal{M}_{1,\ell-1})$$
$$= \prod_{s \in \mathcal{S}_{1,\ell}} P(\mathcal{M}_{1,\ell}(s)|\mathcal{M}_{1,\ell-1}(s^-)). \tag{1.3}$$

Finally, the feature vectors in the image time series $\mathcal{I}$ are also assumed to be conditionally independent on the labels in $\mathcal{M}$:

$$p(\mathcal{I}|\mathcal{M}) = \prod_{k=1}^{K} \prod_{\ell=0}^{L_k} p(\mathcal{I}_{k\ell}|\mathcal{M}_{k\ell}) = \prod_{k=1}^{K} \prod_{\ell=0}^{L_k} \prod_{s \in \mathcal{S}_{k\ell}} p(\mathcal{I}_{k\ell}(s)|\mathcal{M}_{k\ell}(s)), \tag{1.4}$$

where $p(\cdot)$ denotes the PDF of continuous random variables and fields. Again, this assumption is widely accepted in the literature of latent MRF models (Li 2009; Kato and Zerubia 2012).

To ease the notations, in the following, we will simply write the feature vector $\mathcal{I}_{k\ell}(s)$ and the class label $\mathcal{M}_{k\ell}(s)$ of site $s \in \mathcal{S}_{k\ell}$ as x_s and c_s, respectively, dropping the explicit dependence on k and ℓ for the sake of clarity. For this reason, we will explain the formulation of the first proposed method in the case of a series composed of $K = 2$ images $\mathcal{I}_1$ and $\mathcal{I}_2$, acquired by two different sensors and at two different resolutions on the considered area. In this case, two quad-trees in cascade are used. The extension to the case $K > 2$ is straightforward.

The formulation of MPM defined in Hedhli *et al.* (2016) with regard to the case of multitemporal classification of single-sensor multiresolution imagery is generalized here to the case of multisensor data. The MPM decision rule assigns site $s \in \mathcal{S}_{k\ell}$ ($\ell = 0, 1, \ldots, L_k$; $k = 1, 2, \ldots, K$) the class label that maximizes the posterior marginal probability $P(c_s|\mathcal{I})$, i.e. the distribution of its own individual label, given all feature vectors in the image series (Li 2009; Kato and Zerubia 2012). This decision rule is especially advantageous in the case of hierarchical graphs because it penalizes classification errors as a function of the scale at which they occur. Intuitively, an error on a site in the leaves layer only directly affects the corresponding pixel, whereas an error in a single pixel in the root layer may propagate into many erroneously labeled pixels on the leaves layer. MPM correctly penalizes the latter scenario more strongly than the former (Laferté *et al.* 2000).

As proven in Laferté *et al.* (2000) and Hedhli *et al.* (2016), under suitable conditional independence assumptions, the posterior marginal $P(c_s|\mathcal{I})$ can be recursively expressed as a function of the posterior marginal $P(c_{s-}|\mathcal{I})$ of the parent node s^- in the same quad-tree and, in the case $k = 2$, also of the posterior marginal $P(c_{s=}|\mathcal{I})$ of the parent node $s^=$ in the previous quad-tree:

$$
P(c_s|\mathcal{I}) = \begin{cases} \displaystyle\sum_{x_{s-},x_{s=}} P(c_s|c_{s-},c_{s=},\boldsymbol{X}_s)P(c_{s-}|\mathcal{I})P(x_{s=}|\mathcal{I}), & s \in \mathcal{S}_2^* \\ \displaystyle\sum_{x_{s-}} P(c_s|c_{s-},\boldsymbol{X}_s)P(c_{s-}|\mathcal{I}), & s \in \mathcal{S}_1^*, \end{cases}
$$

$$[1.5]$$

where $\mathcal{S}_k^* = \bigcup_{k=1}^{L_k} \mathcal{S}_{k\ell}$ collects all sites except the root in the k-th quad-tree ($k = 1, 2$) and $\boldsymbol{X}_s$ is a vector collecting the features of all of the descendants of site s. Through this formulation, MPM takes into consideration the information conveyed by the input multisensor data within the labeling of each site $s \in \mathcal{S}_2^*$.

1.2.3. *Hierarchical model associated with the second proposed method*

In the second proposed method, the case-specific problem of jointly classifying a multimission, multifrequency (radar X band, radar C band and optical VNIR) and multiresolution series of images acquired by COSMO-SkyMed, RADARSAT-2 and Pléiades is addressed. All of these sensors support multiple spatial resolutions, up to 0.5 m for Pléiades, approximately 1 m for COSMO-SkyMed and 1 m × 2 m for RADARSAT-2.

Let us propose a time series of three images, collected by COSMO-SkyMed, RADARSAT-2 and Pléiades, in the same area, at times close enough to assume land cover stability. A case-specific hierarchical model, again using two quad-trees in cascade, is introduced to generate a supervised classification map at the finest among the spatial resolutions of the input images in the series. Unlike in the case of the hierarchical model of the first proposed approach, in which distinct quad-trees are related to different sensors, in this second approach, for each of the two considered radar sensors, the input image is included in a separate quad-tree according to its spatial resolution (see Figure 1.5). These resolutions are generally expected to be coarser than the finest resolution that is observed through Pléiades. Hence, the input Pléiades data are inserted in the finest resolution layers of both aforementioned quad-trees (see Figure 1.5). The rationale is to both benefit from all input multisensor imagery and to map land cover at the finest resolution available. Empty layers of each of the two quad-trees are filled in with wavelet transforms computed from the Pléiades image included in the leaves layer (see Figure 1.5). The Markovian formulation defined in the previous section, the recursive equations [1.5] and the remarks on the power-of-2 relation among the resolutions of the input images in the series are also valid in this case.

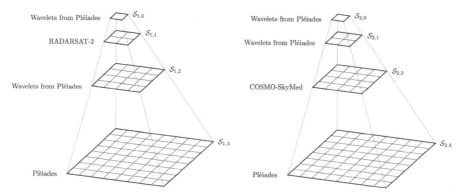

Figure 1.5. *Cascaded quad-trees associated with the second proposed method. In this example, we assume that the input time series includes Pléiades data at a 0.5 m resolution, COSMO-SkyMed spotlight data at a 1 m resolution and RADARSAT-2 data sampled on a 2 m pixel lattice. Accordingly, the Pléiades image is included in the leaves layer of both quad-trees. The COSMO-SkyMed and RADARSAT-2 images are inserted in the intermediate layers of separate quad-trees, according to their resolutions. The empty layers of both quad-trees are filled in with wavelet transforms of the Pléiades imagery*

1.2.4. *Multisensor hierarchical MPM inference*

Equation [1.5] allows us to calculate the posterior marginal $P(c_s|\mathcal{I})$ at each site $s \in \mathcal{S}_2^*$ of the second quad-tree (except the root) recursively, as long as the probabilities $P(c_s|c_{s-}, c_{s=}, \boldsymbol{X}_s)$ become known. In particular, the focus on the second quad-tree is consistent with the cascade approach used within the proposed methods: given the input time series, the output classification map is obtained on the leaves of this second quad-tree (or on the leaves of the last quad-tree in the case of a longer time series).

Specifically, under appropriate assumptions, in Hedhli *et al.* (2016) we proved that, for all $s \in \mathcal{S}_2^*$:

$$P(c_s|c_{s^-}, c_{s^=}, \boldsymbol{X}_s) \propto \frac{P(c_s|c_{s^-}, c_{s^=})P(c_{s^-}|c_{s^=})P(c_{s^=})P(c_s|\boldsymbol{X}_s)}{P(c_s)}, \qquad [1.6]$$

where $P(c_s|c_{s^-}, c_{s^=})$ is the parent–child transition probability across the two quad-trees, $P(c_s)$ is the prior probability, $P(c_{s^-}|c_{s^=})$ is the transition probability between two sites at the same scale and $P(c_s|\boldsymbol{X}_s)$ is the partial posterior marginal probability. Given the obvious constraint $\sum_{c_s} P(c_s|c_{s^-}, c_{s^=}, \boldsymbol{X}_s) = 1$, equation [1.6] determines $P(c_s|c_{s^-}, c_{s^=}, \boldsymbol{X}_s)$ uniquely on all sites $s \in \mathcal{S}_2^*$. To determine these probabilities, the approach developed in Hedhli *et al.* (2016) for the multitemporal single-sensor case is generalized to the multisensor tasks considered here. This process is formalized within three recursive passes across the second quad-tree – one bottom-up and two top-down passes – which are described in the next sections.

1.2.4.1. *Initializing on the first quad-tree*

First, in order to initialize the process, classification is performed using only the data included in the first quad-tree through a classical MPM on a single quad-tree. We refer the reader to Laferté *et al.* (2000) for more detail. Here, we only briefly recall that the algorithm is initialized by choosing the prior distribution on the root of this first quad-tree. In order to favor spatial regularity, this prior is selected here according to a Potts MRF model (Li 2009; Kato and Zerubia 2012). Details can be found in Hedhli *et al.* (2016). From the perspective of the classification of the input series of multisensor images, the key point is that, after this initialization stage, the posterior marginal $P(c_s|\mathcal{I})$ is known for each site $s \in \mathcal{S}_{1,\ell}$ ($\ell = 0, 1, \dots L_1$) of the first quad-tree. Furthermore, $P(c_s|\boldsymbol{X}_s)$ is also obtained as an intermediate byproduct on the same sites.

1.2.4.2. *First top-down pass*

In the first top-down pass, the second quad-tree is swept downward from the root to the leaves to calculate the prior $P(c_s)$ recursively. This prior is initialized in each site $s \in \mathcal{S}_{2,0}$ of the root of the second quad-tree as $P(c_s) = P(c_r|\boldsymbol{X}_r)$, where $r \in \mathcal{S}_{1,0}$ is the site of the root of the first quad-tree with the same spatial location as s. The partial posterior marginal $P(c_r|\boldsymbol{X}_r)$ has been derived in the aforementioned initialization. Then, the top-down pass travels along the other layers until it reaches the leaves ($s \in \mathcal{S}_2^*$):

$$P(c_s) = \sum_{c_{s^-}} P(c_s|c_{s^-})P(c_{s^-}). \qquad [1.7]$$

This formulation encourages parent and children sites to share the same class label, although it does not deterministically enforce this condition. It also implies a model for the statistical relations between labels in consecutive layers. Here, the parent–child transition probability $P(c_s|c_{s-})$ is expressed using the parametric model in Bouman (1991):

$$P(c_s|c_{s-}) = \begin{cases} \theta & \text{if } c_s = c_{s-} \\ \dfrac{1-\theta}{M-1} & \text{otherwise,} \end{cases}$$ [1.8]

where $\theta \in [0,1]$ is a hyperparameter of the method. Experiments conducted in Hedhli et al. (2016) indicated limited sensitivity of the result of MPM on multiple cascaded quad-trees to the value of this hyperparameter. We also note that equation [1.8] implicitly yields a stationary model for the considered transitions, i.e. the probability $P\{c_s = \omega_m | c_{s-} = \omega_n\}$ depends on the pair (ω_m, ω_n) of classes, but not on the specific site location s ($s \in \mathcal{S}_2^*; m, n = 1, 2, \ldots, M$).

After the first top-down pass, the prior $P(c_s)$ is known on every site s of the second quad-tree.

1.2.4.3. Bottom-up pass

To calculate $P(c_s|c_{s-}, c_{s=}, \boldsymbol{X}_s)$ ($s \in \mathcal{S}_2^*$), a bottom-up step traveling through the second quad-tree from the leaves to the root is used. It is based on equation [1.6], in which, besides the priors $P(c_s)$, which are known from the first top-down pass, three further probability distributions are necessary: (i) the transition probabilities at the same scale $P(c_{s-}|c_{s=})$; (ii) the parent–child transition probabilities $P(c_s|c_{s-}, c_{s=})$; and (iii) the partial posterior marginals $P(c_s|\boldsymbol{X}_s)$.

Concerning (i), the algorithm in Bruzzone et al. (1999) is applied to estimate the multitemporal joint probability matrix, i.e. the $M \times M$ matrix J, whose (m, n)-th entry is $J_{mn} = P\{c_{s-} = \omega_m, c_{s=} = \omega_n\}$ ($m, n = 1, 2, \ldots, M$). This technique is based on the expectation maximization (EM) algorithm and addresses the problem of learning these joint probabilities as a parametric estimation task. More details can be found in Hedhli et al. (2016). Once J has been estimated, $P(c_{s-}|c_{s=})$ is derived as an obvious byproduct.

With regard to (ii), the parametric model in equation [1.8] is extended as follows:

$$P(c_s|c_{s-}, c_{s=}) = \begin{cases} \theta & \text{if } c_s = c_{s-} = c_{s=} \\ \phi & \text{if } (c_s = c_{s-} \text{ or } c_s = c_{s=}) \text{ and } c_{s-} \neq c_{s=} \\ \dfrac{1-\theta}{M-1} & \text{if } c_s \neq c_{s-} \text{ and } c_s \neq c_{s=} \text{ and } c_{s-} = c_{s=} \\ \dfrac{1-2\phi}{M-2} & \text{otherwise,} \end{cases}$$ [1.9]

where θ has the same meaning as in equation [1.8] and $\phi \in [0,1]$ is a second hyperparameter.

Concerning (iii), it has been proved that, on all layers except the leaves (Laferté *et al.* 2000):

$$P(c_s|\boldsymbol{X}_s) \propto p(\boldsymbol{x}_s|c_s)P(c_s) \prod_{r \in s^+} \sum_{c_r} \frac{P(c_r|\boldsymbol{X}_r)P(c_r|c_s)}{P(c_r)} \qquad [1.10]$$

for all sites $s \in \mathcal{S}_{2,\ell}, \ell = 0, 1, \ldots, L_2 - 1$. First, $P(c_s|\boldsymbol{X}_s)$ is initialized on the leaves of the second quad-tree by setting $P(c_s|\boldsymbol{X}_s) = P(c_s|\boldsymbol{x}_s) \propto p(\boldsymbol{x}_s|c_s)P(c_s)$ for $s \in \mathcal{S}_{2,L_2}$. Then, $P(c_s|\boldsymbol{X}_s)$ is calculated by using equation [1.10] while sweeping the second quad-tree upward until the root is reached. This recursive process makes use of the pixelwise class-conditional PDF $p(\boldsymbol{x}_s|c_s)$, whose modeling is discussed in section 1.2.5. After the bottom-up pass, $P(c_s|c_{s^-}, c_{s=}, \boldsymbol{X}_s)$ is known on every site s of the second quad-tree.

1.2.4.4. *Second top-down pass*

Finally, based on equation [1.5], the posterior marginal is initialized at the root of the second quad-tree as $P(c_s|\boldsymbol{\mathcal{I}}) = P(c_s|\boldsymbol{X}_s)$ for $s \in \mathcal{S}_{2,0}$. Then, given the probabilities that have been determined or modeled within the previous stages, $P(c_s|\boldsymbol{\mathcal{I}})$ is obtained on all sites $s \in \mathcal{S}_2^*$ of all other layers through equation [1.5], by sweeping the second quad-tree downward in a second top-down pass.

1.2.4.5. *Generation of the output map*

The aforementioned stages lead to the computation of the posterior marginal $P(c_s|\boldsymbol{\mathcal{I}})$ on every site s of the second quad-tree. In principle, site s could directly be given the label $\arg\max_{c_s} P(c_s|\boldsymbol{\mathcal{I}})$, i.e. the label that maximizes $P(c_s|\boldsymbol{\mathcal{I}})$ over the set Ω of classes. However, this strategy is often avoided in the literature of hierarchical MRFs because of its computational burden and of the risk of blocky artifacts (Laferté *et al.* 2000; Voisin *et al.* 2014). As an alternative, the case-specific formulation of the modified Metropolis dynamics (MMD) algorithm (Berthod *et al.* 1996), which was combined with MPM in Hedhli *et al.* (2016) for the case of multitemporal single-sensor classification, is generalized here to the multisensor case. We refer the reader to Hedhli *et al.* (2016) for more detail. In the case of both proposed methods, after this integrated MPM–MMD labeling, the classification result on the leaves of the second quad-tree provides the output classification map at the finest of the observed resolutions.

1.2.5. *Probability density estimation through finite mixtures*

For each class, layer and quad-tree, a finite mixture model (FMM) is used for the corresponding pixelwise class-conditional pdf. This means that the function

$f_{k\ell m} : \boldsymbol{x}_s \mapsto p(\boldsymbol{x}_s | c_s = \omega_m)$ for $s \in \mathcal{S}_{k\ell}$ $(\ell = 0, 1, \dots, L_k; k = 1, 2; m = 1, 2, \dots, M)$ is supposed to belong to the following class of pdfs:

$$\mathcal{F}(g) = \left\{ \sum_{n=1}^{N} \pi_n g(\cdot | \psi_n) : N \in \mathbb{N}, \ \pi_n \in [0, 1], \ \sum_{n=1}^{N} \pi_n = 1, \ \psi_n \in \Psi \right\}$$

[1.11]

where $g(\cdot | \psi)$ is a pdf model depending on a vector $\psi \in \Psi$ of parameters that takes values in a parameter set Ψ, and every function $f(\boldsymbol{x}) = \sum_{n=1}^{N} \pi_n g(\boldsymbol{x} | \boldsymbol{\theta}_n)$ is a convex linear combination of N such pdfs, parameterized by the parameter vectors $\psi_1, \psi_2, \dots, \psi_N \in \Psi$ and weighted by the proportions $\pi_1, \pi_2, \dots, \pi_N$.

This modeling choice is motivated by the remarkable flexibility that FMMs offer in the characterization of data with heterogeneous statistics – a highly desirable property in the application to high spatial resolution remote sensing imagery (Hedhli et al. 2016). In the proposed methods, for each layer of each quad-tree, if the corresponding data are multispectral, then for all class-conditional pdfs, g is chosen to be a multivariate Gaussian, i.e. a Gaussian mixture model is used. In this case, the parameter vector ψ_n of each component obviously includes the related vector mean and covariance matrix $(n = 1, 2, \dots, N)$ (Landgrebe 2003). This model is also extended to the layers populated by wavelet transforms of optical data, consistently with the linearity of the wavelet operators.

On the contrary, for each layer that is populated by SAR data, all class-conditional pdfs are modeled using FMMs in which g is a generalized Gamma distribution, i.e. generalized Gamma mixtures are used. In this case, the parameter vector $\boldsymbol{\theta}_n$ of each n-th component includes a scale parameter and two shape parameters $(n = 1, 2, \dots, N)$. The choice of the generalized Gamma mixture is explained by its accuracy in the application to high spatial resolution SAR imagery (Li et al. 2011; Krylov et al. 2013). Here, we also generalize it – albeit empirically – to the layers populated with wavelet transforms of SAR imagery.

In all of these cases, the FMM parameters are estimated through the stochastic expectation maximization (SEM) algorithm. SEM is an iterative stochastic parameter estimation technique that has been introduced for problems characterized by data incompleteness and that approaches maximum likelihood estimates under suitable assumptions (Celeux et al. 1996). It is separately applied to the training set of each class ω_m in each ℓ-th layer of each k-th quad-tree, to model the corresponding class-conditional pdf $f_{k\ell m}$ $(\ell = 0, 1, \dots, L_k; k = 1, 2; m = 1, 2, \dots, M)$. In the case of the generalized Gamma mixtures for the SAR layers, it is also integrated with the method of log-cumulants (Krylov et al. 2013). Details on this combination can be found in (Moser and Serpico 2009). We recall that SEM also automatically determines the number N of mixture components, for which only an upper bound has to be provided by the operator. This upper bound was set to 10 in all of our experiments.

1.3. Examples of experimental results

1.3.1. *Results of the first method*

To experimentally validate the first method, a time series of two high-resolution images acquired in 2010 over Port-au-Prince, Haiti, has been used. The series was made of an HH-polarized single-look COSMO-SkyMed stripmap image with a 2.5 m pixel spacing (325×400 pixels; see Figure 1.6(a)) and of a GeoEye-1 image with a 2.5 m spatial resolution (see Figure 1.6(b)) and three channels in the visible wavelength range. The time lag between the two acquisitions was a few days. Five main land cover classes were present in the scene: urban, water, vegetation, soil and containers. These classes were defined by an expert photointerpreter who also annotated their training and test samples.

In the approach taken by the first proposed method, the quad-trees are ordered, and consistently with the cascade approach, the output classification map is the result obtained on the leaves of the second quad-tree. Here, the GeoEye-1 and COSMO-SkyMed images were associated with the first and second quad-trees, respectively. The rationale of this choice is to initialize the land cover mapping result using the optical data and to finalize it through the fusion with SAR imagery. In the case of both quad-trees, to fill in the empty levels of the quad-tree, 2D Daubechies wavelets of order 10 were applied (Mallat 2008).

The classification result obtained by the proposed technique (see Figure 1.6(g)) was compared to those generated by several previous approaches to multisensor and/or multiresolution classification. First, to compare with the result of a multiscale but single-sensor approach, the hierarchical MRF on a single quad-tree of Laferté et al. (2000) was applied to classify the image collected by each sensor. In this case, the MPM criterion was also used and the class-conditional pdfs were estimated using SEM together with multivariate Gaussian or generalized Gamma mixtures in the case of optical and SAR data, respectively (see Figure 1.6(c) and (d)). Then, to compare with a multisensor multiscale approach, the algorithm in Voisin et al. (2014) was used. It makes use of a hierarchical MRF on a single quad-tree, whose layers are filled in with both optical and SAR data in a stacked vector fashion. Multisensor fusion is accomplished using multivariate copula functions (see Figure 1.6(e)). Finally, to compare with a multisensor but single-scale approach, the technique in Storvik et al. (2009) was considered after upsampling all of the data to the pixel lattice at the finest resolution. In Storvik et al. (2009), the joint class-conditional distributions of multisensor data are estimated using meta-Gaussian density functions (essentially equivalent to Gaussian copulas) and the maximum likelihood decision rule is applied to generate the output classification map (see Figure 1.6(f)).

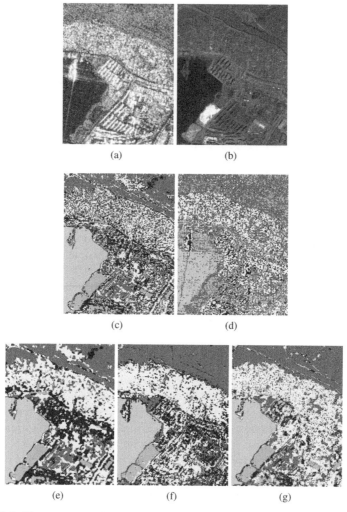

Figure 1.6. *First proposed method. (a) COSMO-SkyMed (©ASI 2010) and (b) GeoEye-1 (©GeoEye 2010) images of the input series. The former is shown after histogram equalization. The R-band of the latter is displayed. Classification maps obtained by separately classifying (c) the GeoEye-1 and (d) the COSMO-SkyMed images through a hierarchical MRF on a single quad-tree. Classification maps generated by (e) the multisensor multiscale method in (Voisin et al. 2014), (f) the multisensor single-scale technique in (Storvik et al. 2009) and (g) the proposed algorithm.*
Color legend: water☐ urban☐ vegetation■ bare soil☐ containers■.
For a color version of this figure, see www.iste.co.uk/atto/change2.zip

First, a visual qualitative inspection of the classification maps generated by the proposed and benchmark techniques suggests that the first proposed algorithm yielded quite accurate results and obtained improvements, compared to the previous methods, especially in the separate multiscale classification of the individual images coming from COSMO-Skymed and GeoEye-1. Specifically, in the results achieved through the use of only the SAR image, roads were discriminated quite accurately, but most other classes were not. In the results obtained through the use of only the optical image, classes that were spatially homogeneous were discriminated more effectively. The proposed technique is able to benefit from both satellite data sources in order to produce a classification output in which most classes in the high-resolution data set are visually well detected. Furthermore, compared to the case of multisensor but single-scale classification through the algorithm described in Storvik *et al.* (2009), the proposed method improved in terms of the spatial regularity of the classification map. This result is interpreted as a consequence of the contextual modeling components that are integrated in the proposed approach and are due to MRF modeling over a quad-tree and wavelet transformation.

	Class-wise accuracies					Overall	Time
	Water	Urban	Vegetation	Bare soil	Containers	accuracy	[s]
Proposed method	100%	78.12%	89.46%	98.78%	47.12%	82.69%	254
(Storvik *et al.* 2009)	99.95%	97.32%	90.81%	96.22%	37.25%	79.44%	298
(Voisin *et al.* 2014)	100%	75.24%	87.16%	98.89%	49.31%	82.12%	668

Table 1.1. *First proposed method: classification accuracies and computation times of the proposed technique and of the previous algorithms in Storvik et al. (2009) and Voisin et al. (2014) on the test set of the time series composed of COSMO-SkyMed and GeoEye-1 images. Computation times refer to an Intel i7 quad-core, 2.40 GHz, 8-GB RAM, 64-bit Linux system*

The effectiveness of the results of the proposed technique and the improvement, compared to those achieved by the algorithm in Storvik *et al.* (2009), are quantitatively confirmed by the classification accuracies on the test samples of the aforementioned classes (see Table 1.1). All considered methods obtained a poor discrimination of the "containers" class, due to its significant overlapping with the "urban" class in the multisensor or multispectral feature space. As a further evolution of the present technique, improvements in the discrimination of this class could be obtained by using texture features. On the one hand, accurate performance on the test samples, quite similar to those achieved by the proposed method, was also obtained by the multisensor multiscale technique in Voisin *et al.* (2014). On the other hand, the proposed algorithm granted improvements over this benchmark approach with regard to the spatial detail in the resulting maps (see Figure 1.6 (e) and (g)) and to the overall computational burden (see Table 1.1). The latter advantage is due to the fact that

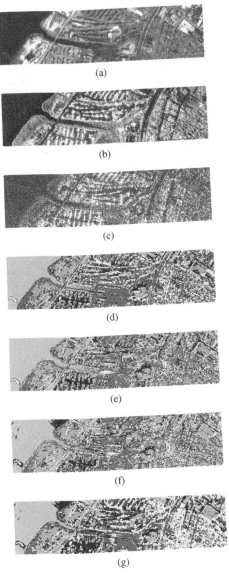

(a)

(b)

(c)

(d)

(e)

(f)

(g)

1.8. *Second proposed method – second test site. (a) Pléiades (©CNES ...ution Airbus DS), (b) COSMO-SkyMed (©ASI 2011) and (c) RADARSAT-2 ...A 2011) images of the input series. The SAR images are shown after histogram ...zation. The R-band of the optical image is displayed. Classification maps ...ed by operating with (d) only Pléiades data, (e) Pléiades and COSMO-SkyMed ...f) Pléiades and RADARSAT-2 data and (g) the proposed technique with all data ...series.*
...egend: water☐ urban☐ vegetation▨ bare soil▨ containers▮.
...olor version of this figure, see www.iste.co.uk/atto/change2.zip

addressing multisensor fusion using multiple quad-trees in cascade can leverage on the time efficiency of the sequential recursive formulation of MPM, without requiring the challenging and possibly time-expensive problem of the modeling of the joint pdf of optical and SAR data. On the contrary, this problem is involved in the approaches in Storvik *et al.* (2009) and Voisin *et al.* (2014), in which copulas and meta-Gaussian densities are used for this purpose.

1.3.2. *Results of the second method*

Two very-high-resolution time series, acquired again over Port-au-Prince, Haiti, were used for experiments with the second proposed method. They both consist of Pléiades pansharpened data at a spatial resolution of 0.5 m (see Figures 1.7(a) and 1.8(a)), of HH-polarized X-band COSMO-SkyMed spotlight data at a resolution of 1 m (see Figures 1.7(b) and 1.8(b)) and of HH-polarized C-band RADARSAT-2 ultrafine data with a pixel spacing of 1.56 m (see Figures 1.7(c) and 1.8(c)). The acquisition dates of the three images in the series were a few days apart from one another. They correspond to two different sites in the Port-au-Prince area, which are shown in Figures 1.7 and 1.8 and are related to 1000×1000 and 2400×600 pixel grids at the finest resolution, respectively. The main classes in the two scenes are the same as in the previous section. Training and test samples associated with the two sites and annotated by an expert photointerpreter were used to train the second proposed method and to quantitatively measure its performance. The pixel grid at a resolution of 0.5 m of the Pléiades image was used as the reference finest resolution, and the RADARSAT-2 image was slightly resampled to a pixel spacing of $4 \cdot 0.5 = 2$ m in order to match the power-of-2 structure associated with the quad-tree (see also Figure 1.5). Antialiasing filtering was applied within this minor downsampling from 1.56 to 2 m, which is expected to have a negligible impact on the classification output, since the resolution ratio between the original and resampled images is close to 1.

In principle, the second proposed method can be applied in two distinct ways that differ in the ordering of the two SAR data sources in the two quad-trees, i.e. the COSMO-SkyMed image in the first quad-tree and the RADARSAT-2 image in the second one or vice versa. Preliminary experiments, which we omit for brevity, indicated that this choice of order did not have relevant impact on the output classification map.

Quite accurate performance was obtained on the test samples by the proposed method in the case of the multimission, multifrequency and multiresolution fusion task addressed in the present experiment (see Table 1.2). The maps obtained from the classification of the compound COSMO-SkyMed/RADARSAT-2/Pléiades time series of the two sites also exhibited remarkable spatial regularity (see Figures 1.7(g) and 1.8(g)). In this experiment, rather low accuracy was also achieved in the case of the "containers" class, again because of its overlapping with the "urban" class in the multisensor feature space.

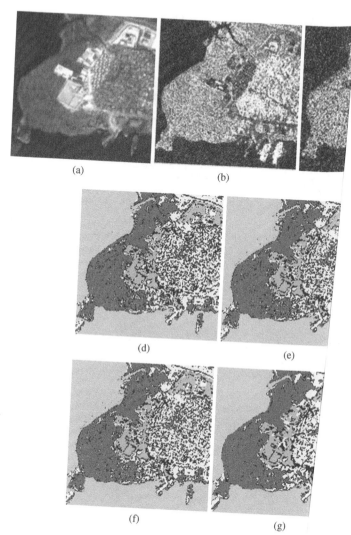

(a)   (b)

(d)   (e)

(f)   (g)

Figure 1.7. *Second proposed method – first test site. (a) Pléia Airbus DS), (b) COSMO-SkyMed (©ASI 2011) and (c) RAL images of the input series. The SAR images are shown after The R-band of the optical image is displayed. Classification ma with (d) only Pléiades data, (e) Pléiades and COSMO-SkyMe RADARSAT-2 data and (g) the proposed technique with all da Color legend: water☐ urban☐ vegetation■ bare soil■ For a color version of this figure, see www.iste.co.uk/atto/cha*

		Class-wise accuracies			Overall
	Water	Urban	Vegetation	Bare soil	Containers	accuracy
Pléiades only	100%	61.66%	81.69%	82.82%	56.72%	76.57%
Pléiades and CS	100%	44.32%	83.54%	74.75%	49.12%	70.34%
Pléiades and RS	92.56%	44.85%	79.85%	78.62%	42.15%	67.60%
Proposed method	90.79%	91.45%	82.59%	81.02%	54.85%	80.14%

Table 1.2. *Second proposed method: classification accuracies on the test set of the time series composed of Pléiades, COSMO-SkyMed (CS) and RADARSAT-2 (RS) images*

In order to explore the capability of the technique to benefit from the synergy of the VNIR optical, X-band radar and C-band radar imagery in the input series in more detail, the aforementioned results were compared to those achieved when (i) only the Pléiades data were used for classification or (ii) the Pléiades data were used in conjunction with only one of the two SAR images (see Table 1.2 and Figures 1.7 and 1.8(d)–(f)). In all such cases, the same classification scheme based on quad-trees, MPM and FMM, as in the proposed method, was applied. We omit the results obtained when only the two SAR images in the series were used because they corresponded to low accuracy values – an expected result in the case of the classification of the aforementioned classes solely with a short series of two SAR images.

The results in Table 1.2 confirm that jointly exploiting all three satellite data sources made it possible to remarkably achieve higher accuracies than when only a subset of these sources was used. When only the Pléiades image was employed, the "water", "vegetation" and "bare soil" classes were discriminated quite accurately but the "urban" class was not. When the second proposed method was applied to these VNIR data, together with both the COSMO-SkyMed and the RADARSAT-2 data, the enhancement in the discrimination of the "urban" class was approximately +30%. Furthermore, in this case, the results were more accurate than those generated by jointly using the Pléiades image along with only one of the two SAR images in the series. This scenario suggests the capability of the second proposed method to benefit from a multimission time series, including multifrequency and multiresolution imagery from current satellite instruments at very high spatial resolution. A drawback in the results of the proposed algorithm was the lower accuracy for the "water" class, compared to when only the Pléiades data or Pléiades and COSMO-SkyMed imagery were employed. The "water" class exhibits a significant texture in the RADARSAT-2 image (see Figure 1.7(c)), and the proposed algorithm does not involve any texture analysis component. The impact of this issue is limited, as the "water" class is discriminated by the proposed algorithm with an accuracy of around 91%. However, extending the method by integrating texture extraction appears to be a promising possible generalization.

1.4. Conclusion

In this chapter, the problem of the generation of a classification map from an input time series composed of multisensor multiresolution remote sensing· images has been discussed. First, the related literature in the area of remote sensing data fusion has been reviewed. Then, an advanced approach based on multiple quad-trees in cascade has been described. It derives from the multisensor generalization of a previous technique focused on the time series of single-sensor data, and addresses the challenging problem of multisensor, multifrequency and multiresolution fusion for classification purposes.

In the framework of this approach, two algorithms have been developed for two different multimodal fusion objectives. In the first one, the general task of jointly classifying a time series of multisensor multiresolution imagery is considered. In the second one, the focus is on the special case of the fusion of multimission data acquired by COSMO-SkyMed, RADARSAT-2 and Pléiades. In the case of both techniques, the fusion task is formalized in the framework of hierarchical probabilistic graphical models – most remarkably hierarchical MRF on cascaded quad-trees. Inference and parameter estimation are addressed through the maximum posterior mode criterion and FMM, respectively.

Examples of experimental results provided by the two proposed algorithms have been shown with regard to high- or very-high-resolution time series associated with case studies in Port-au-Prince, Haiti. The results have suggested that the described algorithms successfully benefit from the data sources in the input multisensor time series, improving the classification result, compared to those obtained using single-mission, single-scale or previous methods in terms of classification accuracy, computation time or spatial regularity.

A major property of the proposed hierarchical Markovian framework is its flexibility. The graphical architecture associated with multiple quad-trees in cascade allows the incorporation of input image sources associated with different sensors, acquisition times and spatial resolutions – jointly. Relevant extensions of this framework may involve the combination with spatial–contextual models within each layer of the quad-trees, or with the intrinsically multiscale structure of CNN (Goodfellow et al. 2016).

1.5. Acknowledgments

The authors would like to thank the Italian Space Agency (ASI), the French Space Agency (CNES) and the Canadian Space Agency (CSA) for providing COSMO-SkyMed, Pléiades and RADARSAT-2 data, respectively. The COSMO-SkyMed and RADARSAT-2 images were procured in the context of the SOAR-ASI 5245 project, framed within the joint ASI-CSA announcement of opportunity.

1.6. References

ALEjaily, A., El Rube, I., Mangoud, M. (2008). Fusion of remote sensing images using contourlet transform. *Innovations and Advanced Techniques in Systems, Computing Sciences and Software Engineering*, pp. 213–218.

Basseville, M., Benveniste, A., Willsky, A. (1992a). Multiscale autoregressive processes I. Schur–Levinson parametrizations. *IEEE Transactions on Signal Processing*, 40(8), 1915–1934.

Basseville, M., Benveniste, A., Willsky, A. (1992b). Multiscale autoregressive processes II. Lattice structures for whitening and modeling. *IEEE Transactions on Signal Processing*, 40(8), 1935–1954.

Benedetti, P., Ienco, D., Gaetano, R., Ose, K., Pensa, R.G., Dupuy, S. (2018). M3fusion: A deep learning architecture for multiscale multimodal multitemporal satellite data fusion. *IEEE Journal of Selected Topics in Applied Earth Observations and Remote Sensing*, 11(12), 4939–4949.

Benz, U. (1999). Supervised fuzzy analysis of single and multichannel SAR data. *IEEE Transactions on Geoscience and Remote Sensing*, 37(2), 1023–1037.

Berthod, M., Kato, Z., Yu, S., Zerubia, J. (1996). Bayesian image classification using Markov random fields. *Image and Vision Computing*, 14(4), 285–295.

Bouman, C. (1991). A multiscale image model for Bayesian image segmentation. Thesis, Purdue University, School of Electrical Engineering.

Brunner, D., Lemoine, G., Bruzzone, L. (2010). Earthquake damage assessment of buildings using VHR optical and SAR imagery. *IEEE Transactions on Geoscience and Remote Sensing*, 48(5), 2403–2420.

Bruzzone, L., Prieto, D.F., Serpico, S. (1999). A neural-statistical approach to multitemporal and multisource remote-sensing image classification. *IEEE Transactions on Geoscience and Remote Sensing*, 37(3), 1350–1359.

Burt, P. (1984). *The Pyramid as a Structure for Efficient Computation*. Springer, Berlin, Heidelberg.

Carvalho, M., Le Saux, B., Trouvé-Peloux, P., Champagnat, F., Almansa, A. (2019). Multitask learning of height and semantics from aerial images. *IEEE Geoscience and Remote Sensing Letters*, pp. 1391–1395.

Celeux, G., Chauveau, D., Diebolt, J. (1996). Stochastic versions of the EM algorithm: An experimental study in the mixture case. *Journal of Statistical Computation and Simulation*, 55(4), 287–314.

Chardin, A. (2000). Modèles énergétiques hiérarchiques pour la résolution des problèmes inverses en analyse d'images: application à la télédétection. PhD Thesis, University of Rennes 1, France.

Chen, Y., Li, C., Ghamisi, P., Jia, X., Gu, Y. (2017). Deep fusion of remote sensing data for accurate classification. *IEEE Geoscience and Remote Sensing Letters*, 14(8), 1253–1257.

Cheng, X., Zheng, Y., Zhang, J., Yang, Z. (2020). Multi-task multi-source deep correlation filter for remote sensing data fusion. *IEEE Journal of Selected Topics in Applied Earth Observations and Remote Sensing*, 13, 3723–3734.

Chibani, Y. and Houacine, A. (2003). Redundant versus orthogonal wavelet decomposition for multisensor image fusion. *Pattern Recognition*, 36(4), 879–887.

Choi, M., Kim, R., Nam, M.-R., Kim, H. (2005). Fusion of multispectral and panchromatic satellite images using the curvelet transform. *IEEE Geoscience and Remote Sensing Letters*, 2(2), 136–140.

Demirel, H. and Anbarjafari, G. (2010). Satellite image resolution enhancement using complex wavelet transform. *IEEE Geoscience and Remote Sensing Letters*, 7(1), 123–126.

Dousset, B. and Gourmelon, F. (2003). Satellite multi-sensor data analysis of urban surface temperatures and landcover. *ISPRS Journal of Photogrammetry and Remote Sensing*, 58(1), 43–54.

Forster, B., Van De Ville, D., Berent, J., Sage, D., Unser, M. (2004). Complex wavelets for extended depth-of-field: A new method for the fusion of multichannel microscopy images. *Microscopy Research and Technique*, 65(1–2), 33–42.

Fukunaga, K. (2013). *Introduction to Statistical Pattern Recognition*. Academic Press, Cambridge, MA.

Gamba, P., Lisini, G., Tomás, L., Almeida, C., Fonseca, L. (2011). Joint VHR-LIDAR classification framework in urban areas using *a priori* knowledge and post processing shape optimization. *IEEE Urban Remote Sensing Event (JURSE)*, pp. 93–96.

Ghamisi, P., Höfle, B., Zhu, X.X. (2016). Hyperspectral and LiDAR data fusion using extinction profiles and deep convolutional neural network. *IEEE Journal of Selected Topics in Applied Earth Observations and Remote Sensing*, 10(6), 3011–3024.

Gómez-Chova, L., Tuia, D., Moser, G., Camps-Valls, G. (2015). Multimodal classification of remote sensing images: A review and future directions. *Proceedings of the IEEE*, 103(9), 1560–1584.

Goodfellow, I., Bengio, Y., Courville, A. (2016). *Deep Learning*. MIT Press, Cambridge, MA.

Graffigne, C., Heitz, F., Perez, P., Preteux, F., Sigelle, M., Zerubia, J. (1995). Hierarchical Markov random field models applied to image analysis: A review. *International Symposium on Optical Science, Engineering, and Instrumentation (SPIE)*, International Society for Optics and Photonics, pp. 2–17.

Hall, D. and Llinas, J. (2001). *Multisensor Data Fusion*. CRC Press, Boca Raton, FL.

Hedhli, I., Moser, G., Zerubia, J., Serpico, S. (2014). New cascade model for hierarchical joint classification of multitemporal, multiresolution and multisensor remote sensing data. *IEEE International Conference on Image Processing (ICIP)*.

Hedhli, I., Moser, G., Serpico, S., Zerubia, J. (2015). New hierarchical joint classification method of SAR-optical multiresolution remote sensing data. *IEEE European Signal Processing Conference*.

Hedhli, I., Moser, G., Zerubia, J., Serpico, S.B. (2016). A new cascade model for the hierarchical joint classification of multitemporal and multiresolution remote sensing data. *IEEE Transactions on Geoscience and Remote Sensing*, 54(11), 6333–6348.

Huang, B. and Song, H. (2012). Spatiotemporal reflectance fusion via sparse representation. *IEEE Transactions on Geoscience and Remote Sensing*, 50(10), 3707–3716.

Iqbal, M., Ghafoor, A., Siddiqui, A. (2013). Satellite image resolution enhancement using dual-tree complex wavelet transform and nonlocal means. *IEEE Geoscience and Remote Sensing Letters*, 10(3), 451–455.

Kato, Z. and Zerubia, J. (2012). *Markov Random Fields in Image Segmentation*. Now Publishers Inc, Hanover, MA.

Krylov, V., Moser, G., Serpico, S., Zerubia, J. (2013). On the method of logarithmic cumulants for parametric probability density function estimation. *IEEE Transactions on Image Processing*, 22(10), 3791–3806.

Laferté, J.-M., Pérez, P., Heitz, F. (2000). Discrete Markov image modeling and inference on the quadtree. *IEEE Transactions on Image Processing*, 9(3), 390–404.

Landgrebe, D. (2003). *Signal Theory Methods in Multispectral Remote Sensing*, vol. 29. John Wiley & Sons, Hoboken, NJ.

Li, S. (2009). *Markov Random Field Modeling in Image Analysis*. Springer Science & Business Media, Berlin, Heidelberg.

Li, H., Manjunath, B., Mitra, S. (1995). Multisensor image fusion using the wavelet transform. *Graphical Models and Image Processing*, 57(3), 235–245.

Li, H.-C., Hong, W., Wu, Y.-R., Fan, P.-Z. (2011). On the empirical-statistical modeling of SAR images with generalized Gamma distribution. *IEEE Journal of Selected Topics in Signal Processing*, 5(3), 386–397.

Mallat, S. (2008). *A Wavelet Tour of Signal Processing*, 3rd edition. Academic Press, Cambridge, MA.

Mas, J. and Flores, J. (2008). The application of artificial neural networks to the analysis of remotely sensed data. *International Journal of Remote Sensing*, 29(3), 617–663.

Minh, D.H.T., Ienco, D., Gaetano, R., Lalande, N., Ndikumana, E., Osman, F., Maurel, P. (2018). Deep recurrent neural networks for winter vegetation quality mapping via multitemporal SAR sentinel-1. *IEEE Geoscience and Remote Sensing Letters*, 15(3), 464–468.

Moser, G. and Serpico, S. (2009). Unsupervised change detection from multichannel SAR data by Markovian data fusion. *IEEE Transactions on Geoscience and Remote Sensing*, 47(7), 2114–2128.

Muñoz-Marí, J., Bovolo, F., Gómez-Chova, L., Bruzzone, L., Camp-Valls, G. (2010). Semisupervised one-class support vector machines for classification of remote sensing data. *IEEE Transactions on Geoscience and Remote Sensing*, 48(8), 3188–3197.

Nelson, J.D.B., Gibberd, A.J., Nafornita, C., Kingsbury, N. (2018). The locally stationary dual-tree complex wavelet model. *Statistics and Computing*, 28(6), 1139–1154.

Nencini, F., Garzelli, A., Baronti, S., Alparone, L. (2007). Remote sensing image fusion using the curvelet transform. *Information Fusion*, 8(2), 143–156.

Nguyen, N., Nasrabadi, N., Tran, T. (2011). Robust multi-sensor classification via joint sparse representation. *International Conference on Information Fusion*.

Pan, S., Wu, J., Zhu, X., Zhang, C., Philip, S.Y. (2015). Joint structure feature exploration and regularization for multi-task graph classification. *IEEE Transactions on Knowledge and Data Engineering*, 28(3), 715–728.

Pérez, P. (1993). Champs markoviens et analyse multirésolution de l'image : application à l'analyse du mouvement. PhD Thesis, University of Rennes 1, France.

Piella, G. (2003). Adaptive wavelets and their applications to image fusion and compression. Thesis, PhD Thesis, University of Amsterdam.

Pohl, C. and van Genderen, J. (1998). Review article – Multisensor image fusion in remote sensing: Concepts, methods and applications. *International Journal of Remote Sensing*, 19(5), 823–854.

Pohl, C. and van Genderen, J. (2014). Remote sensing image fusion: An update in the context of digital earth. *International Journal of Digital Earth*, 7(2), 158–172.

Prendes, J. (2015). New statistical modeling of multi-sensor images with application to change detection. Thesis, PhD Thesis, Université Paris-Sud, France.

Roberts, J., van Aardt, J., Ahmed, F. (2008). Assessment of image fusion procedures using entropy, image quality, and multispectral classification. *Journal of Applied Remote Sensing*, 2(1), 023522 [Online]. Available at: https://doi.org/10.1117/1.2945910.

Rockinger, O. (1996). Pixel-level fusion of image sequences using wavelet frames. *Proceedings of the 16th Leeds Applied Shape Research Workshop*, Leeds University Press, Citeseer.

Serpico, S., Dellepiane, S., Boni, G., Moser, G., Angiati, E., Rudari, R. (2012). Information extraction from remote sensing images for flood monitoring and damage evaluation. *Proceedings of the IEEE*, 100(10), 2946–2970.

Shah, V., Younan, N., King, R. (2008). An efficient pan-sharpening method via a combined adaptive PCA approach and contourlets. *IEEE Transactions on Geoscience and Remote Sensing*, 46(5), 1323–1335.

Storvik, B., Storvik, G., Fjortoft, R. (2009). On the combination of multisensor data using meta-Gaussian distributions. *IEEE Transactions on Geoscience and Remote Sensing*, 47(7), 2372–2379.

Stroppiana, D., Azar, R., Calo, F., Pepe, A., Imperatore, P., Boschetti, M., Silva, J., Brivio, P., Lanari, R. (2015). Remote sensing of burned area: A fuzzy-based framework for joint processing of optical and microwave data. *IEEE Geoscience and Remote Sensing Symposium (IGARSS)*, pp. 1409–1412.

Ulaby, F. and Long, D.G. (2015). *Microwave Radar and Radiometric Remote Sensing*. Artech House, Boston, MA.

Vivone, G., Alparone, L., Chanussot, J., Dalla Mura, M., Garzelli, A., Licciardi, G., Restaino, R., Wald, L. (2015). A critical comparison among pansharpening algorithms. *IEEE Transactions on Geoscience and Remote Sensing*, 53(5), 2565–2586.

Voisin, A. (2012). Classification supervisée d'images d'observation de la Terre à haute résolution par utilisation de méthodes markoviennes. Thesis, PhD Thesis, University of Nice Sophia Antipolis, France.

Voisin, A., Krylov, V., Moser, G., Serpico, S., Zerubia, J. (2012). Multichannel hierarchical image classification using multivariate copulas. *IS&T/SPIE Electronic Imaging*, International Society for Optics and Photonics, Bellingham, WN.

Voisin, A., Krylov, V., Moser, G., Serpico, S., Zerubia, J. (2014). Supervised classification of multi-sensor and multi-resolution remote sensing images with a hierarchical copula-based approach. *IEEE Transactions on Geoscience and Remote Sensing*, 52(6), 3346–3358.

Wald, L. (1999). Some terms of reference in data fusion. *IEEE Transactions on Geoscience and Remote Sensing*, 37(3), 1190–1193.

Waltz, E. and Llinas, J. (1990). *Multisensor Data Fusion*, vol. 685. Artech House, Boston, MA.

Wang, D. and Liang, S. (2014). Improving LAI mapping by integrating MODIS and CYCLOPES LAI products using optimal interpolation. *IEEE Journal of Selected Topics in Applied Earth Observations and Remote Sensing*, 7(2), 445–457.

Waske, B. and van der Linden, S. (2008). Classifying multilevel imagery from SAR and optical sensors by decision fusion. *IEEE Transactions on Geoscience and Remote Sensing*, 46(5), 1457–1466.

Willsky, A. (2002). Multiresolution Markov models for signal and image processing. *Proceedings of the IEEE*, 90(8), 1396–1458.

Yang, B., Li, S., Sun, F. (2007). Image fusion using nonsubsampled contourlet transform. *IEEE International Conference on Image and Graphics*, pp. 719–724.

Zhang, Y. and Hong, G. (2005). An IHS and wavelet integrated approach to improve pan-sharpening visual quality of natural colour IKONOS and QuickBird images. *Information Fusion*, 6(3), 225–234.

Zhang, G. and Kingsbury, N. (2015). Variational Bayesian image restoration with group-sparse modeling of wavelet coefficients. *Digital Signal Processing: A Review Journal*, 47, 157–168.

2

Pixel-based Classification Techniques for Satellite Image Time Series

Charlotte PELLETIER[1] and Silvia VALERO[2]

[1] *IRISA Laboratory UMR 6074, Université Bretagne Sud, Lorient, France*
[2] *CESBIO Laboratory UMR 5126, University of Toulouse, France*

2.1. Introduction

Satellite image time series have proven to be an effective tool for monitoring vegetation dynamics, resources and the effects of climate change. These multitemporal data offer frequent and consistent information on what the Earth's land cover looks like. Recent advances in remote sensing technology have resulted in the acquisition of new satellite image time series (SITS) rendered in high spatial, spectral and temporal resolution. New Earth Observation (EO) missions, such as Landsat-8 or Sentinel-1 and -2, acquire time series that differ significantly from previous datasets. Indeed, their analysis is a Big Data challenge due to the quantity of data, for example, 12 TB per day for the European Sentinel programme.

To automatically extract information about the biophysical cover of the Earth's surface (namely land cover), machine learning and more specifically supervised learning, is the most significant approach used. When applied to multitemporal remote sensing data, its goal is to associate a target label with each temporal profile pixel.

Change Detection and Image Time Series Analysis 2,
coordinated by Abdourrahmane M. ATTO, Francesca BOVOLO and Lorenzo BRUZZONE.
© ISTE Ltd 2021.

Supervised classifiers use *a priori* information about the data to train a model that is able to extract and recognize relevant features. The trained model is then used to label each pixel in the image scene. The classification of a remote sensing scene differs from a classical classification computer vision task, which aims to categorize all pixels in an image into a single class.

The high-dimensional spectro-spatio-temporal representation of the SITS data opens up new challenges and problems for supervised classification algorithms. Example constraints are the irregular temporal sampling because of the presence of artifacts (clouds, cloud shadows or saturated pixels) and the presence of mixed pixels that are due to the medium spatial resolution of these datasets.

Other crucial prerequisites for successfully training a classification model are the selection of a suitable classification algorithm, as well as the availability of quality and representative labeled training samples. A significant quantity of labeled samples is also a key requirement for the classification of these high-dimensional datasets.

Furthermore, applying a supervised classification algorithm requires the determination of a suitable input feature representation. Traditionally, human knowledge has been used to supervise the feature engineering step, which extracts and selects relevant features from the data. This manual feature engineering process and the construction of a large high-quality reference dataset are usually the two most time-consuming tasks for supervised classification tasks.

By contrast, in the last few years, promising classification strategies based on deep learning automatically generated important features. The use of deep learning approaches saves feature engineering costs, but in return it requires important expertise in network architecture engineering. It also needs a larger amount of labeled data to train the models, which is not always available in remote sensing classification applications.

This chapter addresses the above-mentioned key issues in the classification of SITS by presenting an overview of supervised classification algorithms proposed in the literature. It focuses on pixel-wise methods without considering the spatial context.

We begin by introducing some fundamentals about supervised classification in the context of remote sensing applications. Section 2.2 also includes a description of some key data preprocessing steps and the classical evaluation procedure based on the confusion matrix. Section 2.3 overviews three well-established classification algorithms massively used for SITS classification (Gómez *et al.* 2016): support vector machines, random forests and k-nearest neighbors. Section 2.4 presents several classification approaches proposing low-dimensional temporal feature representations of EO time series. We describe the phenological temporal features extracted from vegetation indices (Valero *et al.* 2016), bag-of-words approaches (Bailly *et al.* 2016) and shapelet methods. Finally, section 2.5 details the main deep learning networks recently used for the classification of EO time series, i.e., temporal convolutional neural networks (Pelletier *et al.* 2019; Zhong *et al.* 2019) and recurrent neural networks (and their variants) (Ienco *et al.* 2017; Rußwurm and Körner 2017).

2.2. Basic concepts in supervised remote sensing classification

The goal of supervised learning is for the algorithm to automatically learn rules to predict the labels of new samples. The set of rules is learned from reference data, which is an essential component for developing robust supervised machine learning algorithms. Reference data is described by a feature vector extracted from the satellite data and a reference label. The reference label denotes the class to be predicted.

The quality of the reference dataset is vital for supervised classifiers, and even the most powerful algorithms can be rendered useless when they use inadequate, inaccurate or irrelevant data. Accordingly, the preparation of reference data is one of the most essential steps in supervised classification. The amount and the quality of available reference data in remote sensing represent important constraints for the choice of an appropriate classification scheme (input data, classifier, nomenclature, etc.). In general, the quality of such a dataset depends on the quality of the reference labels and the quality of features describing the data.

In this section, we will overview how to prepare the satellite and reference datasets. Then, we will present some key considerations for training supervised classification algorithms. Finally, we will describe how to evaluate a classification result.

2.2.1. *Preparing data before it is fed into classification algorithms*

Data preparation should result in an accurate reference dataset, which is ready to be used by a machine learning algorithm to uncover insights and/or make predictions. Challenging and time-consuming, this task involves the preparation of satellite data and reference labels as detailed in the following.

2.2.1.1. *Satellite data*

Preparing satellite data implies costly preprocessing operations. The goal of this preparation is to correct for sensor- and platform-specific distortions of data. The set of preparation tasks is especially important for the analysis of multitemporal images, since satellite images composing SITS are acquired on different time periods. This requires special attention because each preparation procedure further alters the data from their original values and can thus increase the potential to introduce errors. Optical satellite data preprocessing involves geometric and radiometric calibration corrections, whereas radar data requires speckle filtering.

One of the most popular preprocessing steps is the imputation of missing values. SITS data indeed have irregular temporal sampling introduced by cloud cover, acquisitions from different orbit tracks and/or sensor geometry artifacts. In addition, optical images from several geographical areas are affected differently by clouds and thus present various irregular temporal samplings. Most of the classification algorithms require that all input samples have the same feature vector dimension, but they do not efficiently deal with missing values themselves. The most common way to handle missing values consists of filling-in approximations. Those methods are called "gap filling" or "imputation" methods. Although different techniques are proposed in the literature, classical weighted linear interpolation is the most used one for large-scale studies (Inglada *et al.* 2015). Data normalization is another important preprocessing step needed by most of the algorithms to align all features on the same scale. This scaling procedure consists of standardizing the range of each feature independently (Pelletier *et al.* 2019, section 3.3.3).

Once preprocessing is completed, the second most important preparation step is the transformation of the preprocessed data into a feature representation that is as suitable as possible for learning.

The SITS data offers a natural time-based representation of the data, which is used in most classification tasks. The use of all available images helps classification algorithms to handle high class intra-variability, i.e. classes with different modes, and also low class inter-variability, i.e. two classes that have strong similarity. On the contrary, the use of few satellite images might prevent the recognition of different classes that have a similar appearance at a given time. For example, using only images acquired during summer makes the recognition of winter crops impossible. Furthermore, the selection of a subset of images is not a straightforward task and it might result in a loss of valuable information.

For this reason, a suitable feature representation is the raw data. The classification algorithms are thus fed with all of the satellite images contained in the sequence. Another possible representation can be obtained by computing new features. They are used to either enrich the raw data representation or create a new feature representation. On EO data, these additional features can be divided into three main categories: (1) spectral features that combine information from different spectral bands, for example, the normalized difference vegetation index (NDVI) for optical images (Mróz and Sobieraj 2004; Silleos *et al.* 2006) or the ratios of two polarimetries for radar images; (2) spatial features that use pixel neighborhood, for example, geometry, texture, morphological operations, attribute profiles (Haralick 1979; Trias-Sanz 2006; Blaschke 2010; Ghamisi *et al.* 2014) and (3) temporal features (Bailly *et al.* 2016; Valero *et al.* 2016).

In remote sensing tasks, the extraction of feature representations from time series has been tackled in two opposite ways: (1) feature engineering and (2) feature learning. Feature engineering is the process of precomputing manually handcrafted features by using domain knowledge. It creates new useful features by either combining existing features or adding external features extracted from auxiliary data. On the contrary, feature learning relies on the use of learning methods to automatically discover important features from the data. An example of feature learning are deep learning algorithms where feature extraction is embedded in the architecture network (see section 2.5).

2.2.1.2. *Reference labels*

One of the major bottlenecks for supervised algorithms is the collection of a substantial number of high-quality reference label data. In remote sensing, reference labels are typically extracted from ground field campaigns or from aerial photography interpretation. These manual labeling approaches are not feasible to obtain large reference datasets required by the most efficient algorithms. Indeed, manual intervention is expensive and requires domain expertise, which results in a limited number of labeled data.

To increase the quantity of labeled data, we can extract reference labels from large governmental databases, existing past land cover maps or crowd-sourcing systems. However, they usually contain numerous labeling issues due to misregistration, update delay or land cover complexity. This results in the presence of class label noise, i.e. a wrong label assignment, in the reference data. Correct labeling is extremely important when applying supervised learning algorithms, as the presence of incorrectly labeled data will have a negative impact on the training outcome (Pelletier *et al.* 2017). Accordingly, a data cleaning process to reduce class label noise can improve training performance.

2.2.1.3. *Split procedure into training, testing and validation datasets*

Traditionally, reference data is divided into three disjoint sets: training, validation and testing. Training data is used to tune the parameters of classifier models, which learn discriminative patterns from input data and make predictions for new data. The validation set is used to tune model hyperparameters, which are all user-defined parameters that can be set arbitrarily before starting the training step. Finally, testing data is used to evaluate the accuracy and efficiency of the trained model by predicting new unlabeled examples.

Ideally, training, validation and testing data belong to disjoint sets in order to ensure that there is no bias in reported accuracy. However, the scarcity of labeled samples in remote sensing applications often prevents obtaining three independent datasets with a sufficient number of samples. In this situation, it is possible to omit the validation set. The training dataset then serves for training and tuning the model hyperparameters by using a resampling procedure named cross-validation. For example, the best known approach, the k-fold cross-validation, divides training instances into k-independent partitions. Then, k models are recursively trained using $k - 1$ partitions for different hyperparameter values and evaluated on the remaining partition. The hyperparameter configuration that obtained the highest average performance is stored to train a final model with the whole training dataset.

When splitting the reference dataset into disjoint sets, the proportion of each data subset can be driven by many factors, including the size of the original dataset. There are also various strategies that can be used to split the data into different subsets. The most common approach is the stratified random sampling procedure, where samples are randomly selected within each class. This approach ensures that the class frequency distribution is approximately equal within the three sets. Ideally, testing data is expected to preserve the same distribution as the training data.

When working with reference data created from labeled polygons, it is important to pay attention to not include the samples coming from a same polygon in the same subset. The high correlation of these samples can indeed introduce a bias and cover some overfitting issues. To mitigate this issue, each polygon can be randomly assigned to one subset. Figure 2.1(b) depicts this solution, where each color (green, yellow and red) corresponds to one subset. We refer to this strategy as a split at the polygon level. Another solution is to split the study area into independent areas. Each area is then associated with the training, validation or testing subsets. Figure 2.1(c) shows this solution by using a grid. There is a space between the grid cells to ensure that a polygon is not cut between several cells. This solution is preferred when exploiting both temporal and spatial structures of the SITS data (Rußwurm and Körner 2018).

(a) labeled dataset   (b) split at random at the   (c) grid split
                                    polygon level

Figure 2.1. *Possible split procedures in training (in green), validation (in yellow) and testing (in red) sets. For a color version of this figure, see www.iste.co.uk/atto/change2.zip*

In remote sensing applications, it is common to work with class imbalanced datasets, which complicates the recognition of the minority classes. Moreover, the class distribution of the testing data will directly impact some accuracy metrics, as will be shown in section 2.2.3. To increase the importance of minority classes, some applications require balancing the number of samples for each class. In order to reduce the impact of class imbalance problems, the solutions are to limit the number of samples for each class or to slightly modify the classification algorithms (e.g. changing the cost function used in deep learning algorithms).

2.2.2. *Key considerations when training supervised classifiers*

Remote sensing applications usually involve complex classification problems requiring the use of a large amount of training samples. However, the quality of the training data, as well as the choice of input features, is in many instances substantially more important than the quantity.

2.2.2.1. *Quality of training data*

Getting sufficient high-quality training data is one of the biggest challenges of remote sensing applications. The quality of the training dataset is directly related to the representativeness and diversity of the data. Training data should be an accurate representation of the population, otherwise the lack of representativeness often results in models not generalizing properly on the dataset that they are not trained on. For example, a scarce labeled dataset located in a specific geographic area may lack the landscape variability that is required to train an accurate classifier model on a larger area.

To increase the chances of building reliable models, training data must contain discriminative and diverse information capturing the problem's complexity. Ideally, training data must be a good approximation of the true sample distribution. When reference labels are described by polygons, the diversity constraint should not be forgotten. Indeed, labeled samples only corresponding to correlated pure pixels inside a polygon will have a very low diversity, which may result in poor classification results for polygon edges.

A strategy to increase the diversity of the training dataset is to increase the number of samples or polygons. However, large training sets often include redundant, non-representative or noisy samples. There is a trade-off between the quantity and quality of training samples, which has a direct influence on the classifier performance.

2.2.2.2. *The curse of dimensionality*

Features used as input data in the classification problem directly influence the trained models and their corresponding results. Suitable and discriminative features achieve more flexible and less complex trained models, which usually imply better results. Consequently, determining which features are useful for the classification problem is an important step that usually requires expert knowledge.

The raw intensity image values of SITS acquired at high temporal resolution provide a huge cube of features. The classification of this datacube involves classification problems with high-dimensional spaces. Typically, a high feature dimension may induce the Hughes phenomenon, also known as the curse of dimensionality. This phenomenon implies that at some point, the accuracy of classification algorithms tends to deteriorate in high-dimensional spaces, due to a limitation in the number of training samples.

Accordingly, feature and date selection methodologies have been studied in SITS classification applications. This selection of relevant features is even more important when the number of training samples is low. Featuring engineering strategies have also been proposed to study how spectral, spatial or temporal features could be incorporated as input data in classification problems. However, the incorporation of additional features does not always increase the classification performance (Pelletier *et al.* 2016). One risk is to end up with too many features adding complexity to the problem and not generalizing well.

In practice, two further constraints must be considered for the selection of the number of input features: the quantity of training samples used during the learning stage and the classifier choice.

2.2.2.3. *How much training data do I need?*

The classical trade-off between quality and quantity also exists in remote sensing applications. Accordingly, "How much training data do I need?" is one of the most common questions when using supervised classifiers. There is no magical solution to answer this question. Traditionally, the amount of training data needed to train a model depends on the complexity of the problem to be solved and on the chosen classification algorithm. Information about the number of classes, input features or model parameters helps to estimate the required number of samples.

In general, models trained on large diverse datasets generalize better on unseen data and avoid the above-mentioned curse of dimensionality. Furthermore, large training datasets help prevent the classical overfitting problem described in section 2.2.2.4.

When reference data comes from polygons, it is important to evaluate the quantity of reference data in terms of polygons rather than samples. As a polygon delineates a homogeneous area, the pixels composing a single polygon are highly correlated with similar spectral features. Accordingly, the use of training samples extracted from few polygons can lead to low variability description for a single class.

In order to measure how well a trained model generalizes, a solution is to evaluate how the model performs on different training and testing sets several times. If the prediction results have a high variance, it could indicate that the number of training samples is too low.

2.2.2.4. *Overfitting, underfitting and the bias-variance trade-off*

One of the main difficulties of the training step is to achieve the trade-off between a too simple and a too complex model. Ideally, a classification model should fit the training data well and be able to correctly predict the labels of new samples unused during the training step. However, it is possible to learn a model that perfectly fits the training data without being able to generalize. The underlying issue is known as the bias-variance trade-off.

The bias measures how close, on average over several different training sets, the predicted values are to their reference labels. Models with high bias pay little attention to the training data and oversimplify the model, usually resulting in poor results. This situation is known as underfitting. In contrast, models fitting the training data very well have low bias, which can result in models that only work well with training datasets.

The variance is a measure of how "stable" the predictive values are. Given small fluctuations in the training set, a model with low variance will tend to produce low varying performances.

Ideally, the training stage aims to minimize both the bias and variance of the model. However, decreasing the bias increases the variance of the models. Models with high variance pay a lot of attention to training data and do not generalize on data that they have not encountered before. The situation where the model fits the data that it has been trained on perfectly and performs poorly on new data is known as overfitting. The risk of overfitting is high when the training dataset contains a relatively small number of samples.

In most situations, increasing the amount of training data adds diversity and it reduces model generalization error. At the same time, it becomes increasingly difficult to adjust the model to each training sample when the training set grows.

2.2.3. *Performance evaluation of supervised classifiers*

A classification evaluation consists of quantifying the quality of a trained model by predicting the labels of unseen testing samples. The labels predicted by a trained model (Figure 2.2(b)) are then compared with the labels of the testing samples extracted from the reference data considered as ground truth data (Figure 2.2(a)).

The comparison of the model's predictions with the reference labels in the form of a contingency table is known as the confusion matrix. Figure 2.3 depicts the confusion matrix computed on the example in Figure 2.2. It provides a more detailed insight into the model's performance. In this double-entry table, the sum of each row represents the number of occurrences of a `real` class of the reference data and the sum of each column corresponds to the number of occurrences of the model's `predicted` class.

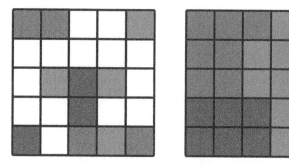

(a) Reference data   (b) Classification algorithm predictions

Figure 2.2. *(Right) A predicted classification map with three classes. (Left) The related ground truth from which the test samples are extracted. For a color version of this figure, see www.iste.co.uk/atto/change2.zip*

predicted

		2	1	0
real		0	3	1
		1	1	2

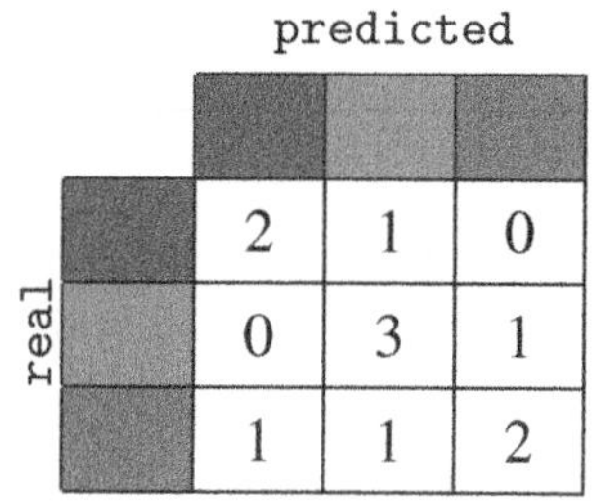

Figure 2.3. *Confusion matrix example. For a color version of this figure, see www.iste.co.uk/atto/change2.zip*

The diagonal elements represent the number of samples that have been correctly predicted by the classification algorithm (seven in the example). To avoid bias in the evaluation results, the reference dataset should be representative of the true sample distribution (Congalton and Green 2008).

To evaluate the performance of classification models, a set of metrics can be computed from the confusion matrix for binary and multiclass classification problems.

2.2.3.1. *Classical evaluation metrics*

Let us denote by C a confusion matrix computed for a classification problem with K classes:

real \ predicted	1	2	$\cdots$	$\cdots$	j	$\cdots$	K
1	c_{11}	c_{12}	$\cdots$	$\cdots$	c_{1j}	$\cdots$	c_{1K}
2	c_{21}	c_{22}	$\cdots$	$\cdots$	c_{2j}	$\cdots$	c_{2K}
$\vdots$	$\vdots$	$\vdots$	$\vdots$	$\vdots$	$\vdots$	$\vdots$	$\vdots$
i	c_{i1}	c_{i2}	$\cdots$	$\cdots$	c_{ij}	$\cdots$	c_{iK}
$\vdots$	$\vdots$	$\vdots$	$\vdots$	$\vdots$	$\vdots$	$\vdots$	$\vdots$
$\vdots$	$\vdots$	$\vdots$	$\vdots$	$\vdots$	$\vdots$	$\vdots$	$\vdots$
K	c_{K1}	c_{K2}	$\cdots$	$\cdots$	c_{Kj}	$\cdots$	c_{KK}

Each c_{ij} coefficient represents the number of test samples that belong to class i and are predicted as class j by the classification model.

Overall accuracy is the most simple measure that corresponds to the percentage of correctly classified test samples. This global measure can be directly computed by considering the trace of the confusion matrix:

$$OA = \frac{1}{N} \sum_{i=1}^{K} c_{ii}, \qquad [2.1]$$

where $N = \sum_{i=1}^{K} \sum_{j=1}^{K} c_{ij}$ is the total number of test samples.

The Kappa coefficient is probably the second most common global metric used by the remote sensing community:

$$\text{Kappa} = \frac{OA - p_h}{1 - p_h}, \qquad [2.2]$$

where $p_h = \frac{1}{N^2} \sum_{i=1}^{K} \left(\sum_{j=1}^{K} c_{ij} \right) \left(\sum_{j=1}^{K} c_{ji} \right)$ is the percentage of correct predictions attributed to randomness. Landis and Koch (1977) provide a scale for interpreting the Kappa coefficient as a function of its value. For example, a Kappa value above 0.81 corresponds to an "almost perfect" agreement between testing samples and predictions. There are several criticisms against the use of the Kappa: (1) it is highly correlated with overall accuracy (Stehman 1997; Liu *et al.* 2007), (2) it is highly dependent on class prevalence (as overall accuracy) (Foody 2020) and (3) it is difficult to interpret (Pontius Jr and Millones 2011).

Such global measures are often insufficient to perform a quality assessment of the predictions, particularly when the number of samples per class composing the testing dataset is imbalanced. These measures do not consider class distributions and classification costs.

To overcome this issue, per class measures are often used to complement the evaluation. For multiclass classification problems, the user's accuracy UA_i and the producer's accuracy PA_i of class i are computed as follows:

$$UA_i = \frac{c_{ii}}{\sum_{j=1}^{K} c_{ji}},$$
[2.3]

$$PA_i = \frac{c_{ii}}{\sum_{j=1}^{K} c_{ij}},$$
[2.4]

The class user's accuracy (also named precision) is the percentage of samples correctly predicted for this class, with respect to all of the predictions done for this class, whereas the class producer's accuracy (also named recall) is the percentage of reference data correctly predicted for this class. When a trade-off between the user's accuracy and producer's accuracy is desired, both metrics can be merged into one, namely a F-Score or F_1-measure, by computing the harmonic mean:

$$\text{F-score}_i = 2\frac{UA_i \times PA_i}{UA_i + PA_i}.$$
[2.5]

The evaluation metrics presented above provide an evaluation of the trained model, without considering the spatial organization of the data. In that case, the evaluation is biased towards the most frequent elements of the testing dataset. On the contrary, less importance is given to the less frequent elements of the reference that usually represent salient points or specific objects such as roads, rivers, hedges or crop edges in the scene. To perfect the evaluation, it is thus possible to also assess the quality of the classification map produced by the trained model. This spatial evaluation has two main goals: (1) ensuring the geometric quality of the predictions and (2) discovering regions with poor prediction performance (and further analyzing them). When abundant and evenly distributed reference data is available, spatial metrics such as (mean) Intersection over Union (IoU) can complete the evaluation. On the contrary, when only scarce reference data is available, unsupervised approaches, relying, for example, on an accurate position of the edges of produced objects, can be used to evaluate the ability of classification models to keep salient attributes (Derksen et al. 2019).

2.2.3.2. Evaluation of uncertainty in classification performances

Confidence intervals are a way of quantifying the uncertainty of the classifier predictions. The traditional confidence interval at 95% indicates that there is a 95% likelihood that the interval encompasses the true model accuracy.

Let us denote by $\overline{acc}$ the average accuracy (e.g. the average overall accuracy) computed for $nruns$ random train/test splits of the reference data, and by σ_{acc} the corresponding standard deviation. The confidence interval at $x\%$ can be expressed as follows:

$$\overline{acc} \pm t_{x\%}\frac{\sigma_{acc}}{\sqrt{nruns}},$$
[2.6]

where the value of $t_{x\%}$ depends on the value of x, as well as on the value of $nruns$. If the value of $nruns$ is small ($nruns \leqslant 25$), $t_{x\%}$ can be estimated by using Student's law; otherwise, we can assume that the classifier accuracy is normally distributed and the classical z value from a two-tailed statistic test can be used (*e.g.*, $t_{95\%} = z_{95\%} = 1.96$).

2.3. Traditional classification algorithms

The first classification methodologies proposed for EO time series were based on parametric classifiers. Classifiers such as maximum likelihood, Gaussian mixture models or discriminant analysis have been tested in the remote sensing literature (DeFries and Townshend 1994; Jia *et al.* 2014; Radoux *et al.* 2014). These approaches assume that the data comes from a specific distribution, for example, a normal distribution. The distribution assumption imposes fixed boundaries on decision functions of classifiers that might fail to take the intra-class variability of each class into account (Hubert-Moy *et al.* 2001).

This limitation explains why non-parametric approaches are nowadays favored for the classification of EO time series (Gómez *et al.* 2016). In this section, we describe three well-established classification algorithms applied to EO time series: support vector machines (SVM) (Mountrakis *et al.* 2011), Random forests (Belgiu and Drăguţ 2016) and k-nearest neighbor (k-NN) (Thanh Noi and Kappas 2018).

SVM and random forests are machine learning techniques, which require building a model that is able to correctly predict the labels of unobserved samples. In contrast, k-NN is referred to as an instance-based machine learning algorithm, which simply stores the training dataset instead of learning a model. This is a lazy learning algorithm that delays the prediction until a new unobserved sample has to be classified. As detailed in section 2.2.1, remote sensing works have applied these algorithms on the original time series and feature-based representations. In this section, we especially focus on how these algorithms work.

2.3.1. *Support vector machines*

The SVM algorithm is a choice classifier for the remote sensing community (Pal and Mather 2005; Mountrakis *et al.* 2011) with successful applications for the classification of optical (Dash *et al.* 2007; Carrão *et al.* 2008) and radar (Tan *et al.* 2007; Son *et al.* 2018) SITS data. SVMs are well known for their effectiveness in high-dimensional spaces, even in cases where the number of features is greater than the number of observations. However, its overfitting robustness mainly depends on the tuning of the SVM hyperparameters, which is not always straightforward.

SVM was initially designed for binary classification problems dealing with linearly separable data (Vapnik 1995, 1998). As an example, Figure 2.4 shows a binary classification task aiming to separate blue samples from green ones. Figure 2.4(a) shows an example where data are linearly separable, whereas Figure 2.4(b) shows a nonlinearly separable example.

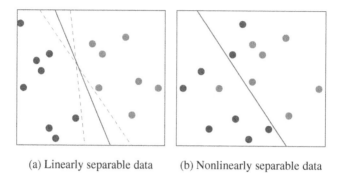

(a) Linearly separable data   (b) Nonlinearly separable data

Figure 2.4. *A binary classification example, which aims to separate blue samples from green ones. Red dot lines are possible decision functions. For a color version of this figure, see www.iste.co.uk/atto/change2.zip*

Although the linear case is seldom present in real classification tasks, it helps to introduce the SVM principle and its key characteristics. Hence, before generalizing to nonlinear problems, the principles of the linear SVM classifier are first described for a binary classification task. Second, we introduce the concept of the soft margin for almost linearly separable data and then describe the kernel trick used in the nonlinear SVM. Finally, the extension of SVM to solve multi-class classification problems is presented.

2.3.1.1. *Hard-margin linear SVM for linearly separable data*

The goal of SVM is to find a decision boundary that divides the two sets of samples. The decision boundary is a line in a two-dimensional space, a plane in a three-dimensional space and generally speaking, a hyperplane in a d-dimensional space (i.e. a flat affine subspace of dimension $d - 1$). As shown in Figure 2.4(a), there are an infinity of decision functions represented by the red dashed lines that can correctly split linearly separable data. Theoretically, the optimal solution is the one that maximizes the distance to the closest data samples from both classes.

Another example of a binary linear classification problem is presented in Figure 2.5, where the optimal linear decision boundary separating blue and green classes is highlighted in red. Let us assign the label $+1$ to green samples and -1 to blue samples. Let $\mathbf{x} \in \mathbb{R}^p$ be a sample represented by a feature vector composed of p features. The optimal linear decision boundary function highlighted in red is defined by the parameter vector $\mathbf{w}$ and the bias b such that $\mathbf{w}^T\mathbf{x} + b = 0$.

Theoretically, the perpendicular distance between a sample and the hyperplane is known as the margin. A big margin reduces the risk of overfitting of the SVM model and thus helps to improve its generalization to new samples. Hence, the optimal decision hyperplane is the one that maximizes the margin. When the data are linearly separable, the minimum distance between the decision boundary and the closest samples is the hard margin. It is represented by the black arrow in Figure 2.5.

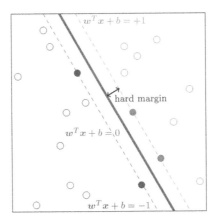

Figure 2.5. *Illustration of hard margin principle when data are linearly separable. For a color version of this figure, see www.iste.co.uk/atto/change2.zip*

Rephrasing the previous ideas, the SVM aims to find the parameter vector $\mathbf{w}$ and bias b that maximizes the margin. Solving this problem relies on the statistical learning theory (Vapnik 1995, 1998). Let $\{(\mathbf{x}_i, y_i)_{i=1}^{n}\}$ be a dataset of n training samples where each sample $\mathbf{x}_i \in \mathbb{R}^p$ is represented by a feature vector composed of p features with the associated label y_i. Formally, the parameter vector $\mathbf{w}$ and the bias b are given by solving the following primal problem:

$$\min_{\mathbf{w}, b} \frac{1}{2} \|\mathbf{w}\|^2 \text{ subject to } y_i(\mathbf{w}^T \mathbf{x}_i + b) \geqslant 1, i = 1, ..., n. \qquad [2.7]$$

Let sgn be the sign function. The following classification function f can be used to predict the label of an unobserved sample $\mathbf{x} \in \mathbb{R}^p$:

$$f(\mathbf{x}) = sgn(\mathbf{w}^T \mathbf{x} + b). \qquad [2.8]$$

In the case of Figure 2.5, if $\mathbf{w}^T \mathbf{x} + b > 0$, then $f(\mathbf{x}) = +1$, which implies that $\mathbf{x}$ is classified as a green sample. Otherwise, $f(\mathbf{x}) = -1$ as $\mathbf{w}^T \mathbf{x} + b < 0$, resulting in $\mathbf{x}$ being classified as a blue sample.

The optimization problem under constraints defined by equation [2.7] is a quadratic problem. Assuming linearly separable data, the problem is convex and admits a unique optimal solution. The convergence of SVM is thus guaranteed. This constrained optimization problem has the following Lagrangian dual formulation:

$$\mathcal{L}(\mathbf{w}, b, \boldsymbol{\alpha}) = \frac{1}{2}\|\mathbf{w}\|^2 - \sum_{i=1}^{n} \alpha_i \left(y_i \left(w^T \mathbf{x}_i + b \right) - 1 \right),$$ [2.9]

where $\alpha_i \geqslant 0$ are the Lagrangian multipliers associated with each constraint of equation [2.7]. The SVM optimal solution is then determined by seeking the saddle point of the Lagrangian function $\mathcal{L}$. Note that this constrained optimization problem satisfies the Karush, Kuhn and Tucker (KKT) conditions: stationarity, complementary slackness, primal feasibility and dual feasibility. The training samples for which the Lagrangian multipliers α_i are not zero are called the support vectors, denoted by $\mathcal{V}$ in the following. In Figure 2.5, the support vectors are the blue and green filled circle samples that belong to the blue and green dashed lines. The other samples have a zero Lagrangian multiplier, i.e. $\alpha_i = 0$, and thus are not used to solve the SVM problem. The classification function f can be rewritten as:

$$f(\mathbf{x}) = sgn\left(\sum_{\mathbf{x}_i \in \mathcal{V}} \alpha_i y_i \left(\mathbf{x}^T \mathbf{x}_i \right) + b \right).$$ [2.10]

2.3.1.2. *Soft-margin linear SVM for almost linearly separable data*

In real-world application scenarios, datasets are corrupted by noise and outliers. This leads to nonlinear classification problems where the above-described strategy is not a solution. Hence, the concept of the soft margin has been proposed by Cortes and Vapnik (1995). In this case, the construction of the optimal hyperplane accepts classification training errors.

Figure 2.6 illustrates another binary classification task where the samples are not perfectly linearly separable. It shows that the green sample p_1 is misclassified by the optimal linear decision boundary depicted in red. To allow some training errors, the idea is to include a penalty term in equation [2.7]. After adding these positive penalties, the decision hyperplane correctly splits a maximum number of training samples by minimizing the classification errors.

These positive penalties are known as slack variables ξ. They penalize misclassified training samples: the further a sample is from its margin, the higher its slack variable is. In Figure 2.6, the slack variable ξ_1, depicted by the black arrow, is associated with sample p_1, which is located between both dashed green and blue lines.

The aim of soft-margin SVM remains unchanged: maximizing the margin. If the sample $\mathbf{x}_i$ belongs to the correct side of the margin, then the associated slack variable ξ_i is zero. Otherwise, the slack variable ξ_i corresponds to the perpendicular distance between $\mathbf{x}_i$ and the margin. Formally, the values $\mathbf{w}$ and b are given by solving the following new primal problem:

$$\min_{\mathbf{w},b,\xi} \frac{1}{2}\|\mathbf{w}\|^2 + C\sum_{i=1}^{n}\xi_i$$

$$\text{with } y_i(\mathbf{w}^T\mathbf{x}_i + b) \geqslant 1 - \xi_i \text{ and } \xi_i \geqslant 0, i = 1, ..., n, \qquad [2.11]$$

where C is a user-defined regularization hyperparameter. It defines the trade-off between the influence of the slack variables and the margin width. A small C value favors a large margin by authorizing some misclassification errors, whereas a big C value limits the number of misclassification errors resulting in a small margin.

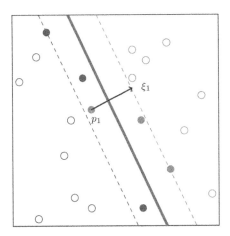

Figure 2.6. *Illustration of a slack variable in the case of nonlinearly separable data. The slack variable ξ_1 associated with the green sample p_1 corresponds to the perpendicular distance between p_1 and the support of the green class is denoted by the dashed line of the same color. For a color version of this figure, see www.iste.co.uk/atto/change2.zip*

Note that the previous equation is equivalent to equation [2.7] when all of the slack variables are zero. Consequently, it can also be solved with a Lagrangian dual formulation:

$$\mathcal{L}(\mathbf{w}, b, \boldsymbol{\alpha}, \boldsymbol{\beta}) = \frac{1}{2}\|\mathbf{w}\|^2 + C\sum_{i}^{n}\xi_i$$

$$- \sum_{i=1}^{n}\alpha_i\Big(y_i\left(\mathbf{w}^T\mathbf{x}_i + b\right) - 1\Big) - \sum_{i=1}^{n}\beta_i\xi_i, \qquad [2.12]$$

where $\alpha_i \geqslant 0$ and $\beta_i \geqslant 0$ are the Lagrangian multipliers.

2.3.1.3. *Nonlinear SVM and the kernel trick*

Another famous solution to address nonlinearly separable classification problems is to find a nonlinear decision hyperplane. Within the SVM formulation, this can be simply performed by embedding the data in a higher-dimensional space where a linear decision boundary might be found. To do so, a nonlinear transformation is applied to the data by using a kernel function (Müller *et al.* 2001; Schölkopf and Smola 2002). This is known as the kernel trick: the dot product from equations [2.8] and [2.10] is replaced by a similarity measure, without increasing the algorithmic complexity.

More specifically, a kernel is a function K that associates with each pair of samples $(\mathbf{x}_i, \mathbf{x}_j)$ a measure of reciprocal influence, such as a distance, a similarity measure or correlation. A kernel function should respect the conditions of Mercer's theorem. In particular, the kernel K should be positive, i.e. the Gram matrix[1] associated with K should be a symmetric positive definite matrix. The classification function of equation [2.10] can be expressed as follows:

$$f(\mathbf{x}) = sgn \left(\sum_{\mathbf{x}_i \in \mathcal{V}} \alpha_i y_i K(\mathbf{x}, \mathbf{x}_i) + b \right). \qquad [2.13]$$

Through a misuse of language, a non-use of the kernel is known as the linear kernel. The dot product is performed in the initial space without applying any embedding: $K_{linear}(\mathbf{x}_i, \mathbf{x}_j) = \mathbf{x}_i^T \mathbf{x}_j$, as in equation [2.8].

Numerous kernel functions have been proposed in the literature (Schölkopf and Smola 2002). The radial basis function (RBF) is one of the most widely used kernels for the classification of EO time series (Mountrakis *et al.* 2011; Pelletier *et al.* 2016; Karasiak *et al.* 2019): $K_{RBF}(\mathbf{x}_i, \mathbf{x}_j) = e^{-\gamma \|\mathbf{x}_i - \mathbf{x}_j\|^2}$, where $\gamma > 0$ is the hyperparameter that controls the standard deviation. There also exist some attempts to develop kernels dedicated to EO time series (Camps-Valls *et al.* 2008). Besides the mentioned kernels, the signal processing community proposed the global alignment kernel (Cuturi *et al.* 2007) as a specific kernel for time series. To our knowledge, this kernel has not been used by the remote sensing community yet.

2.3.1.4. *From binary to multiclass problems*

A multiclass classification problem can be solved by reducing it to multiple binary classification tasks, on which binary SVM classifiers can be trained. The classifier ensemble is then used to predict new unobserved data, by either using a majority vote or by estimating *a posteriori* probabilities.

---

1. The Gram matrix for the data $\{\mathbf{x}_1, \cdots, \mathbf{x}_i, \cdots, \mathbf{x}_n\}$ is the squared matrix $G \in \mathbb{R}^{n \times n}$, for which the coefficients are defined as follows: $G_{ij} = K(\mathbf{x}_i, \mathbf{x}_j)$ for $1 \leqslant i, j \leqslant n$, with K as the kernel function.

Two different strategies have been proposed in the multiclass classification literature (Hsu and Lin 2002): (1) one-against-all and (2) one-against-one. The one-against-all approach trains a model for each class: the positive samples are the ones of the current class, whereas the negative samples are the ones of all of the other classes. The second approach, one-against-one, trains a model for each pair of classes. This last approach thus requires more models to train, but their convergence is usually faster than for the one-against-all approach.

2.3.1.5. *Hyperparameter tuning*

SVM models require the setting of hyperparameters such as C and γ, which cannot be directly learned. As a bad setting might lead to poor classification performance, a manual choice of the hyperparameter values is not recommended. Hence, hyperparameters need to be tuned carefully before training the model. To find a suitable configuration, the most time-consuming strategy, as well as the most comprehensive one, is the grid search. The main idea is to create a grid of hyperparameter values and to evaluate all of the configurations using a k-fold cross-validation procedure (see section 2.2.1.3). The configuration that gives the best performance is then selected.

2.3.2. *Random forests*

The random forest is a machine learning algorithm, which is based on the well-known binary decision tree classifier. Its specificity is to build its own decision rule by combining the predictions made by many binary decision trees. This ensemble method is probably the most widely used supervised algorithm for SITS classification (Belgiu and Drăguţ 2016). Its popularity is explained by several reasons: it can handle the SITS high-dimensional space (Pelletier *et al.* 2016), its parameters are easy to set (Pal 2005; Rodríguez-Galiano *et al.* 2012), they are able to deal with high data variability present in large geographical areas (Inglada *et al.* 2017) and they are robust to the presence of some mislabeled training data (Pelletier *et al.* 2017).

Traditionally, classification approaches based on a random forest considered the complete SITS data as input. They do not capture the temporal structures contained in the data. In the literature, some random forest variants have thus been proposed to make the most of the temporal structure of time series in their final predictions. Although they have not been applied to EO data yet, two promising approaches are proximity forest (Lucas *et al.* 2019) and TS-CHIEF (Shifaz *et al.* 2020). We will not present these variants further in this chapter.

In the following, the construction of a binary decision tree classifier is first described. Then, the random forest methodology used for constructing an ensemble of binary decision trees is presented.

2.3.2.1. *Binary decision tree*

Decision trees summarize a set of decision rules into a hierarchical tree structure. They provide an intuitive graphical representation of the learned decision rules. Figure 2.7 shows an example binary decision tree. This tree can be used to perform a crop-type classification based on agricultural calendar features.

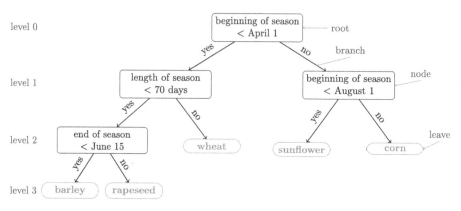

Figure 2.7. *An example binary decision tree, which classifies five crop-type classes based on three agricultural calendar characteristics. For a color version of this figure, see www.iste.co.uk/atto/change2.zip*

The tree is composed of a set of nodes, shown as black and orange rectangles in Figure 2.7. The root is the topmost node of the tree, which is the only one without a parent. Located at the bottom of the tree, terminal nodes are labeled with decisions. In the example of Figure 2.7, these leave nodes are depicted in orange and they denote the predicted crop type. The inner nodes are defined by the joint choice of a feature (e.g. beginning of season, length of season or end of season) and an associated test, i.e. below or above a given threshold. The depth of a node, also named the level, is defined by starting at zero from the root node.

To make a new prediction, a sample is passed through the built tree until it reaches a leave node. At each node, a test is performed on the sample. The sample goes to either the left or the right branch depending on the test result. Considering the example tree of Figure 2.7, a sample whose growing season starts between the 1st of April and the 1st of August will be classified as sunflower.

The "knowledge" encoded into the hierarchical tree structure is learned through the training process. Theoretically, a tree is constructed by analyzing training examples through a top-down approach. The strategy consists of choosing the feature at each step that best splits the set of training samples. Figure 2.8 illustrates the principle of building a binary decision tree through a training process. It shows a binary classification problem (blue vs. green) in a two-dimensional space (X^1 and X^2

features). Figure 2.8(a) shows how the construction starts by considering all of the training samples in the root node. The next recursive steps look for the best partition rules, which recursively split the current training samples into two most homogeneous subsets.

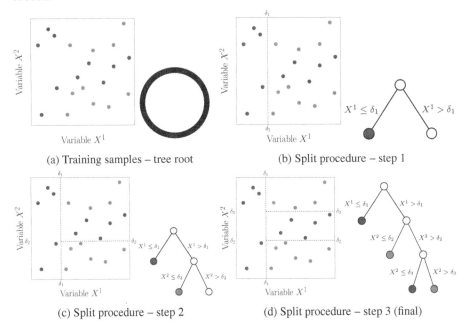

(a) Training samples – tree root

(b) Split procedure – step 1

(c) Split procedure – step 2

(d) Split procedure – step 3 (final)

Figure 2.8. *Principle of building a binary decision tree for a binary classification problem in a two-dimensional feature space. For a color version of this figure, see www.iste.co.uk/atto/change2.zip*

At each iteration, the algorithm evaluates which is the best feature to split the tree node on. This evaluation is based on an impurity measure I, which quantifies the homogeneity of the labels at the node. A node with multiple classes is impure, whereas a node with only one class is pure. The strategy is to select the split maximizing the information gain ΔI, which measures the purity gained when a parent node P is split into two descendant nodes P_l and P_r. Considering that the n samples contained in P are split into n_l and n_r samples, the change in impurity is computed as follows:

$$\Delta I(P, P_l, P_r) = I(P) - \left(\frac{n_l}{n} I(P_l) + \frac{n_r}{n} I(P_r) \right).$$ [2.14]

Some decision tree algorithms such as ID3 and C4.5 have proposed entropy as an impurity measure (Quinlan 1986, 1993). Another well-known impurity measure is the Gini index, which has shown its special interest in the classification and regression trees (Breiman *et al.* 1984) used by the random forest algorithm (Breiman 2001). It measures the probability of a particular sample being wrongly classified when it is randomly chosen. Let m_k denote the number of samples that belong to class k in the node P, hence $n = \sum_{k=1}^{K} m_k$, where K represents the total number of classes. The Gini index is expressed as follows:

$$I_{Gini}(P) = 1 - \sum_{k=1}^{K} \left(\frac{m_k}{n}\right)^2 . \qquad [2.15]$$

An example of a splitting step is shown in Figure 2.8(b), where training samples that have an X^1 value below δ_1 go to the left branch of the tree, whereas the others go to the right branch. After this split, the left child node is pure, i.e. it only contains samples that belong to the blue class. Figure 2.8(c) illustrates how the recursive procedure only continues for the right branch. The construction ends when two terminal nodes are created, as depicted by Figure 2.8(d).

As building a tree until its maximal depth (completely pure terminal nodes) might lead to overfitting the training data, the recursive splitting process often uses a stopping criterion that limits the tree growth. It also speeds up the training process by stopping the tree construction early. One of the following user-predefined criteria can be used:

– a maximal depth is reached;

– the number of samples in a node is below a given threshold;

– the node variance does not decrease between the parent node and child nodes below a given threshold.

2.3.2.2. *From tree to forest*

Decision trees are not usually extremely accurate classifiers. However, their decisions are easy to understand and explain. Besides, the training time complexity of such classifiers is quasi-linear with the number of training samples n ($O(n \cdot log(n))$). Despite these advantages, they can be extremely sensitive to small perturbations in the data, which results in low generalization. To increase the overall performance of an individual tree, Breiman (2001) proposed the random forest algorithm that builds an ensemble of decision trees. Considering a forest of trees, the prediction of an unobserved sample is obtained by applying a majority vote on the tree ensemble. Generally speaking, the use of an ensemble approach has the following advantages (Dieterich 2000):

– increasing the overall performance;

– increasing the generalization capacity of the final classifier that is thus less dependent on finding a suboptimal solution;

– solving complex classification problems that would not have been solved by a single classification algorithm.

The random forest performance is directly related to the performance of each individual tree classifier belonging to the forest. Ideally, each tree should commit few errors, i.e. have a low bias. However, if all of the trees make the same predictions, the use of an ensemble is obsolete. It is therefore important to ensure diversity among the ensemble, i.e. the trees should be weakly correlated by making dissimilar predictions on a same training dataset (Ueda and Nakano 1996).

To produce a pool of non-correlated trees presenting high diversity, the random forest algorithm relies on two main randomization processes: (1) random feature selection (Ho 1998; Bryll *et al.* 2003) and (2) the bagging (bootstrap aggregating) strategy (Breiman 1996).

The idea of random feature selection is to evaluate only a subset of features at each node split. This subset is selected at random without replacement. The evaluation of fewer splits reduces the training time for building one tree and increases the diversity among the trees. The second process to increase the ensemble diversity is to build each tree on a bootstrap sample that is obtained by resampling with replacement n samples among the n training samples (Efron and Tibshirani 1994). Hence, each tree is built on a variation of the training set.

2.3.2.3. *Hyperparameter setting*

The training of a random forest model requires the setting of at least two main hyperparameters: the number of trees and the number of features randomly selected at each node.

The number of trees is usually easy to set as the random forest generalization accuracy increases with the number of trees and then reaches a plateau (Probst and Boulesteix 2017). As the model training time grows linearly with the number of trees, it can be set to a computationally manageable value that ensures a good generalization. Several studies show that a few hundred trees is usually sufficient (Rodríguez-Galiano *et al.* 2012; Pelletier *et al.* 2016).

Regarding the number of features randomly selected at each node, a default value to the square root of the total number of features is usually recommended (Breiman 2001). A small gain in accuracy has been observed when the value of this hyperparameter is cross-validated (Cutler *et al.* 2007; Rodríguez-Galiano *et al.* 2012).

Finally, a stopping criterion such as a maximum depth not to be exceeded and/or a minimum number of samples to split can also be set. As long as the tree is deep enough, the setting of such stopping criteria has a low influence on the classification performance (Pelletier *et al.* 2016)

2.3.2.4. *Random forest for data analysis*

Besides good classification results and fast training, various data analyses can be performed with a trained random forest model. For example, it is able to output the vector of class probability for each sample or compute an outlier score.

The random forest is also able to compute an unbiased generalization error, named the out-of-bag (OOB) error, without using any testing samples. This is possible due to the use of the bootstrap sample. As the samples used to build a tree are selected with replacements, one-third of the samples are not used for building each tree. They are the OOB samples. The OOB error corresponds to the percentage of misclassified OOB samples.

Last, the random forest is able to compute how significant each input feature is. This feature importance score is usually computed by the mean decrease in accuracy (MDA) (Breiman 2001). MDA measures the increase in the OOB error for each feature by randomly permuting its values in all of the nodes where it is used. The higher the feature importance score, the more the feature contributes to the forest decision. The remote sensing community has massively used feature importance scores to perform feature selection (Genuer et al. 2010) and thus reduces the risk of the curse of dimensionality. Traditionally, the community uses the recursive feature elimination (RFE) algorithm, for which the practitioner defines the number of features to retain in the final feature representation. Based on the feature importance scores, RFE recursively removes some subsets of useless features from the feature representation.

2.3.3. k-nearest neighbor

The k-nearest neighbor (k-NN) algorithm is one of the simplest machine learning algorithms. In contrast to the two previous algorithms, k-NN does not have a training step resulting in an explicit model. The main idea of the k-NN algorithm is to predict the class of a new sample $\mathbf{x}$ by matching it with the most similar samples from the training set. The majority class of the closest samples is associated with $\mathbf{x}$. Despite its simplicity, there exist significant applications to EO time series (Gupta and Rajan 2010; Petitjean et al. 2012; Baumann et al. 2017; Belgiu and Csillik 2018).

In practice, the k-NN algorithm can be applied on feature-based representations of time series. However, its main interest is to be able to exploit the temporal structure of time series data. This is possible since k-NN can compare temporal representations by using specific similarity measures that align the series.

In the following, we describe the k-NN algorithm and one of the most well-established time-based similarity measures to be used with it: dynamic time warping (DTW). DTW is also the most common similarity measure used by the remote sensing community. Any reader interested in time-based similarity measures may refer to Lines and Bagnall (2015), where 11 temporal similarity measures are reviewed, including DTW.

2.3.3.1. The k-nearest neighbor algorithm

Let $\mathbf{x}$ be a new sample to be classified and $\{(\mathbf{x}_i, y_i)_{i=1}^{n}\}$ be a dataset of n training samples, where each sample $\mathbf{x}_i \in \mathbb{R}^p$ is represented by a feature vector composed of

p features with the associated label y_i. The k-NN algorithm is composed of three main steps:

1) compute the distance of $\mathbf{x}$ to each training sample $\mathbf{x}_i$: $\delta(\mathbf{x}, \mathbf{x}_i), i = 1, \cdots, n$;

2) sort all the distances $\delta(\mathbf{x}, \mathbf{x}_i)$ in ascending order;

3) associate with $\mathbf{x}$, the label y that is the most frequent class in the $\mathbf{x}_i$ samples that have the k smallest distances $\delta(\mathbf{x}, \mathbf{x}_i)^2$.

Besides the choice of the similarity measure $\delta(\mathbf{x}, \mathbf{x}_i)$, the k parameter is a crucial hyperparameter for the k-NN algorithm. The value of k determines the number of samples that are considered to take the classification decision. A small k value leads to a local decision and a complex model that might present a high variance, and thus a risk of overfitting. On the contrary, a large k value induces a global decision and a simple model that might have a high bias. The tuning of k is usually performed by a k-fold cross-validation[3].

As a naive implementation of the k-NN algorithm requires a full scan of the training data to classify each test sample, one main drawback of this approach is its prohibitive computational time when the number of training samples is high.

2.3.3.2. *Dynamic time warping*

Dynamic time warping (DTW) is a well-known similarity measure, which computes the distance between two temporal sequences (Sakoe and Chiba 1978). The idea is to find the optimal alignment between two time series by authorizing some temporal shifts. Figure 2.9 shows an example with two temporal profiles representing a vegetation index, the normalized difference vegetation index (NDVI). The green lines represent the alignment used by the Euclidean distance or DTW. For both similarity measures, the difference between the two time series corresponds to the cumulative sum of these green lines. Despite the slight shift in time, Figure 2.9(b) shows that DTW is able to match the elements of the two time series efficiently. On the contrary, the Euclidean distance fails to capture the temporal shifts.

The minimization of the temporal shifting effect when computing the similarity is of particular interest when comparing EO time series. Indeed, various agricultural practices or changes in weather conditions shift and slightly distort temporal profiles, which are thus harder to compare. Another advantage for remote sensing applications is that DTW does not require time series of the same length. It is thus possible to compare time series presenting different temporal samplings.

---

2. In a case of equality, several strategies are possible, such as randomly drawing a class among the ones that are majority, increasing the value of k from 1 (but the equality issue might persist), or using the distances to the training samples to weigh the majority voting rule (the closest samples have more weight).

3. Here, k is the number of folds for the cross-validation; see section 2.2.1.3. It is not linked to the k hyperparameter of k-NN.

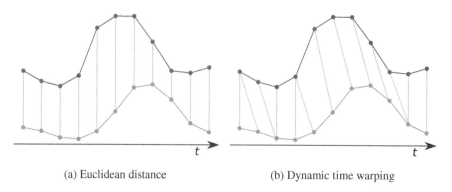

(a) Euclidean distance   (b) Dynamic time warping

Figure 2.9. *Similarity measures between two normalized difference vegetation index profiles. The green lines represent the mapping between elements of the two time series. (To show the alignments displayed in green, the bottom time series has been shifted vertically). For a color version of this figure, see www.iste.co.uk/atto/change2.zip*

Theoretically, DTW computes a cost alignment matrix to determine an optimal global alignment between two time series that can be converted into a similarity measure. Let $S = <s_1, \cdots, s_{|S|}>$ and $T = <t_1, \cdots, t_{|T|}>$ be two univariate time series of length $|S|$ and $|T|$, respectively. Let $\delta(s_i, t_j)$ be the distance between the time points s_i and t_j (usually the Euclidean distance). DTW recursively computes the cost of the optimal alignment between the time series S and T in a matrix $D \in \mathbb{R}^{|S| \times |T|}$ as follows:

$$D(s_i, t_j) = \delta(s_i, t_j) + \min \begin{cases} D(s_{i-1}, t_{j-1}) \\ D(s_i, t_{j-1}) \\ D(s_{i-1}, t_j) \end{cases} \qquad [2.16]$$

The similarity between S and T is then given by the last cumulative element of the cost matrix: $DTW(S, T) = D(s_{|S|}, t_{|T|})$. Figure 2.10 shows the cost matrix D for two time series represented in blue and orange. It also highlights the warping path in green, which contains the optimal alignment. The right figure also shows the matching between the elements of both time series. Each element of the blue time series is linked at least to one element of the orange time series (and *vice versa*).

To handle the specificity of the EO time series data, the remote sensing community have applied two DTW variants. Instead of using DTW for univariate time series, (Petitjean *et al.* 2012) evaluate a multivariate version of the DTW for the analysis of optical SITS. The second variant, named time-weighted dynamic time warping (TWDTW), deals with the irregular temporal sampling of EO time series (Maus *et al.* 2016). This second variant adds a temporal cost while computing the cost matrix in equation [2.16]. This temporal cost depends on the elapsed time between two elements of the time series.

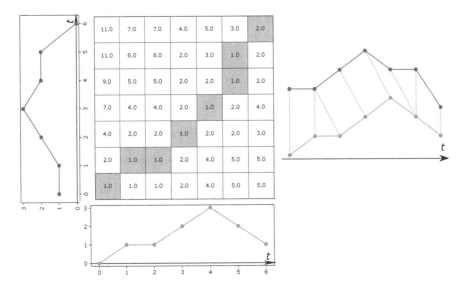

Figure 2.10. *An example DTW cost matrix for two time series. The warping path in green displays the optimal alignment. The resulting alignment is also shown in green on the right. For a color version of this figure, see www.iste.co.uk/atto/change2.zip*

One issue of the DTW is authorizing an element of a time series to match an unlimited number of elements in the other time series. It can lead to a pathological mapping, which reduces the quality of the alignment. To mitigate this issue, the calculations in the cost matrix D (equation [2.16]) are only performed for elements s_i and t_j, which are not too time-distant from each other (Petitjean *et al.* 2012). This solution is known as the temporal warping window. It also reduces the high quadratic computational complexity of DTW with the time series lengths $O(|S| \times |T|)$, and thus speeds up the computation.

2.4. Classification strategies based on temporal feature representations

In the literature, most classification studies have proposed considering the original EO time series data as the most significant feature representation. Traditionally, this raw time-based representation is used as input data for the classification algorithms (Gómez *et al.* 2016) presented in section 2.3. For example, random forests have been applied to optical SITS for land cover mapping (Inglada *et al.* 2017) or the SVM classifier has been used for mapping forest tree species (Karasiak *et al.* 2019).

Despite the accurate results obtained by the original SITS, this time-based representation might not be tailored for remote sensing applications involving scarce reference label datasets. In this situation, classification algorithms might become sensitive to the curse of dimensionality (see section 2.2.2.2). To mitigate this issue, the dimension of the problem can simply be reduced by selecting some key image dates. For example, summer crops can be distinguished from winter crops by carefully selecting images acquired during the two seasons (Rodríguez-Galiano *et al.* 2012). Unfortunately, the selection of key dates is not as straightforward and might result in a loss of valuable information for classification algorithms. Indeed, key dates might change from one year to another due to various factors, such as the climate change, urbanization processes, weather conditions and agricultural practices.

One of the most powerful strategies to reduce the dimensionality of the data is to transform the original EO time series into a meaningful low-dimensional feature-based representation. The training of the traditional machine learning algorithms can then be performed on this new representation. Ideally, a low-dimensional temporal feature representation will capture the temporal structure of the time series. The extraction of such representations from EO data receives growing interest due to the high revisit time of new satellites, which now acquire dense time series at a medium spatial resolution.

Moreover, the temporal structure of SITS is not considered by traditional classification algorithms when its raw time-based representation is used as input data to the classification process. The order of the images has no influence on the model, nor on the results. In other words, a shuffle of the input images in the series would result in the same trained model, and thus the same accuracy performance.

In this section, we describe classification strategies based on temporal feature representation. These approaches reduce the dimension of the data and incorporate information about the temporal structure of SITS data in the classification process. We first present relevant approaches based on the extraction of the phenological information. Then, we briefly describe two promising classification strategies based on dictionary and shapelets.

2.4.1. *Phenology-based classification approaches*

SITS acquired by optical sensors are widely used to monitor vegetation phenology, which is the description of periodic plant life cycle events across the growing season. Phenological features can help the classification system discriminate between land cover classes that evolve over time, such as the numerous forms of vegetation that are subject to seasonal changes (Matton *et al.* 2015; Waldner *et al.* 2015; Valero *et al.* 2016). The phenology-based feature representation is then used to feed common classification algorithms, such as random forests or SVM.

To depict key stages and dates of the growing cycle, phenological features are traditionally extracted from a vegetation index or from some biophysical vegetation parameters. From the temporal description of the vegetation cycle, some features can easily be derived to characterize the phenology. The easiest strategy is to apply basic statistics to extract significant values from temporal profiles, including the maximum, the amplitude or the average (Pittman *et al.* 2010; Arvor *et al.* 2011; Matton *et al.* 2015; Valero *et al.* 2016). However, this approach cannot deal with time series corrupted by noise due to clouds (and their shadows), dust, aerosols or varying atmospheric conditions.

Hence, more robust methods based on curve fitting have been proposed in the literature. The general idea is to fit a well-known curve, for example, a double logistic, to each vegetation temporal profile (Jönsson and Eklundh 2002; Zhang *et al.* 2003; Beck *et al.* 2006; Eerens *et al.* 2014; Pelletier *et al.* 2016).

To perform such a fitting, the most popular tool is the TIMESAT software (Jönsson and Eklundh 2004; Eklundh and Jönsson 2015, 2016), which extracts 11 phenological parameters, including the beginning of the growing season, its peak and its length. It is possible to fit three well-known curves: asymmetric Gaussian function, double logistic function or Savitzky–Golay filtering, which smoothes the data. The main advantage of TIMESAT is its robustness to noise. However, the used fitting strategy requires time series with a regular temporal sampling, representing at least one complete year. Due to these requirements, this phenological-based feature representation has been mainly used on low–medium spatial resolution time series, such as the one provided by AVHRR or MODIS sensors, to extract seasonality information and produce map land cover (Clark *et al.* 2010; Zhang *et al.* 2013; Jia *et al.* 2014).

2.4.2. *Dictionary-based classification approaches*

The basic idea of dictionary-based approaches is to transform the time series into a "bag-of-words" representation, which is used as input data by a general-purpose classifier. Based on the training samples, these approaches learn a set of representative words, the dictionary. Once the dictionary is defined, each time series is represented by a histogram of word counts. This new representation is then used as input by the final classification algorithm. More specifically, a standard dictionary-based classification approach involves the following four steps (Lin *et al.* 2012; Schäfer 2015):

1) breaking up the time series into subseries, i.e. continuous parts of the time series;

2) using a quantization technique to discretize each subseries into words, which are discovered during this step;

3) building a feature vector, usually a histogram of word counts;

4) training a classification algorithm on the extracted feature vectors.

Because of their ability to reduce inherent noise and find discriminative patterns in time series with repetitive behaviors (Schäfer 2015), dictionary-based approaches are appealing for the classification of EO time series data. However, only limited investigations have been performed to date. This might be due to the novelty of dictionary-based approaches and the use of short EO time series at medium spatial resolution datasets in most research studies. Furthermore, the irregular temporal sampling might also explain why dictionary-based approaches are not used much. Nevertheless, two approaches have been proposed.

Recently, Bailly *et al.* (2016) have proposed a bag-of-words model for the classification of MODIS time series. They used an adaptation of the popular scale-invariant feature transform (SIFT) for time series (Bailly 2018). The goal is to extract scale- and rotation-invariant local features, which are also robust to noise. The generated features are then transformed into words in order to represent time series by word histograms. Finally, an SVM classifier is trained on the resulting histograms.

A more recent dictionary-based strategy has been applied to a time series composed of Landsat-8 images (Schäfer 2016). The method combines two dictionary-based methods: Word eXtrAction for time SEries cLassification (WEASEL) (Schäfer and Leser 2017a) and Multivariate Unsupervised Symbols and dErivatives (MUSE) (Schäfer and Leser 2017b). It first extracts discriminative features by using a variant of the symbolic Fourier approximation (SFA) (Schäfer and Högqvist 2012). The computed Fourier coefficients are then discretized into words in each dimension of the multivariate time series. Besides the word counts traditionally used to form the feature vector, the WEASEL+MUSE approach also uses bi-grams of words that consider the order in which the words occur. This step generates a big feature space that is reduced by using a statistical feature selection technique, a chi-squared test. Then, a final logistic regression classifer is applied.

Although other efficient dictionary-based approaches such as bag-of-SFA-symbols (BOSS) (Schäfer 2015) exist in the time series literature, the remote sensing community has not explored them yet.

2.4.3. *Shapelet-based classification approaches*

Shapelet-based classification approaches have successfully been applied by the machine learning community to time series classification. First introduced by Ye and Keogh (2009), shapelets are small subseries that are informative or discriminative for a certain class. The intuition behind shapelets is that only some subseries from the complete time series are helpful in characterizing each class. Compared to dictionary-based approaches, a shapelet-based representation does not consider the occurrence of the subseries in a time series. In fact, it only accounts for the presence or absence of the shapelet somewhere in a whole time series. Moreover, shapelets have the advantage of being easy to interpret by domain experts.

To our knowledge, shapelets have only been explored once by the remote sensing community for monitoring rubber plantation expansion (Ye *et al.* 2018). This might be explained by the lack of dense time series acquired at high spatial resolution. It is probably also due to the late development of a multivariate version and the prohibitive computational time of the initial shapelet discovery step, which is quadratic with the number of training time series samples n and quartic with the length of time series ℓ: $(O(n^2\ell^4))$. However, the recent research trends for shapelets include a speedup of the shapelet discovery phase (Rakthanmanon and Keogh 2013; Grabocka *et al.* 2014; Karlsson *et al.* 2016), which might open up new research paths for the remote sensing community.

We briefly present here the noteworthy algorithm: shapelet transform (Lines *et al.* 2012; Hills *et al.* 2013). The algorithm involves the following three main steps. First, it extracts the best K shapelets of the training data. Second, it transforms the data using the K best shapelets. Finally, the shapelet transform algorithm trains an ensemble of eight classifiers, including SVM and random forests.

The important and interesting step of the shapelet transform algorithm is the data transformation based on shapelets. The idea of shapelet transformation is to compute distances between the time series and the shapelets. The distance between a shapelet of length l and a time series is the minimum distance of a shapelet with all subseries of the same length l, which are extracted from the time series. In the new representation, each feature corresponds to the distance between a time series and one shapelet. For a dataset composed of n time series of length ℓ, the shapelet transformation thus computes a matrix of distances of size $\mathbb{R}^{n \times K}$. If K is lower than ℓ, then it might be interpreted as a dimension reduction.

2.5. Deep learning approaches

Encouraged by the latest developments in machine learning and computer vision, deep learning approaches have successfully been applied to EO data (Ball *et al.* 2017; Zhu *et al.* 2017; Ma *et al.* 2019). These techniques offer new opportunities for classification tasks, whose main advantage is to automate the extraction of a discriminative and informative feature representation. Thus, there is no need for feature engineering. In the context of EO time series analysis, the exploration of deep methodologies is still a young, but swiftly evolving research area (Rußwurm *et al.* 2020).

Given the temporal structure of SITS data, the first remote sensing approaches have explored the use of deep recurrent neural network (RNN) architectures, which effectively handle sequential data. RNNs have thus been the most investigated architecture for the classification of optical (Ienco *et al.* 2017; Rußwurm and Körner 2017) and radar (Minh *et al.* 2018; Ndikumana *et al.* 2018) EO time series.

These works usually use the raw SITS data as input, for which the spatial and/or spectral dimensions are not considered. However, another well-known deep learning approach, convolutional neural network (CNN), is intrinsically designed for extracting spatial features from two-dimensional image data. Hence, CNNs have been combined with RNN to extract spatio-temporal feature representation. Research works in remote sensing include the merging of spatial and temporal representations (Benedetti *et al.* 2018; Interdonato *et al.* 2019), the consecutive learning of temporal and spatial representations (Garnot *et al.* 2019b) and the use of dedicated architecture such as ConvLSTM (Rußwurm and Körner 2018). The use of the spatial structure of SITS lies outside the scope of this chapter and is thus not elaborated further.

More recently, CNNs have been adapted to make the most of the temporal structure of time series (Ismail Fawaz *et al.* 2019). The main difference with CNN used for two-dimensional image data is the use of one-dimensional convolution applied to the temporal dimension of the data. They have also been applied successfully to SITS data (Pelletier *et al.* 2019; Zhong *et al.* 2019).

In this chapter, we focus on how the two well-established one-dimensional CNN and RNN work. We do not cover the most recent advances, including the use of attention mechanisms[4], for which there are only few recent applications to EO time series (Ienco *et al.* 2019; Garnot *et al.* 2019a; Rußwurm and Körner 2019).

Before describing both CNN and RNN, we begin this section by briefly introducing deep neural network theory.

2.5.1. *Introduction to deep learning*

The multilayer perceptron (MLP) network is the most simple (deep) neural network classifier. Consequently, to introduce the main concepts of deep learning algorithms, we first describe MLP for multiclass classification problems. Then, we describe some basis for training a deep neural network.

2.5.1.1. *Multilayer perceptron*

Multilayer perceptron (MLP) is a class of feedforward network composed of fully connected neurons in multiple layers. Figure 2.11 shows an example MLP classification network composed of four layers: the first layer in green represents the inputs, the last one in red the outputs and the two middle layers in blue are the hidden layers. Each layer is composed of several units, the so-called neurons. The input layer size depends on the dimensions of the input data. The output layer is composed of as many neurons as there are classes to be identified. The number of hidden layers and the number of neurons need to be decided by the user.

---

4. An attention mechanism computes importance scores to weight each input element. Proposed initially by Bahdanau *et al.* (2015) for RNN architecture, it has been adapted to fully connected networks with transformers (Vaswani *et al.* 2017).

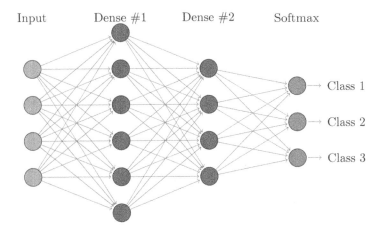

Input   Dense #1   Dense #2   Softmax

Figure 2.11. *An example multilayer perceptron (MLP) classifier composed of two dense layers and one softmax layer, as presented in Pelletier* et al. *(2019). For a color version of this figure, see www.iste.co.uk/atto/change2.zip*

In an MLP network, the hidden layers are dense layers, in which a neuron is connected to all of the neurons in the previous layer. Formally, the outputs of a dense layer l are known as the activation map, which is denoted by $A^{[l]}$. Theoretically, these maps are obtained through a two-step calculation. First, it computes a linear combination of the input activations $A^{[l-1]}$, which are the outputs of layer $l-1$. Second, it applies a nonlinear activation function $g^{[l]}$ to the linear combination. This computation can be written as follows:

$$A^{[l]} = g^{[l]}(W^{[l]}A^{[l-1]} + b^{[l]}),$$ [2.17]

where $W^{[l]}$ and $b^{[l]}$ are the weights and the biases of the layer l that need to be learned, respectively. The input of the first layer $A^{[0]}$ is the input data. To learn a complex nonlinear decision function, the use of a nonlinear function g is vital. It allows the hidden layers to perform nonlinear transformations of the network inputs. The most used nonlinear function is the rectified linear units (ReLU) function (Krizhevsky *et al.* 2012), computed as ReLU$(z) = \max(0, z)$. Other classical activation functions are sigmoidal functions, such as tangent hyperbolic and logistic functions.

The cascade of several dense layers usually ends with the traditional softmax layer. This last layer is a specific layer composed of K neurons for a classification problem of K classes. For a given sample $\mathbf{x}$, it ensures that (1) the output values range between 0 and 1 and (2) the sum of the K outputs is equal to 1. Furthermore, the output values can be interpreted as a class probability vector of $\mathbf{x}$, which is used to predict its label.

Formally, the probability of predicting class y, given the sample $\mathbf{x}$ is computed as follows:

$$p(y = j|\mathbf{x}) = \frac{e^{t_j}}{\sum_{i=1}^{K} e^{t_i}}, \quad\quad\quad [2.18]$$

where t_i is the result of the linear combination for the i-th neuron, i.e. $t_i = W_i^{[L]} A^{[L-1]} + b_i^{[L]}$.

Training an MLP classifier corresponds to finding the values of the model parameters $\mathbf{W} = \{W^{[l]}\}_{l=1}^{L}$ and $\mathbf{b} = \{b^{[l]}\}_{l=1}^{L}$ that will minimize a classification cost function. This process, known as empirical risk minimization, is composed of two steps: (1) the forward propagation step that passes down the training data through the network to calculate the different activation values and (2) the backpropagation step that reverses the process and updates the model parameters. Let $\{(\mathbf{x}_i, y_i)_{i=1}^{n}\}$ be a dataset of n training samples, where each sample $\mathbf{x}_i \in \mathbb{R}^p$ is represented by a feature vector composed of p features with the associated label y_i.

During the forward propagation step, the training samples are passed through the network to compute the cost function $\mathcal{J}$, which is defined as the average of the classification errors committed on the training sample:

$$\mathcal{J}(\mathbf{W}, \mathbf{b}) = \frac{1}{n} \sum_{\mathbf{x}_i} \mathcal{L}(\hat{y}_i, y_i), \qu\quad\quad [2.19]$$

where $\hat{y}_i$ corresponds to the model predictions. The loss function $\mathcal{L}(\hat{y}_i, y_i)$ is usually expressed for a multiclass classification problem as the cross-entropy loss:

$$\mathcal{L}(\hat{y}_i, y_i) = - \sum_{y \in \{1, \cdots, C\}} \mathbb{1}\{y = y_i\} log(p(y|\mathbf{x}_i)) \quad\quad [2.20]$$

$$= -log(p(y_i|\mathbf{x}_i)), \quad\quad\quad [2.21]$$

where $p(y_i|\mathbf{x}_i)$ represents the probability of predicting the true class y_i for the sample $\mathbf{x}_i$. As mentioned above, this probability value is obtained by equation [2.18].

During the backpropagation step, the common gradient descent technique is used. It first computes the gradient of the cost function using the chain rule, with respect to each individual weight and bias parameter. It then updates the parameter by following the opposite direction to the gradient, in order to minimize the cost function:

$$W^{[l]} = W^{[l-1]} - \alpha \frac{\partial \mathcal{J}}{\partial W^{[l-1]}}, \quad\quad\quad [2.22]$$

$$b^{[l]} = b^{[l-1]} - \alpha \frac{\partial \mathcal{J}}{\partial b^{[l-1]}}. \quad\quad\quad [2.23]$$

The hyperparameter α, known as the learning rate, controls how much the model parameters are modified with respect to the gradient. If the value of α is too small, many iterations will be required for the network to converge and learning may be stuck in a local minimum. Conversely, if α is too large, learning may overshoot the minimum and even diverge. The correct setting of the learning rate is thus crucial to ensure the convergence to a minimum of the cost function defined by equation [2.19] in a reasonable amount of time.

2.5.1.2. *Basic knowledge for training a deep neural network*

The key idea of deep learning networks is the stacking of many layers, which can be trained with a huge quantity of labeled data. Besides the non-trivial choice of the architecture, training a deep network is not straightforward. Indeed, training a complex network with thousands of neurons packaged in multiple layers can involve two main problems: (1) an endless training time and (2) a lack of generalization due to overfitting.

The traditional gradient descent algorithm is not really time efficient. Indeed, it requires processing all of the training data in the network before applying the gradient descent. The model parameters are thus not updated often, resulting in a network that improves slowly. Hence, the gradient descent algorithm is in practice applied on batches, where a batch is a small subset of the training dataset. In this case, the network parameters are updated after successive forward and backward propagation steps applied on the different batches. The network improves more quickly, resulting in a training speedup. The batch size is a hyperparameter that sets the trade-off between the speed and the stability of the learning process.

As mentioned above, the long training time of the network can also be reduced by selecting a large learning rate α during the backward propagation step, at the cost of diverging. Instead of training the network with a static learning rate as in equations [2.22] and [2.23], a good solution is to use an optimizer that varies the value of the learning rate during the training for each parameter and at each iteration. One of the most commonly used ones is Adam (adaptive moment optimization) (Kingma and Ba 2014), which stores an exponentially decaying average of past squared gradients and past gradients as in the momentum method (Sutskever *et al.* 2013).

Long training times can also be explained by the "vanishing gradient" problem. In a multilayer network, the gradients in the earlier layers are calculated as products of derivatives of each following layer. Therefore, those gradients can quickly approach zero when the number of layers increases. This results in a negligible change in the values of network parameters during the training process. It makes the network hard and long to train. To mitigate this issue, a solution is to use an appropriate activation function g that does not cause small derivatives, such as ReLU (Krizhevsky *et al.* 2012). Another solution is the use of residual connections that allow a direct flow of the gradient via a shortcut linear connection to the next layer (He *et al.* 2016).

Moreover, a deep network may be affected by the "exploding gradient" problem, for which gradients explode. In practice, this situation is easier to solve by using gradient clipping where gradients cannot exceed a user-defined threshold.

Finally, to help the training of the network and to control overfitting, several regularization techniques are also traditionally used, such as $\mathcal{L}_2$-regularization on the weights, dropout (Srivastava *et al.* 2014) and batch-normalization (Ioffe and Szegedy 2015). We do not further elaborate on these techniques.

2.5.2. *Convolutional neural networks*

A convolutional neural network (CNN) is a type of deep feedforward artificial neural network initially designed for working with images. Although CNNs are mostly used in two-dimensional datasets, they can be easily extended to one- and three-dimensional problems. The main novelty of CNN is the use of convolutional layers instead of fully-connected layers, such as in MLP. Convolutional layers consist of a set of convolution filters, which enable the extraction of complex features. In a multilayer CNN, earlier CNN layers extract basic features such as corners, edges or lines. Conversely, deeper layers apply convolutions on these low-level features to create high-level features describing complex shapes.

A convolution filter is an array of weights, which is slid through the input data in order to highlight discriminative areas. It is a three-dimensional array for colored images, whereas it is a two-dimensional array for multivariate time series. The convolution filter size of the last dimension is usually equal to the number of features of the input activation map. The filter is used in a convolution process, which computes, at each location, the sum of products between the input data and the filter[5].

The novelty of CNN is to learn the weights of the convolution filters during network training. Ideally, the training process looks for filter weights extracting the most informative and relevant features for a given classification problem. It assumes that filters can be useful in different parts of the inputs. Besides the feature extraction based on convolutional layers, a classical CNN architecture is also composed of (at least) a softmax layer for classification purposes.

Figure 2.12 shows, on the right, an input p-multivariate time series of length T. The left array displays the result of sliding the orange filter through the whole input. This convolution process outputs a univariate time series.

The size of the outputs depends on the size of the input and also on two other hyperparameters – the stride and the padding. The stride corresponds to the amount

---

5. The so-called convolution is technically a cross-correlation in CNN. Indeed, a true convolution should first reverse the filter before sliding it through the input data.

by which the filter is shifted between two convolutions. In the example in Figure 2.12, the stride is set to 1, meaning that convolution is applied at each instant. The padding is used to avoid a loss of information at the input borders where convolutions cannot be applied. It usually adds values (e.g. zeros) at the borders.

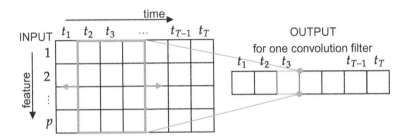

Figure 2.12. *Output of the convolution between a p-multivariate time series of length T. The one-dimensional convolution filter depicted in orange is a univariate time series of length T. For a color version of this figure, see www.iste.co.uk/atto/change2. zip*

Besides convolutional layers, CNN also uses pooling layers, which are usually interleaved between successive convolutional layers. The objective of pooling layers is to down-sample activation maps produced by convolutional layers. An advantage of integrating pooling layers between convolution layers is to reduce the location dependence of the features in the activation maps. Besides, pooling layers reduce the output complexity, speed up the computation and decrease the risk of overfitting. For example, the max pooling layer outputs the maximum value over a window of fixed length and on each activation.

Although initially designed for image classification, recent research showed that CNN is also effective for time series classification (Ismail Fawaz *et al.* 2019). In remote sensing, temporal CNN, which apply one-dimensional CNN convolutions in the temporal dimension, have also demonstrated their relevance for SITS classification (Pelletier *et al.* 2019; Zhong *et al.* 2019). Figure 2.13 displays an example of a temporal CNN (Pelletier *et al.* 2019) that contains three convolutional layers, one dense layer and the final softmax layer to output the predictions (see section 2.5.1.1). We note here a main difference with traditional architectures used for image classification: the absence of pooling layers. Compared with image classification where local pooling is used to extract features robust to change in position and scale, the location and the amplitude of the temporal features can be crucial for SITS classification. Accordingly, CNN architectures applied on time series do not use local pooling layers to avoid a loss in the location of the feature. They still might insert a global pooling layer after a set of convolutional layers (Ismail Fawaz *et al.* 2019).

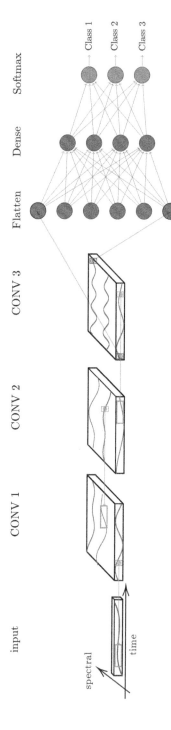

Figure 2.13. *Temporal convolutional neural network (TempCNN), as presented in Pelletier et al. (2019). For a color version of this figure, see www.iste.co.uk/atto/change2.zip*

2.5.3. *Recurrent neural networks*

Recurrent neural networks (RNN) are a type of neural network commonly used for processing time series datasets. Originally developed for dense time series such as text, music or DNA sequencing, they have also been explored for the classification of EO time series datasets (Ienco *et al.* 2017; Rußwurm and Körner 2017; Minh *et al.* 2018; Ndikumana *et al.* 2018). The success of RNN is due to their ability to model short-term dependencies by learning features shared across the different positions of a time series. In the classification context, the complex features learned by RNN architectures are used to feed a softmax layer that output the predicted label. For multiclass classification problems, the traditional cost function used by RNN classifiers is the cross-entropy loss defined in equation [2.19]. Furthermore, they are also able to accept time series inputs of different lengths.

Instead of using fully connected layers to transform the data, RNN has a looping mechanism that reuses past activations from previous time series elements to make better predictions. RNNs memorize what happened earlier in the series by exploiting the information contained in the representations of previous time series elements. This memory, also known as the hidden state, is computed for each time series element.

The recurrent layers, which are the hidden layers, can be organized in various architectures to form different RNNs. In the following, we first describe how a simple RNN works. Later, two variants of the RNN algorithm – long short-term memory (LSTM) and gated recurrent unit (GRU) – explored by the remote sensing community are presented.

2.5.3.1. *A simple recurrent neural network model*

Hidden layers of RNNs consist of recurrent cells whose states are affected by both the past hidden state and the current input with feedback connections. In the following, we describe the structure of a recurrent cell. Then, we present RNN architectures currently used for time series classification.

Let $\mathbf{x} = <x_1, \cdots, x_t, \cdots, x_T>$ be a time series of length T. At time t, a recurrent cell takes the input x_t and updates the hidden state h_{t-1} to h_t. Considering W and b as the trainable weight and bias parameters shared across time, respectively, and g as a nonlinear activation function, the current hidden state h_t can be expressed as follows:

$$h_t = g(W[h_{t-1}, x_t] + b). \tag{2.24}$$

The operator $[\cdots]$ concatenates the inputs h_{t-1} and x_t.

Figure 2.14 displays an example of a recurrent cell, where g corresponds to the most classical and widely used activation function, the hyperbolic tangent *tanh* function. Compared to the classical layer operation described in equation [2.17], the cell output depends not only on the current element x_t, but also on the information coming from previous time instants and stored in h_{t-1}. This operation described by equation [2.24] is applied to each element of the input time series.

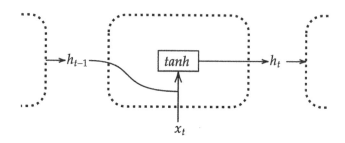

Figure 2.14. *Classical recurrent neural network (RNN) cell structure*

As previously, the W and b parameters need to be learned during the training of the network. It is performed by the "backpropagation through time" strategy, which is actually a specific case of back propagation in recurrent neural networks.

For a time series classification problem, two main RNN architectures are usually applied: many-to-one and many-to-many. Figure 2.15 shows both architecture configurations. Figure 2.15(a) illustrates the many-to-one architecture, which learns how to encode the most relevant parts of the input time series into a single output h_T. The many-to-many architecture, shown in Figure 2.15(b), generates a sequence of outputs $\mathbf{h} = \{h_1, \cdots, h_T\}$ from the input time series. In the classification context, the output of both RNN architectures can be used by the softmax layer to compute the class probability vector. The hidden state vector $\mathbf{h}$ outputted by a many-to-many configuration can also be used to stack several recurrent layers thus training a deep RNN model.

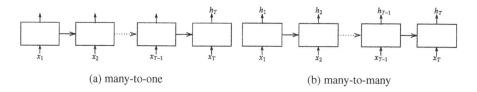

(a) many-to-one   (b) many-to-many

Figure 2.15. *Many-to-one and many-to-many RNN architectures*

Some RNNs also propose a bidirectional variant of the recurrent cell (Schuster and Paliwal 1997). It uses two hidden states for both past and future information. The output of the bidirectional cell is simply the concatenation of past and future states.

2.5.3.2. *RNN variants*

Traditional RNNs have difficulties training time series with long temporal dependencies. Indeed, they fail in extracting important features between long time-distant elements. The main cause is the vanishing gradient problem encountered during the backpropagation step and is presented in section 2.5.1. To mitigate this issue, two variant RNN cells have been proposed in the literature: long short-term memory (LSTM) (Hochreiter and Schmidhuber 1997) and gated recurrent unit (GRU) (Cho *et al.* 2014; Chung *et al.* 2014).

LSTM cells are an old well-established variant of the classical recurrent cell in Figure 2.14. Their hidden states are computed in a different way, in order to consider and store long time information for a current output. To do so, LSTM cells introduce a cell state c_t and use internal mechanisms named the gates. The cell state transports the long temporal dependencies through the cell, whereas the gates decide the amount of information to use or remove from the cell state. Figure 2.16 displays an LSTM cell composed of the cell state c_t and the three classical gates, which are known as the forget Γ_f, input Γ_i and output Γ_o gates.

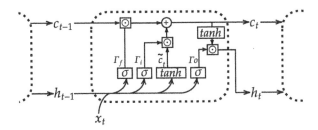

Figure 2.16. *Long short-term memory (LSTM) cell*

The three gates output the results of a linear combination followed by a nonlinear activation function, which is traditionally the sigmoid function. A gate thus outputs a value between 0 and 1 that corresponds to the amount of information that will flow throughout the gate. The operation is described for the three gates by the following equations:

$$\Gamma_f = \sigma(W_f[h_{t-1}, x_t] + b_f), \tag{2.25}$$

$$\Gamma_i = \sigma(W_i[h_{t-1}, x_t] + b_i), \tag{2.26}$$

$$\Gamma_o = \sigma(W_o[h_{t-1}, x_t] + b_o). \tag{2.27}$$

Given a specific cell, the hidden state h_t is computed by equation [2.28], where $\odot$ is the element-wise multiplication, also known as the Hadamard product. The hidden state depends on the output gate Γ_o and the current cell state c_t. The output gate is used to decide which amount of the new cell state will be carried out in the next cell, i.e. the new hidden state. The $tanh$ function is used here to increase or decrease the hidden state value.

$$h_t = \Gamma_o \odot tanh(c_t)$$ [2.28]

The other two gates Γ_f and Γ_i are used to compute the current cell state. The forget gate Γ_f decides how much information will be thrown away from the cell state. As shown in equation [2.25], this gate considers the previous hidden state h_{t-1} and the current input element x_t. If the output of Γ_f is 1, then the information is kept in the cell state. Similarly, the input gate Γ_i decides the amount of new information that will be stored in the cell state c_t.

The result of the input gate is combined through an element-wise multiplication with the candidate value $\tilde{c}_t$. As depicted by equation [2.29], this candidate value is generated by applying a hyperbolic tangent function to the previous hidden state h_{t-1} and the current input element x_t.

$$\tilde{c}_t = tanh(W_c[h_{t-1}, x_t] + b_c)$$ [2.29]

Finally, the content of the cell state is updated by adding the information from the forget and input gates as follows:

$$c_t = \Gamma_i \odot \tilde{c}_t + \Gamma_f \odot c_{t-1}$$ [2.30]

To improve the capacity of LSTM to detect important features between distant elements, a common LSTM variant adds "peephole connections" (Gers and Schmidhuber 2000). In this version, the gates not only depend on the previous hidden state h_{t-1}, but also look at the previous cell state c_{t-1}.

The structure of LSTM cells drastically reduces the risk of the vanishing gradient issue faced in classical RNN cells. Moreover, the incorporation of the cell state and gates allows the relevant information from the past to be carried over to the future instants. However, the complex structure of the LSTM cell has led to several variants, including the well-known gated recurrent unit (GRU), which is depicted in Figure 2.17.

GRU simplifies the LSTM cell structure by using fewer gates and no cell state. More specifically, the GRU cell includes two gates described by equations [2.31] and [2.32]. The update gate Γ_u determines the amount of information to carry out from the past, whereas the reset gate Γ_r decides how much of the previous information should be dropped.

$$\Gamma_u = \sigma(W_u[h_{t-1}, x_t] + b_u)$$ [2.31]

$$\Gamma_r = \sigma(W_r[h_{t-1}, x_t] + b_r)$$ [2.32]

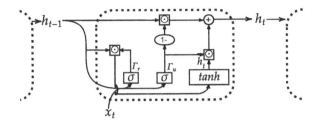

Figure 2.17. *Gated recurrent unit (GRU) cell*

To save the relevant information from the past, the current hidden state content $\tilde{h}_t$ described in equation [2.33] is proposed in a GRU cell. It is determined by using the reset gate. Finally, the hidden state content h_t is updated by using the update gate Γ_u and the previous and current hidden state contents h_{t-1} and $\widetilde{h(t)}$, as depicted in equation [2.34].

$$\tilde{h}_t = tanh(W_c[\Gamma_r \odot \tilde{h}_{t-1}, x_t] + b_c) \tag{2.33}$$

$$h_t = \Gamma_u \odot \tilde{h}_t + (1 - \Gamma_u) \odot h_{t-1} \tag{2.34}$$

The use of two gates in GRU, against three in LSTM, leads to a smaller number of trainable parameters and thus a decrease in training time.

2.6. References

Arvor, D., Jonathan, M., Meirelles, M.S.P., Dubreuil, V., Durieux, L. (2011). Classification of MODIS EVI time series for crop mapping in the state of Mato Grosso, Brazil. *International Journal of Remote Sensing*, 32(22), 7847–7871.

Bahdanau, D., Cho, K., Bengio, Y. (2015). Neural machine translation by jointly learning to align and translate. *3rd International Conference on Learning Representations, ICLR 2015*, San Diego, USA, May 7–9.

Bailly, A. (2018). Time series classification algorithms with applications in remote sensing. Thesis, PhD Thesis, Université Bretagne Sud.

Bailly, A., Arvor, D., Chapel, L., Tavenard, R. (2016). Classification of MODIS time series with dense bag-of-temporal-SIFT-words: Application to cropland mapping in the Brazilian Amazon. *IEEE International Geoscience and Remote Sensing Symposium (IGARSS)*, pp. 2300–2303.

Ball, J.E., Anderson, D.T., Chan, C.S. (2017). Comprehensive survey of deep learning in remote sensing: Theories, tools, and challenges for the community. *Journal of Applied Remote Sensing*, 11(4), 042609.

Baumann, M., Ozdogan, M., Richardson, A.D., Radeloff, V.C. (2017). Phenology from Landsat when data is scarce: Using MODIS and Dynamic Time-Warping to combine multi-year Landsat imagery to derive annual phenology curves. *International Journal of Applied Earth Observation and Geoinformation*, 54, 72–83.

Beck, P.S.A., Atzberger, C., Høgda, K.A., Johansen, B., Skidmore, A.K. (2006). Improved monitoring of vegetation dynamics at very high latitudes: A new method using MODIS NDVI. *Remote Sensing of Environment*, 100(3), 321–334.

Belgiu, M. and Csillik, O. (2018). Sentinel-2 cropland mapping using pixel-based and object-based time-weighted dynamic time warping analysis. *Remote Sensing of Environment*, 204, 509–523.

Belgiu, M. and Drăguţ, L. (2016). Random forest in remote sensing: A review of applications and future directions. *ISPRS Journal of Photogrammetry and Remote Sensing*, 114, 24–31.

Benedetti, P., Ienco, D., Gaetano, R., Ose, K., Pensa, R.G., Dupuy, S. (2018). M3-fusion: A deep learning architecture for multiscale multimodal multitemporal satellite data fusion. *IEEE Journal of Selected Topics in Applied Earth Observations and Remote Sensing*, 11(12), 4939–4949.

Blaschke, T. (2010). Object based image analysis for remote sensing. *ISPRS Journal of Photogrammetry and Remote Sensing*, 65(1), 2–16.

Breiman, L. (1996). Bagging predictors. *Machine Learning*, 24(2), 123–140.

Breiman, L. (2001). Random forests. *Machine Learning*, 45(1), 5–32.

Breiman, L., Friedman, J., Stone, C.J., Olshen, R. (1984). *Classification and Regression Trees*. Taylor & Francis, Oxfordshire.

Bryll, R., Gutierrez-Osuna, R., Quek, F. (2003). Attribute bagging: Improving accuracy of classifier ensembles by using random feature subsets. *Pattern Recognition*, 36(6), 1291–1302.

Camps-Valls, G., Gómez-Chova, L., Muñoz-Marí, J., Rojo-Álvarez, J.L., Martínez-Ramón, M. (2008). Kernel-based framework for multitemporal and multisource remote sensing data classification and change detection. *IEEE Transactions on Geoscience and Remote Sensing*, 46(6), 1822–1835.

Carrão, H., Gonçalves, P., Caetano, M. (2008). Contribution of multispectral and multitemporal information from MODIS images to land cover classification. *Remote Sensing of Environment*, 112(3), 986–997.

Cho, K., van Merriënboer, B., Bahdanau, D., Bengio, Y. (2014). On the properties of neural machine translation: Encoder–decoder approaches. *Proceedings of SSST-8, Eighth Workshop on Syntax, Semantics and Structure in Statistical Translation*, pp. 103–111.

Chung, J., Gulcehre, C., Cho, K., Bengio, Y. (2014). Empirical evaluation of gated recurrent neural networks on sequence modeling. *NIPS 2014 Workshop on Deep Learning*, December.

Clark, M.L., Aide, T.M., Grau, H.R., Riner, G. (2010). A scalable approach to mapping annual land cover at 250 m using MODIS time series data: A case study in the Dry Chaco ecoregion of South America. *Remote Sensing of Environment*, 114(11), 2816–2832.

Congalton, R.G. and Green, K. (2008). *Assessing the Accuracy of Remotely Sensed Data: Principles and Practices*. CRC Press, Boca Raton, FL.

Cortes, C. and Vapnik, V.N. (1995). Support-vector networks. *Machine Learning*, 20(3), 273–297.

Cutler, D.R., Edwards Jr., T.C., Beard, K.H., Cutler, A., Hess, K.T., Gibson, J., Lawler, J.J. (2007). Random forests for classification in ecology. *Ecology*, 88(11), 2783–2792.

Cuturi, M., Vert, J.-P., Birkenes, O., Matsui, T. (2007). A kernel for time series based on global alignments. *IEEE International Conference on Acoustics, Speech and Signal Processing, ICASSP'07*, 2, II–413.

Dash, J., Mathur, A., Foody, G.M., Curran, P.J., Chipman, J.W., Lillesand, T.M. (2007). Land cover classification using multi-temporal MERIS vegetation indices. *International Journal of Remote Sensing*, 28(6), 1137–1159.

DeFries, R.S. and Townshend, J.R.G. (1994). NDVI-derived land cover classifications at a global scale. *International Journal of Remote Sensing*, 15(17), 3567–3586.

Derksen, D., Inglada, J., Michel, J. (2019). A metric for evaluating the geometric quality of land cover maps generated with contextual features from high-dimensional satellite image time series without dense reference data. *Remote Sensing*, 11(16), 1929.

Dietterich, T.G. (2000). Ensemble methods in machine learning. *International Workshop on Multiple Classifier Systems*, Springer, Berlin, Heidelberg.

Eerens, H., Haesen, D., Rembold, F., Urbano, F., Tote, C., Bydekerke, L. (2014). Image time series processing for agriculture monitoring. *Environmental Modelling & Software*, 53, 154–162.

Efron, B. and Tibshirani, R.J. (1994). *An Introduction to the Bootstrap*. CRC Press, Boca Raton, FL.

Eklundh, L. and Jönsson, P. (2015). TIMESAT: A software package for time series processing and assessment of vegetation dynamics. *Remote Sensing Time Series*, Springer, Cham.

Eklundh, L. and Jönsson, P. (2016). TIMESAT for processing time series data from satellite sensors for land surface monitoring. *Multitemporal Remote Sensing*, Springer, Cham.

Foody, G.M. (2020). Explaining the unsuitability of the kappa coefficient in the assessment and comparison of the accuracy of thematic maps obtained by image classification. *Remote Sensing of Environment*, 239, 111630.

Garnot, V.S.F., Landrieu, L., Giordano, S., Chehata, N. (2019a). Satellite image time series classification with pixel-set encoders and temporal self-attention. arXiv preprint:1911.07757.

Garnot, V.S.F., Landrieu, L., Giordano, S., Chehata, N. (2019b). Time-space tradeoff in deep learning models for crop classification on satellite multi-spectral image time series. *IEEE International Geoscience and Remote Sensing Symposium (IGARSS)*, pp. 6247–6250.

Genuer, R., Poggi, J.-M., Tuleau-Malot, C. (2010). Variable selection using random forests. *Pattern Recognition Letters*, 31(14), 2225–2236.

Gers, F.A. and Schmidhuber, J. (2000). Recurrent nets that time and count. *Proceedings of the IEEE-INNS-ENNS International Joint Conference on Neural Networks. IJCNN 2000. Neural Computing: New Challenges and Perspectives for the New Millennium*, 3, 189–194.

Ghamisi, P., Dalla Mura, M., Benediktsson, J.A. (2014). A survey on spectral–spatial classification techniques based on attribute profiles. *IEEE Transactions on Geoscience and Remote Sensing*, 53(5), 2335–2353.

Gómez, C., White, J.C., Wulder, M.A. (2016). Optical remotely sensed time series data for land cover classification: A review. *ISPRS Journal of Photogrammetry and Remote Sensing*, 116, 55–72.

Grabocka, J., Schilling, N., Wistuba, M., Schmidt-Thieme, L. (2014). Learning time series shapelets. *Proceedings of the 20th ACM SIGKDD International Conference on Knowledge Discovery and Data Mining*, pp. 392–401.

Gupta, S. and Rajan, K. (2010). Temporal signature matching for land cover classification. *International Society for Photogrammetry and Remote Sensing – Technical Commission VIII Symposium*, Kyoto, Japan.

Haralick, R.M. (1979). Statistical and structural approaches to texture. *Proceedings of the IEEE*, 67(5), 786–804.

He, K., Zhang, X., Ren, S., Sun, J. (2016). Deep residual learning for image recognition. *Proceedings of the IEEE Conference on Computer Vision and Pattern Recognition*, pp. 770–778.

Hills, J., Lines, J., Baranauskas, E., Mapp, J., Bagnall, A. (2014). Classification of time series by shapelet transformation. *Data Mining and Knowledge Discovery*, 28(4), 851–881.

Ho, T.K. (1998). The random subspace method for constructing decision forests, *IEEE Transactions on Pattern Analysis and Machine Intelligence*, 20(8), 832–844.

Hochreiter, S. and Schmidhuber, J. (1997). Long short-term memory. *Neural Computation*, 9(8), 1735–1780.

Hsu, C.-W. and Lin, C.-J. (2002). A comparison of methods for multiclass Support Vector Machines. *IEEE Transactions on Neural Networks*, 13(2), 415–425.

Hubert-Moy, L., Cotonnec, A., Le Du, L., Chardin, A., Pérez, P. (2001). A comparison of parametric classification procedures of remotely sensed data applied on different landscape units. *Remote Sensing of Environment*, 75(2), 174–187.

Ienco, D., Gaetano, R., Dupaquier, C., Maurel, P. (2017). Land cover classification via multitemporal spatial data by deep recurrent neural networks. *IEEE Geoscience and Remote Sensing Letters*, 14(10), 1685–1689.

Ienco, D., Interdonato, R., Gaetano, R., Minh, D.H.T. (2019). Combining Sentinel-1 and Sentinel-2 satellite image time series for land cover mapping via a multi-source deep learning architecture. *ISPRS Journal of Photogrammetry and Remote Sensing*, 158, 11–22.

Inglada, J., Arias, M., Tardy, B., Hagolle, O., Valero, S., Morin, D., Dedieu, G., Sepulcre, G., Bontemps, S., Defourny, P., Koetz, B. (2015). Assessment of an operational system for crop type map production using high temporal and spatial resolution satellite optical imagery. *Remote Sensing*, 7(9), 12356–12379.

Inglada, J., Vincent, A., Arias, M., Tardy, B., Morin, D., Rodes, I. (2017). Operational high resolution land cover map production at the country scale using satellite image time series. *Remote Sensing*, 9(1), 95.

Interdonato, R., Ienco, D., Gaetano, R., Ose, K. (2019). DuPLO: A DUal view Point deep Learning architecture for time series classificatiOn. *ISPRS Journal of Photogrammetry and Remote Sensing*, 149, 91–104.

Ioffe, S. and Szegedy, C. (2015). Batch normalization: Accelerating deep network training by reducing internal covariate shift. *International Conference on Machine Learning*, pp. 448–456.

Ismail Fawaz, H., Forestier, G., Weber, J., Idoumghar, L., Muller, P.-A. (2019). Deep learning for time series classification: A review. *Data Mining and Knowledge Discovery*, 33(4), 917–963.

Jia, K., Liang, S., Wei, X., Yao, Y., Su, Y., Jiang, B., Wang, X. (2014). Land cover classification of Landsat data with phenological features extracted from time series MODIS NDVI data. *Remote Sensing*, 6(11), 11518–11532.

Jönsson, P. and Eklundh, L. (2002). Seasonality extraction by function fitting to time series of satellite sensor data. *IEEE Transactions on Geoscience and Remote Sensing*, 40(8), 1824–1832.

Jönsson, P. and Eklundh, L. (2004). TIMESAT – A program for analyzing time series of satellite sensor data. *Computers & Geosciences*, 30(8), 833–845.

Karasiak, N., Dejoux, J.-F., Fauvel, M., Willm, J., Monteil, C., Sheeren, D. (2019). Statistical stability and spatial instability in mapping forest tree species by comparing 9 years of satellite image time series. *Remote Sensing*, 11(21), 2512.

Karlsson, I., Papapetrou, P., Boström, H. (2016). Generalized random shapelet forests. *Data Mining and Knowledge Discovery*, 30(5), 1053–1085.

Kingma, D.P. and Ba, J. (2014). Adam: A method for stochastic optimization. *International Conference on Learning Representations (ICLR)*.

Krizhevsky, A., Sutskever, I., Hinton, G.E. (2012). Imagenet classification with deep convolutional neural networks. *Advances in Neural Information Processing Systems*, pp. 1097–1105.

Landis, J.R. and Koch, G.G. (1977). The measurement of observer agreement for categorical data. *Biometrics*, 33(1), 159–174.

Lin, J., Khade, R., Li, Y. (2012). Rotation-invariant similarity in time series using bag-of-patterns representation. *Journal of Intelligent Information Systems*, 39(2), 287–315.

Lines, J. and Bagnall, A. (2015). Time series classification with ensembles of elastic distance measures. *Data Mining and Knowledge Discovery*, 29(3), 565–592.

Lines, J., Davis, L.M., Hills, J., Bagnall, A. (2012). A shapelet transform for time series classification. *Proceedings of the 18th ACM SIGKDD International Conference on Knowledge Discovery and Data Mining*, pp. 289–297.

Liu, C., Frazier, P., Kumar, L. (2007). Comparative assessment of the measures of thematic classification accuracy. *Remote Sensing of Environment*, 107(4), 606–616.

Lucas, B., Shifaz, A., Pelletier, C., O'Neill, L., Zaidi, N., Goethals, B., Petitjean, F., Webb, G.I. (2019). Proximity forest: An effective and scalable distance-based classifier for time series. *Data Mining and Knowledge Discovery*, 33(3), 607–635.

Ma, L., Liu, Y., Zhang, X., Ye, Y., Yin, G., Johnson, B.A. (2019). Deep learning in remote sensing applications: A meta-analysis and review. *ISPRS Journal of Photogrammetry and Remote Sensing*, 152, 166–177.

Matton, N., Sepulcre, G., Waldner, F., Valero, S., Morin, D., Inglada, J., Arias, M., Bontemps, S., Koetz, B., Defourny, P. (2015). An automated method for annual cropland mapping along the season for various globally-distributed agrosystems using high spatial and temporal resolution time series. *Remote Sensing*, 7(10), 13208–13232.

Maus, V., Câmara, G., Cartaxo, R., Sanchez, A., Ramos, F.M., De Queiroz, G.R. (2016). A time-weighted dynamic time warping method for land-use and land-cover mapping. *IEEE Journal of Selected Topics in Applied Earth Observations and Remote Sensing*, 9(8), 3729–3739.

Minh, D.H.T., Ienco, D., Gaetano, R., Lalande, N., Ndikumana, E., Osman, F., Maurel, P. (2018). Deep recurrent neural networks for winter vegetation quality mapping via multitemporal SAR Sentinel-1. *IEEE Geoscience and Remote Sensing Letters*, 15(3), 464–468.

Mountrakis, G., Im, J., Ogole, C. (2011). Support vector machines in remote sensing: A review. *ISPRS Journal of Photogrammetry and Remote Sensing*, 66(3), 247–259.

Mróz, M. and Sobieraj, A. (2004). Comparison of several vegetation indices calculated on the basis of a seasonal SPOT XS time series, and their suitability for land cover and agricultural crop identification. *Technical Sciences*, 7, 39–66.

Müller, K.-R., Mika, S., Rätsch, G., Tsuda, K., Schölkopf, B. (2001). An introduction to kernel-based learning algorithms. *IEEE Transactions on Neural Networks*, 12(2), 181.

Ndikumana, E., Ho Tong Minh, D., Baghdadi, N., Courault, D., Hossard, L. (2018). Deep recurrent neural network for agricultural classification using multitemporal SAR Sentinel-1 for Camargue, France. *Remote Sensing*, 10(8), 1217.

Pal, M. (2005). Random forest classifier for remote sensing classification, *International Journal of Remote Sensing*, 26(1), 217–222.

Pal, M. and Mather, P. (2005). Support vector machines for classification in remote sensing. *International Journal of Remote Sensing*, 26(5), 1007–1011.

Pelletier, C., Valero, S., Inglada, J., Champion, N., Dedieu, G. (2016). Assessing the robustness of random forests to map land cover with high resolution satellite image time series over large areas. *Remote Sensing of Environment*, 187, 156–168.

Pelletier, C., Valero, S., Inglada, J., Champion, N., Marais Sicre, C., Dedieu, G. (2017). Effect of training class label noise on classification performances for land cover mapping with satellite image time series. *Remote Sensing*, 9(2), 173.

Pelletier, C., Webb, G.I., Petitjean, F. (2019). Temporal convolutional neural network for the classification of satellite image time series. *Remote Sensing*, 11(5), 523.

Petitjean, F., Inglada, J., Gançarski, P. (2012). Satellite image time series analysis under time warping. *IEEE Transactions on Geoscience and Remote Sensing*, 50(8), 3081–3095.

Pittman, K., Hansen, M.C., Becker-Reshef, I., Potapov, P.V., Justice, C.O. (2010). Estimating global cropland extent with multi-year MODIS data. *Remote Sensing*, 2(7), 1844–1863.

Pontius Jr., R.G. and Millones, M. (2011). Death to Kappa: Birth of quantity disagreement and allocation disagreement for accuracy assessment. *International Journal of Remote Sensing*, 32(15), 4407–4429.

Probst, P. and Boulesteix, A.-L. (2017). To tune or not to tune the number of trees in random forest. *The Journal of Machine Learning Research*, 18(1), 6673–6690.

Quinlan, J.R. (1986). Induction of decision trees. *Machine Learning*, 1(1), 81–106.

Quinlan, J.R. (1993). *C4.5: Programs for Machine Learning*, vol. 1. Morgan Kaufmann, Burlington, VT.

Radoux, J., Lamarche, C., Van Bogaert, E., Bontemps, S., Brockmann, C., Defourny, P. (2014). Automated training sample extraction for global land cover mapping. *Remote Sensing*, 6(5), 3965.

Rakthanmanon, T. and Keogh, E. (2013). Fast shapelets: A scalable algorithm for discovering time series shapelets. *Proceedings of the 2013 SIAM International Conference on Data Mining*, SIAM, pp. 668–676.

Rodríguez-Galiano, V.F., Ghimire, B., Rogan, J., Chica-Olmo, M., Rigol-Sanchez, J.P. (2012). An assessment of the effectiveness of a random forest classifier for land-cover classification. *ISPRS Journal of Photogrammetry and Remote Sensing*, 67, 93–104.

Rußwurm, M. and Körner, M. (2017). Temporal vegetation modelling using long short-term memory networks for crop identification from medium-resolution multi-spectral satellite images. *Proceedings of the IEEE Conference on Computer Vision and Pattern Recognition Workshops*, pp. 11–19.

Rußwurm, M. and Körner, M. (2018). Multi-temporal land cover classification with sequential recurrent encoders. *ISPRS International Journal of Geo-Information*, 7(4), 129.

Rußwurm, M. and Körner, M. (2019). Self-attention for raw optical satellite time series classification. arXiv preprint:1910.10536.

Rußwurm, M., Pelletier, C., Zollner, M., Lefèvre, S., Körner, M. (2020). BreizhCrops: A time series dataset for crop type mapping. arXiv preprint:1905.11893.

Sakoe, H. and Chiba, S. (1978). Dynamic programming algorithm optimization for spoken word recognition. *IEEE Transactions on Acoustics, Speech, and Signal Processing*, 26(1), 43–49.

Schäfer, P. (2015). The BOSS is concerned with time series classification in the presence of noise. *Data Mining and Knowledge Discovery*, 29(6), 1505–1530.

Schäfer, P. (2016). Scalable time series classification. *Data Mining and Knowledge Discovery*, 30(5), 1273–1298.

Schäfer, P. and Högqvist, M. (2012). SFA: A symbolic Fourier approximation and index for similarity search in high dimensional datasets. *Proceedings of the 15th International Conference on Extending Database Technology*, pp. 516–527.

Schäfer, P. and Leser, U. (2017a). Fast and accurate time series classification with WEASEL. *Proceedings of the 2017 ACM on Conference on Information and Knowledge Management*, pp. 637–646.

Schäfer, P. and Leser, U. (2017b). Multivariate time series classification with WEASEL+ MUSE. arXiv preprint:1711.11343.

Schölkopf, B. and Smola, A.J. (2002). *Learning with Kernels: Support Vector Machines, Regularization, Optimization, and Beyond.* MIT Press, Cambridge, MA.

Schuster, M. and Paliwal, K.K. (1997). Bidirectional recurrent neural networks. *IEEE Transactions on Signal Processing*, 45(11), 2673–2681.

Shifaz, A., Pelletier, C., Petitjean, F., Webb, G.I. (2020). TS-CHIEF: A scalable and accurate forest algorithm for time series classification. *Data Mining and Knowledge Discovery*, pp. 1–34.

Silleos, N.G., Alexandridis, T.K., Gitas, I.Z., Perakis, K. (2006). Vegetation indices: Advances made in biomass estimation and vegetation monitoring in the last 30 years. *Geocarto International*, 21(4), 21–28.

Son, N.-T., Chen, C.-F., Chen, C.-R., Minh, V.-Q. (2018). Assessment of Sentinel-1A data for rice crop classification using random forests and support vector machines. *Geocarto International*, 33(6), 587–601.

Srivastava, N., Hinton, G., Krizhevsky, A., Sutskever, I., Salakhutdinov, R. (2014). Dropout: A simple way to prevent neural networks from overfitting. *The Journal of Machine Learning Research*, 15(1), 1929–1958.

Stehman, S.V. (1997). Selecting and interpreting measures of thematic classification accuracy. *Remote Sensing of Environment*, 62(1), 77–89.

Sutskever, I., Martens, J., Dahl, G., Hinton, G. (2013). On the importance of initialization and momentum in deep learning. *International Conference on Machine Learning*, pp. 1139–1147.

Tan, C.-P., Koay, J.-Y., Lim, K.-S., Ewe, H.-T., Chuah, H.-T. (2007). Classification of multi-temporal SAR images for rice crops using combined entropy decomposition and support vector machine technique. *Progress in Electromagnetics Research*, 71, 19–39.

Thanh Noi, P. and Kappas, M. (2018). Comparison of random forest, k-nearest neighbor, and support vector machine classifiers for land cover classification using Sentinel-2 imagery. *Sensors*, 18(1), 18.

Trias-Sanz, R. (2006). Texture orientation and period estimator for discriminating between forests, orchards, vineyards, and tilled fields. *IEEE Transactions on Geoscience and Remote Sensing*, 44(10), 2755–2760.

Ueda, N. and Nakano, R. (1996). Generalization error of ensemble estimators. *IEEE International Conference on Neural Networks*, 1, 90–95.

Valero, S., Morin, D., Inglada, J., Sepulcre, G., Arias, M., Hagolle, O., Dedieu, G., Bontemps, S., Defourny, P., Koetz, B. (2016). Production of a dynamic cropland mask by processing remote sensing image series at high temporal and spatial resolutions. *Remote Sensing*, 8(1), 55.

Vapnik, V.N. (1995). *The Nature of Statistical Learning Theory*. Springer Science & Business Media, Berlin, Heidelberg.

Vapnik, V.N. (1998). *Statistical Learning Theory*. Wiley, New York.

Vaswani, A., Shazeer, N., Parmar, N., Uszkoreit, J., Jones, L., Gomez, A.N., Kaiser, Ł., Polosukhin, I. (2017). Attention is all you need. *Advances in Neural Information Processing Systems*, pp. 5998–6008.

Waldner, F., Canto, G.S., Defourny, P. (2015). Automated annual cropland mapping using knowledge-based temporal features. *ISPRS Journal of Photogrammetry and Remote Sensing*, 110, 1–13.

Ye, L. and Keogh, E. (2009). Time series shapelets: A new primitive for data mining. *Proceedings of the 15th ACM SIGKDD International Conference on Knowledge Discovery and Data Mining*, pp. 947–956.

Ye, S., Rogan, J., Sangermano, F. (2018). Monitoring rubber plantation expansion using Landsat data time series and a shapelet-based approach. *ISPRS Journal of Photogrammetry and Remote Sensing*, 136, 134–143.

Zhang, X., Friedl, M.A., Schaaf, C.B., Strahler, A.H., Hodges, J.C.F., Gao, F., Reed, B.C., Huete, A. (2003). Monitoring vegetation phenology using MODIS. *Remote Sensing of Environment*, 84(3), 471–475.

Zhang, M.-Q., Guo, H.-Q., Xie, X., Zhang, T.-T., Ouyang, Z.-T., Zhao, B. (2013). Identification of land-cover characteristics using MODIS time series data: An application in the Yangtze River Estuary. *PloS One*, 8(7), 1–11.

Zhong, L., Hu, L., Zhou, H. (2019). Deep learning based multi-temporal crop classification. *Remote Sensing of Environment*, 221, 430–443.

Zhu, X.X., Tuia, D., Mou, L., Xia, G.-S., Zhang, L., Xu, F., Fraundorfer, F. (2017). Deep learning in remote sensing: A comprehensive review and list of resources. *IEEE Geoscience and Remote Sensing Magazine*, 5(4), 8–36.

3

Semantic Analysis of Satellite Image Time Series

Corneliu Octavian DUMITRU and Mihai DATCU

German Aerospace Center, Oberpfaffenhofen, Germany

During the last years, huge quantities of satellite images are available due to the increased number of Earth observation (EO) sensors. Thanks to this, the acquisition frequency is increasing. Furthermore, the high spatial resolution of the sensors gives access to detailed image structures in order to study the dynamics of the Earth's surface. This is one of the emergent issues in the field of remote sensing imagery processing. The opportunities to compose high-resolution satellite image time series are growing, and the observation of precise spatio-temporal structures in dynamic scenes is getting increasingly more accessible.

3.1. Introduction

In linguistics, "semantics" refers to the meaning of language. In computer science, "semantics" covers aspects of programming languages, metadata or standardization as ontologies. In all these cases, the semantic message is represented as text.

Images as two-dimensional signals recorded by a photographic camera do not have an inherent meaning; they are signatures of the imaged objects, objects that can be described semantically, as having a meaning. Thus, the images can gain meaning only in an annotation, labeling process.

Change Detection and Image Time Series Analysis 2,
coordinated by Abdourrahmane M. ATTO, Francesca BOVOLO and Lorenzo BRUZZONE.
© ISTE Ltd 2021.

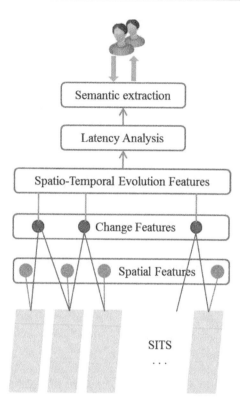

Figure 3.1. *Spatio-temporal evolution patterns depending on the spatial and temporal resolution and scales of the observations. SITS: satellite image time series. For a color version of this figure, see www.iste.co.uk/atto/change2.zip*

This can be manual or supported by machine learning paradigms, and always needs supervision directly by a human or indirectly from pre-existing labeled datasets.

Images need to be decomposed in pixels, regions or a grid partition of patches; one extracts their basic descriptors as color, texture or shape; analyzes their topological properties and further aggregates these elements and associates them to observe objects, shadows or backgrounds, thus creating the semantic description by learning from examples or existing rules.

Earth observation images are acquired by sensors designed to record physical parameters, such as, in the case of PolSAR (Polarimetric Synthetic Aperture Radar), vegetation and water indices in the case of multispectral observations or surface and volume scattering.

Satellite image time series (SITS) are high-complexity multidimensional signals represented in space, time and spectral domain. SITS observe objects and structures and their spatial and temporal evolution, i.e. spatio-temporal evolution patterns. The spatio-temporal evolution patterns can have a wide range of complexity, from simple changes between two observations, as in the example of a flooded area, to the evolution of mega-cities impacting urbanism, traffic networks, water management, agriculture and the overall ecosystem. The nature and consequently the meaning of spatio-temporal evolution patterns depend on the spatial and temporal resolutions of the observations. An airplane is observed with very high-resolution (VHR) sensors at a short temporal scale, while polar ice cover is observed at a lower spatial resolution for extended areas and a long period of time. Figure 3.1 presents examples of spatio-temporal evolution patterns depending on the spatial and temporal resolution and scales of the observations.

In general, spatio-temporal evolution pattern recognition in SITS relies on the appropriate representation and use of knowledge and on the capability of the predictions based on which a system can understand and learn EO image content. SITS can be interpreted as being based on the output of latent pattern detectors. Thus, it is possible to recognize expected objects and their evolution by using a coding procedure that works in space and time. In contrast, the detection of unexpected objects, i.e. anomalies or artifacts not represented in the existing models, usually requires broader spatial contextual analysis needed to reinforce the learning of latent information. These hypotheses are confirmed by the human interaction where unexpected spatio-temporal evolution patterns can be discovered by contextual analysis. SITS analysis is a hierarchic process aiming to link the elementary image descriptors, which bridges the semantic and sensory gaps between low-level image features and high-level concepts describing the meaning of spatio-temporal evolution patterns at semantic understanding. The generic process is depicted in Figure 3.2.

At a low level, elementary spatial and spectral descriptors are extracted from each image. They are indexed in time by the moment of the image acquisition.

The sequence of images in the SITS is analyzed to detect the changes and extract their features. These are also indexed in time by the moment and the intervals between the image acquisitions. This step is mainly based on the utilization of similarity measures.

Further, these elementary features are jointly analyzed and aggregated to form the spatio-temporal evolution patterns. This is achieved using methods of pattern recognition or time series analysis such as clustering or Markov estimation.

Since the observations are noisy and affected by disturbance factors, as atmospheric or illumination variability, a latency analysis is needed to filter the relevant spatio-temporal evolution patterns. The methods applied are from the class of generative models or information theoretic algorithms.

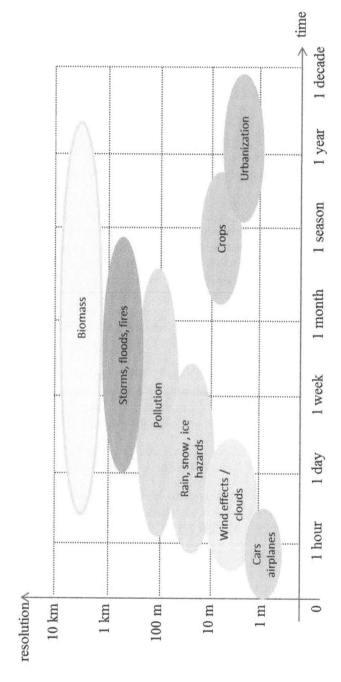

Figure 3.2. *Change processes linked to the phenomena occurring in an STIS that have different time scales. For example, airplane appearances are evanescent structures characterized by short time scales, while buildings (urban areas) are stable structures characterized by relatively long time scales. The change processes related to agricultural developments such as plant growth or harvest phenomena are at various time scales. All these changes depend on the resolution of the SITS. For a color version of this figure, see www.iste.co.uk/atto/change2.zip*

The highest abstraction, the semantics of spatio-temporal evolution patterns, is obtained in the machine learning process, either via active learning in human–machine interaction or using pre-existing annotated datasets. The overall paradigm can also be modeled by deep architectures.

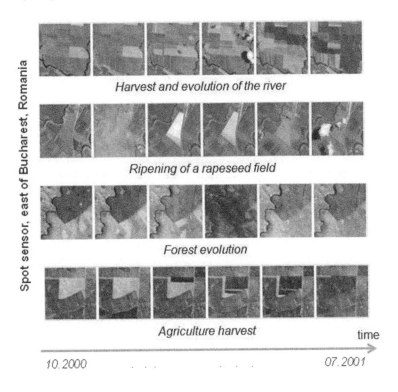

Figure 3.3. *Evolution of four classes extracted from the SITS over the east of Bucharest acquired by SPOT satellite (ADAM project 2003). For a color version of this figure, see www.iste.co.uk/atto/change2.zip*

3.1.1. *Typical SITS examples*

Monitoring the land cover/land use evolution is necessary for understanding the changes and transformations of the areas in the short or long time. Nowadays, large data collections have been created using images provided by high-, medium- or low-resolution images (e.g. LANDSAT, Sentinel-1, Sentinel-2, SPOT, TerraSAR-X and WorldView), which have been identified as satellite image time series (SITS) that can provide significant knowledge about the Earth's surface dynamics.

In order to build a reliable SITS, a number of aspects should be taken into account, such as selection of the appropriate satellite and area of investigation; image cleaning and removal of artifacts and geometric and radiometric corrections.

Further in this section, some examples of SITS are shown. Figure 3.3 presents the evolution of four classes (harvest and evolution of the river, ripening of a rapeseed field, forest evolution, and agriculture harvest) over a year between October 15, 2000, and July 27, 2001. The SITS is composed of SPOT-1, -2 and -4 multispectral images with three bands and a spatial resolution of 20 m. The covered area is a rural area located in the east of Bucharest, Romania (DLR and CNES cooperation 2016).

Another example over Bucharest is presented in Figure 3.4, where the images from LANDSAT multispectral satellite were used to create the SITS (Landsat 2020). The SITS is composed of multispectral images with seven bands and has a spatial resolution of 30 m. In this figure, we present the evolution of three classes and we extracted from this SITS 12 significant examples for the period between July 16, 1991, and October 4, 2006. These classes show the changes in the area over time, such as a reduction of the agricultural area and the appearance of new houses or a new lake.

Similar examples are displayed in the next two figures for the SAR (synthetic aperture radar) satellite images. In both cases, the TerraSAR-X images are used with a spatial resolution of 2.9 m. In the first case, the covered area is Sendai in Japan, affected in March 11, 2011, by a tsunami, and the second case is the area of the Elbe River in Germany, affected by floods in June 15, 2013 (TerraSAR-X 2020).

Figure 3.5 presents six classes and their evolution before and after the tsunami. For some of them (e.g. airport, channels, shore), we can see the changes over time and the return to their original state.

Similar results are presented in Figure 3.6, for the case of flooding, where five classes are selected and the changes between pre- and post-event are visible.

3.1.2. *Irregular acquisitions*

In most cases, for multispectral SITS, the acquisitions of the images are affected by the weather conditions and by snow in winter (in the case of monitoring of the agriculture seasons). Taking into account these situations plus the revisit period of satellite (from 2 to 6 days), in most cases, will encounter irregular acquisitions. In the case of SAR images, the only influence will be from the revisit period of the satellite. Concerning the previous examples, in the following three figures, we present the irregular acquisition in the cases of SPOT (Figure 3.7), Landsat (Figure 3.8) and TerraSAR-X (Figure 3.9).

For the historical data from the archive, the creation of SITS depends on the availability of previous acquisitions.

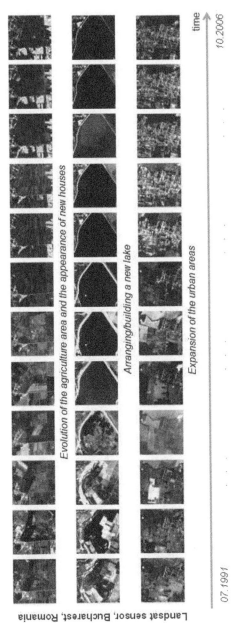

Figure 3.4. *Evolution of three classes extracted from the SITS over the center of Bucharest, acquired by LANDSAT satellite. For a color version of this figure, see www.iste.co.uk/atto/change2.zip*

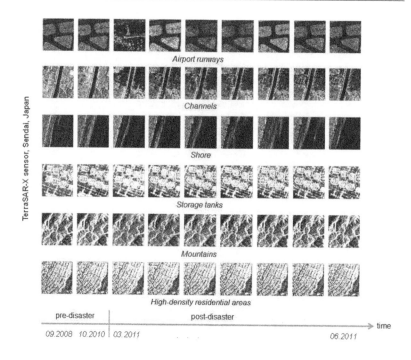

Figure 3.5. *Evolution of the selected classes extracted from the SITS over the area affected by the tsunami in Sendai, Japan, acquired by TerraSAR-X satellite (TELEIOS project 2013)*

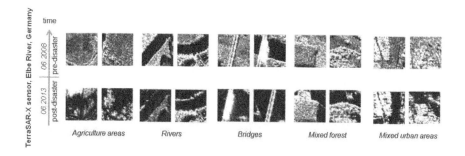

Figure 3.6. *Evolution of the selected classes extracted from the two images over the area affected by floods in Germany, acquired by TerraSAR-X satellite*

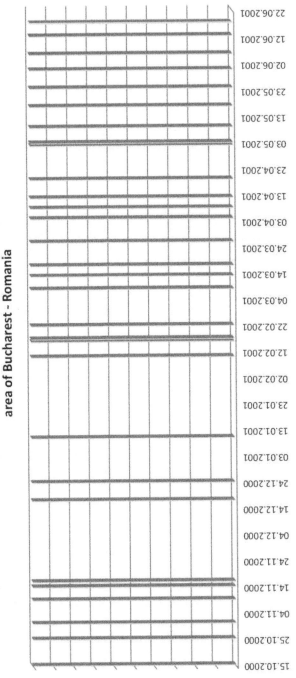

Figure 3.7. *Acquisition dates of cloud-free SPOT images. The horizontal axis represents acquisition time, which is irregularly sampled. For a color version of this figure, see www.iste.co.uk/atto/change2.zip*

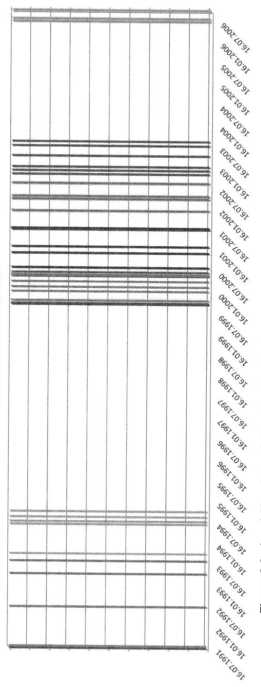

Figure 3.8. *Acquisition dates of cloud-free Landsat images. The horizontal axis represents acquisition time, which is irregularly sampled. For a color version of this figure, see www.iste.co.uk/atto/change2.zip*

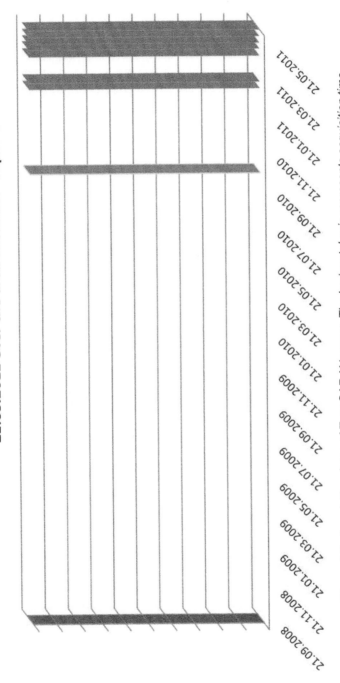

Figure 3.9. *Acquisition dates of TerraSAR-X images. The horizontal axis represents acquisition time, which is irregularly sampled. For a color version of this figure, see www.iste.co.uk/atto/change2.zip*

3.1.3. *The chapter structure*

This chapter is organized into six main sections. Section 3.2 explains the need for semantics in EO SITS, while section 3.3 describes the similarities metrics. Section 3.4 presents typical feature methods used for the SITS. Section 3.5 contains the classification methods for SITS, and section 3.6 summarizes our conclusions and future work. The chapter ends with acknowledgments and a list of references.

This chapter proposes a number of algorithms developed and tested during different projects for different SITS acquired by the multispectral and SAR sensors. In conclusion, we will try to provide some suggestions to be taken into account to efficiently analyze EO SITS.

3.2. Why are semantics needed in SITS?

Earth cover is continuously changing. Causes and factors are many, from humidity after rain to the evolution of vegetation or human activities. The changes can be continuous and periodic as the evolution of natural vegetation may show discontinuities, for example agricultural crops can be flooded or disappear due to human work (e.g. construction of a road).

EO multi-temporal images are difficult to be obtained under identical conditions. Atmospheric conditions, sun position and look angles affect the radiometric calibration. Sensor look angle or sun position influences the perspective and shadows of the observed objects. If multi-temporal observations are obtained by different EO sensors, then the spatial resolution or the wavelengths of the recorded images may differ.

SITS are at the convergence of a multitude of causes and factors; therefore, the extraction of relevant meaningful information needs the definition of a specific taxonomy and semantics. The meaning of SITS information may refer both to conceptual aspects, such as classifications, as well as physical entities.

The taxonomy is defining the evolution of the image spatial structures, i.e. pixels, regions or image patches.

The time series of radiometric information, for example, spectral indices for multispectral images or backscatter coefficients for SAR data, carry information on the periodicity of vegetation evolution, crops management and the identification of anomalies, such as late spring snowfall. The information is related to physical quantities like the vegetation index and the NDVI (normalized difference vegetation index).

The spectral signatures of single EO images are not discriminatory enough for various classes of land cover types, mainly in the case of vegetation. However, the temporal evolution of the spectral signatures is an important descriptor of land cover. Thus, the time series at the pixel level are used for land cover classification mainly for natural vegetation and agriculture.

At the image region level, the classification change/no-change is the simplest semantic concept. A more elaborate classification is in change classes, i.e. assigning a new semantics to the pair of labels of two or multiple observations.

The most specific and challenging meaning assignment regards the evolution patterns. These are multidimensional patterns in space, time, sensing wavelengths and extracted physical quantities.

With the advent of deep learning, SITS may also analyze at the patch (cubelets) level and the images are partied in a spatio-temporal grid, typically of the order of 100 x 100 x 100 pixels. Each cublet may be assigned multiple semantic labels.

3.3. Similarity metrics

SITS analysis, at its basis, compares observations at different time moments. The comparison can be directly of the image pixels or of local image features. Therefore, both the image feature and the chosen metric influence the results. This section discusses the most popular metrics and their properties relative to SITS analysis.

The Lp norm is popular mainly by the use of L2, the Euclidian distance, and L1, the Manhattan norm. In terms of change detection, the L2 norm is sensitive to the data calibration and observation noise. Used for regularization, the L1 norm favors sparsity, while the L2 norm favors small values, i.e. a Guassianity assumption. Other norms are heuristically applied, estimating the value of p with experiments adapted to particular cases.

The angular distance is one of the most robust similarity measures at risk of changing due to radiometric correction inaccuracy and atmospheric effects.

The Hausdorff distance is used for the comparison of object shapes.

The Kullback–Leibler divergence is used to compare the probabilistic models of two observations, i.e. their probability distributions. This enables the multi-sensor multi-temporal analysis, for example, of multispectral and SAR images. In the case of first-order statistics, the information is primarily radiometric, and for the second-order statistics, the changes of spatial structures are also measured.

Mutual information is a strong measure for the assessment of statistical independence. It applies to the multi-sensor multi-temporal analysis.

The normalized compression distance (NCD) is the most unbiased similarity measure. It directly compares the observations without any intermediate feature extraction or use of metrics. It is probably the most powerful similarity metric for semantic extraction.

3.4. Feature methods

Early works mainly focused on analyzing the dynamic patterns of vegetation. Since 2000, increasingly more methods are developed to analyze the evolution of SITS.

The methods start with a hierarchical Bayesian modeling of SITS information content, which enables users to link spatio-temporal structures to their specific interests (Heas and Datcu 2005).

The Gibbs Markov random fields and auto-binominal Gibbs random filed models are applied to characterize the spatio-temporal structures (Gueguen 2007). This is followed by a spatio-temporal indexing based on the compression method. The normalized sufficient compression distance was proposed in order to assess the quantity of relevant information that an object provides to another, and based on this, an indexing compression spatio-temporal pattern was used to extract the relevant information from SITS (Gueguen 2007).

A frequent sequential pattern extraction method is found in Julea *et al.* (2011), where the temporal evolution is extracted at the pixel level.

A dynamic time warping (Petitjean and Weber 2014) is a good solution in the case of irregular sampling and the need to compare pairs of SITS with different number of samples.

More recently, the auto-encoders began to be used increasingly more often as methods to extract features (Dumitru *et al.* 2019).

3.5. Classification methods

With increasing satellite image acquisition rates and image resolution, both image content and temporal patterns are becoming quite diverse, which makes an automatic or at least semi-automatic interpretation of large satellite volumes an increasingly more stringent and demanding technique.

Among few practical implementations of such systems, there are not too many solutions to solve such problems. A very popular satellite image search system is the Tomnod (2018) from Digital Globe or Google Earth (2020) with its related tools.

In the EO, we speak of LandEX (Stepinski *et al.* 2014), GeoIRIS (Shyu *et al.* 2007) and IKONA (Boujemaa 2001), which are dedicated to the indexation of large volumes of image data. However, these systems can only be used for direct queries, and we set aside the intrinsic dependencies in the data that are needed to model more complex classes. The KIM (knowledge-driven information mining) (Datcu *et al.* 2003) system uses the Bayesian hierarchical information representation to link the image content to the user semantic interpretation. To further evolve and to reduce existing limitations of the previous systems, other systems have been developed: the TELEIOS prototype (TELEIOS project 2013), the Earth Observation Librarian (EOLib) system for the ground segment of TerraSAR-X (EOLib project 2018) and now the CANDELA platform (CANDELA project 2020) for the Copernicus data (Copernicus Sentinels Scientific Data Hub 2020), to be operated on CreoDIAS.

3.5.1. *Active learning*

Various cascaded classifiers have been developed and applied, as well as achieved remarkable efficiency regarding object detection in computer vision (Viola and Jones 2004; Wu *et al.* 2008). Contrary to this, in EO, cascaded classifiers have not been exploited like this until the work of Blanchart (2011).

As reported in the literature, as one of the best supervised classifiers, the SVM (support vector machine) is used as a basic element in the cascaded active learning method. The reason why the SVM was chosen is because it can efficiently manage high-dimensional feature vectors while preserving a high level of accuracy. In addition, it has good generalization capability, even for nonlinearly separable cases. To learn about a good SVM, sufficient training samples are required, which is not trivial for practical cases (Cui 2014).

The cascaded active learning approach is developed to manage the increasing volumes of satellite image archives; it allows fast annotation and the discovery of hidden patterns in multi-temporal satellite images.

Active machine learning is the paradigm when the machine is interactively interrogating a user (expert) to label new data points with the desired outputs. It has the major advantage of learning with extremely few training samples.

Cascaded learning implemented on the EOLib and CANDELA systems is based on a hierarchical top-down processing scheme for object retrieval in a high volume of satellite images. The algorithm learns, via a multistage active learning process, a cascade of classifiers each working at a certain scale on a patch-based representation of images. At each stage of the hierarchy, the user eliminates large parts of images considered to be non-relevant, with the purpose of setting the focus at the finest scales on more promising and as spatially limited as possible areas. The scheme is based on the fact that, by reducing the size of the patch size (e.g. 128x128 pixels to 64x64 pixels, etc.), the properties of the targeted object can be better captured. The cascaded hierarchy is introduced to compensate for the extra computational burden incurred by diminishing the size of the patch, which causes an explosion of the number of patches to process. This strategy (Blanchart 2011) proposed a cascade active learning algorithm to build a classifier based on SVM at each level of the hierarchy and to provide a new multiple instance learning algorithm to automatically propagate the training examples from one level of the hierarchy to the other.

3.5.2. *Relevance feedback*

Often, in many publications, the SVM is associated with RF (relevance feedback) (Ferecatu *et al.* 2004; Costache and Datcu 2007).

The RF method embedded into the search systems should be very fast and maximize the quality of the results based on user interaction. Normally, an RF method has two main components: one for learning and one for selection. At every step, the system learns about the desired class based on the feedback given by the user, by marking the images/patches as "relevant" (meaning similar to the class that is searched for) or as "irrelevant" (meaning the class is not of interest). Given the current estimation of the desired class, the user chooses the images/patches that are asked for in order to provide feedback during the next step. The learning task is very difficult in the context of RF because the training examples are rare and imbalanced, to which is added the real-time operation.

3.5.3. *Compression-based pattern recognition*

Another perspective is the supervised approach of a k-NN (nearest neighbors) algorithm based on the NCD (normalized compression distance) metric. These approaches avoid aspects like complicated data modeling and parameters estimation. The NCD has an important advantage: it does not use features and compares the intrinsic data information.

The NCD is a way of measuring the similarity between two arbitrary objects; it is obtained by approximating the notion of Kolmogorov complexity as real-world compressors and normalizes the information distance. The FCD (fast compression distance) is an accelerating version of the NCD; it avoids computing the full compression concept (Cerra and Datcu 2012). It is demonstrated to be fast without skipping the joint compression step, which shows better performance compared to the NCD (Li *et al.* 2004). The idea behind this is to use the LZW (Lempel–Ziv–Welch) algorithm in order to extract a dictionary from each image patch and to encode it in ascending order into a string. The FCD is defined as an operation that takes into account the joint number of patterns within two dictionaries (Yao 2019).

Essentially, when applied to a single set of patches, the scope of the NCD is to generate a distance matrix that contains similarity grades between pairwise objects. This metric considers the length of the shortest binary program used to transform two items into each other. The similarity between two objects is directly proportional with the difficulty to transform them into each other. Two objects are deemed close if we can significantly "compress" one, given the information in the other, the idea being that if two pieces are more similar, then we can more succinctly describe one, given the other (Coca *et al.* 2018).

The CompLearn Toolkit (2003) is an open-source suite of simple utilities that we can use to apply compression techniques to the process of discovering and learning patterns in completely different domains. In fact, this method is so general that it requires no background knowledge about any particular subject area. There are no domain-specific parameters to set, only a handful of general settings.

The NCD distance is considered to be the distance metric implied in the k-NN classifier since the classification process of new cases is based on a similarity measure (Coca *et al.* 2019).

3.5.4. *Latent Dirichlet allocation*

LDA (latent Dirichlet allocation) (Blei *et al.* 2003) has been developed in natural language processing to discover meaningful topics within a corpus of text documents. It has been later used for various applications in the computer vision and remote sensing domains, such as for the semantic classification of PolSAR images (Tanase 2016), land-cover categorization by a fusion of SAR and multispectral image data (Fernandez-Beltran *et al.* 2018) and the dynamic evolution of the Earth's surface (Vaduva *et al.* 2013a).

In order to apply LDA to each image, this is modeled as a bag-of-words (BoW), a dictionary-based model representing each image with the occurrence of the words within a dictionary (Bahmanyar 2015). LDA discovers an intermediate level of representation of the data known as "topics" in a BoW framework. In image analogy, "topics" are often referred to as visual topics and are used to create a map-like representation of an area by assigning the maximum probable topic for every single word, where words are vectorized pixel values in very small image patches. This method is applied to EO images (e.g. Sentinel-1 images acquired in the polar area for two consecutive years, 2018 and 2019) (Karmakar *et al.* 2020) to create interpretable topic representation maps, each topic being identified by a unique color and representing latent structure of the data.

Vaduva *et al.* (2013b) highlight the evolution of the Earth's surface by using attributes of change which are computed in order to show the land dynamic evolution over time by analyzing consecutive images. Based on these attributes, the generative process of the LDA model is able to latently discover classes of evolution whose semantics is defined by similar dynamic evolutions in time of different regions.

We can say that the LDA model is able to discover a wide range of evolutions of the classes over time (e.g. land cover and land use classes) (Vaduva *et al.* 2013a; Karmakar *et al.* 2020).

3.6. Conclusion

Typical examples of changes are presented in Figures 3.10 and 3.11. In these figures, we can see changes that occur over the years (appearance or disappearance of objects/classes) and changes that occur from one month to another or from one season to another.

Using two practical methods presented in the previous section, Figure 3.12 presents the results for a selected area from a Sentinel-1 image over the area of Belgica Bank in Greenland. The results show how this area can be analyzed with the help of SITS and how important the semantics are in order to understand the changes that occur over time. In addition to this, Figure 3.13 shows the link between the two methods and how semantic labels can be represented by topics.

Given that active learning is a supervised method that requires user interaction (user experience is very important for defining semantic labels) and LDA is unsupervised, this connection between them can be very important for the generalization and creation of benchmark datasets.

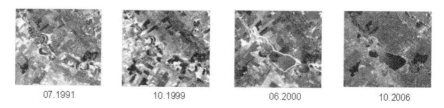

07.1991   10.1999   06.2000   10.2006

Figure 3.10. *Evolution of an area near Bucharest in Romania between July 1991 and October 2006 acquired by Landsat sensor. The images shows the appearance of a recreational lake in 2000 (where before this was agricultural land) and the surrounding area's new houses. For a color version of this figure, see www.iste.co.uk/ atto/change2.zip*

With the advent of EO technology, mainly in the areas of multispectral and SAR missions, the Earth's surface is frequently and continuously imaged at a global scale. Thus, SITS are now becoming the most important EO data product. SITS are an essential asset in multidisciplinary EO applications and valorization domains.

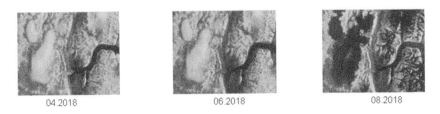

Figure 3.11. *Evolution of another area in Greenland between April 2018 and August 2018, acquired this time by the Sentinel-1 sensor. The images show the evolution of the area covered by mountains, snow and a glacier over the winter and summer season, where the snow starts to melt in summer. For a color version of this figure, see www.iste.co.uk/atto/change2.zip*

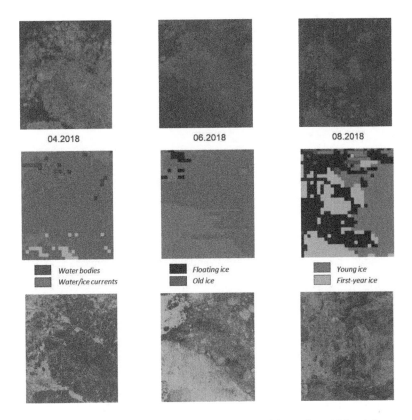

Figure 3.12. *(Top) Evolution of an area in Greenland from the old ice into pancake ice (broken ice). This areas is analyzed using two of the methods: (middle) the active learning method and (bottom) the LDA method. For a color version of this figure, see www.iste.co.uk/atto/change2.zip*

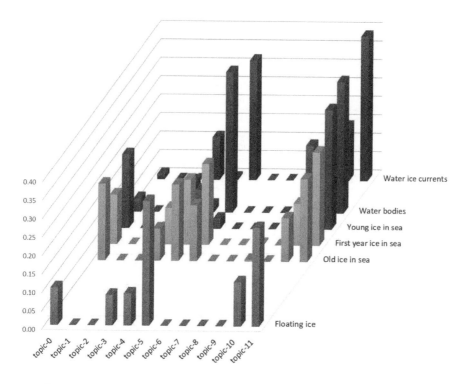

Figure 3.13. *The link between the two methods (active learning and LDA) and how the topics are distributed inside a semantic class (Karmakar et al. 2020). For a color version of this figure, see www.iste.co.uk/atto/change2.zip*

SITS semantics are important in the communication of meaning from the observed Earth dynamic process to the applications and valorization services.

However, the SITS analysis poses many challenges, among which are irregular temporal observations, mainly with optical sensors, radiometric and geometric precise calibration, the different sensing modalities in the case of multi-sensor observations or the lack of reference and training data, mainly in the case of dynamic evolution processes. To overcome these challenges, appropriate selection of the methodology to be applied is needed. A few suggestions are as follows:

– for multispectral observations, the radiometric calibration and atmospheric effects can be reduced using angular distances for change analysis;

– the analysis performed at the image patch level reduces the sensitivity of the geometric calibration, i.e. co-registration;

– the multi-sensor SITS analysis and semantic similarities can be obtained with the use of statistical and information theoretic methods, as used for Bayesian learning, mutual information and NCD-based algorithms;

– the generative models can support the discovery of complex, meaningful, spatio-temporal evolution patterns, as in the case of LDA, which can be a suggestion for semantic annotations;

– semantic annotations can be optioned by the active learning process.

3.7. Acknowledgments

The contribution results from this chapter were partially supported by ESA under the KIM project, by the European Commission under the FP7 TELEIOS project and by the CNES-DLR cooperation. Regarding the satellite images used here, these were provided by the TerraSAR-X Science Service System (under the MTH 1118 proposal), by the French Space Agency (under the ADAM project) and downloaded from NASA Landsat science or from the Copernicus Sentinels Scientific Data Hub.

3.8. References

ADAM Project (2003). Kalideos Adam : assimilation de données par agro-modélisation [Online]. Available at: https://adam.kalideos.fr/drupal/fr.

Bahmanyar, R. (2015). Conception and assessment of semantic feature descriptors for Earth observation images. PhD Thesis, Technical University Munich [Online]. Available at: https://mediatum.ub.tum.de/1283359.

Blanchart, P. (2011). Fast learning methods adapted to the user specificities: Application to Earth observation image information mining. PhD Thesis, École Doctorale d'Informatique, Télécommunications et Électronique de Paris, Télécom ParisTech.

Blei, D., Ng, A., Jordan, M. (2003). Latent Dirichlet allocation. *Journal of Machine Learning Research*, 3, 993–1022.

Boujemaa, N. (2001). Ikona: Interactive specific and generic image retrieval. *MMCBIR*.

CANDELA Project (2020). Candela [Online]. Available at: http://www.candela-h2020.eu/.

Cerra, D. and Datcu, M. (2012). A fast compression-based similarity measure with applications to content-based image retrieval. *Journal of Visual Communication and Image Representation*, 23, 293–302.

Coca, M., Anghel, A., Datcu, M. (2018). Normalized compression distance for SAR image change detection. *IGARSS*, 5784–5787.

Coca, M., Anghel, A., Datcu, M. (2019). Unbiased seamless SAR image change detection based on normalized compression distance. *IEEE Journal of Selected Topics in Applied Earth Observations and Remote Sensing*, 12(7), 2088–2096.

Copernicus Sentinels Scientific Data Hub (2020). Copernicus Open Access Hub [Online]. Available at: https://scihub.copernicus.eu/.

Costache, M. and Datcu, M. (2007). Learning – Unlearning for mining high resolution EO images. *IEEE International Geoscience and Remote Sensing Symposium, IGARSS*, 4761–4764.

Cui, S. (2014). Spatial and temporal SAR image information mining. PhD Thesis, University of Siegen [Online]. Available at: https://dspace.ub.uni-siegen.de/handle/ubsi/823.

Datcu, M., Daschiel, H., Pelizzari, A., Quartulli, M., Galoppo, A., Colapicchioni, A., Pastori, M., Seidel, K., Marchetti, P., D'Elia, S. (2003). Information mining in remote sensing image archives: System concepts. *IEEE TGRS*, 41(12), 2923–2936.

DLR and CNES Cooperation (2016). DLR [Online]. Available at: https://www.dlr.de/content/en/articles/news/2016/20160602_dlr-and-cnes-renew-their-framework-agreement-for-bilateral-cooperation_18064.html.

Dumitru, C., Andrei, V., Schwarz, G., Datcu, M. (2019). Machine learning for sea ice monitoring from satellites. *The International Archives of the Photogrammetry, Remote Sensing and Spatial Information Sciences*, XLII-2/W16, 83–89 [Online]. Available at: https://www.int-arch-photogramm-remote-sens-spatial-inf-sci.net/XLII-2-W16/83/2019/isprs-archives-XLII-2-W16-83-2019.pdf.

EOLib Project (2018). EOLIB [Online]. Available at: http://wiki.services.eoportal.org/tiki-index.php?page=EOLib.

Ferecatu, M., Crucianu, M., Boujemaa, N. (2004). Retrieval of difficult image classes using svd-based relevance feedback. *The 6th ACM SIGMM International Workshop on Multimedia Information Retrieval*, 23–30.

Fernandez-Beltran, R., Haut, J.M., Paoletti, M.E., Plaza, J., Plaza, A., Pla, F. (2018). Multimodal probabilistic latent semantic analysis for Sentinel-1 and Sentinel-2 image fusion. *IEEE GRSL*, 15(9), 1347–1351.

Google Earth (2020). Google Earth [Online]. Available at: https://www.google.de/maps.

Gueguen, L. (2007). Extraction d'information et compression conjointes des séries temporelles d'images satellitaires. PhD Thesis, École Nationale Supérieure des Télécommunications.

Heas, P. and Datcu, M. (2005). Modeling trajectory of dynamic clusters in image time series for spatio-temporal reasoning. *IEEE Transactions on Geoscience and Remote Sensing*, 43(5), 1635–1647.

Julea, A., Méger, N., Bolon, P., Rigotti, C., Doin, M.-P., Lasserre, C., Trouvé, E., Lazarescu, V. (2011). Unsupervised spatiotemporal mining of satellite image time series using grouped frequent sequential patterns. *IEEE Transactions on Geoscience and Remote Sensing*, 49(4), 1417–1430.

Karmakar, C., Dumitru, C.O., Schwarz, G., Datcu, M. (2020). Feature-free explainable data mining in SAR images using latent Dirichlet allocation. *IEEE Journal of Selected Topics in Applied Earth Observations and Remote Sensing*, 14, 676–689.

Landsat (2020). Landsat Science [Online]. Available at: https://landsat.gsfc.nasa.gov/data/.

Li, E., Chen, X., Li, X., Ma, B., Vitanyi, P. (2004). The similarity metric. *IEEE Transaction of Information Theory*, 50, 5804–5807.

Petitjean, F. and Weber, J. (2014). Efficient satellite image time series analysis under time warping. *IEEE Geoscience and Remote Sensing Letters*, 11, 1143–1147.

Shyu, C., Klaric, M., Scott, G., Barb, A., Davis, C., Palaniappan, K. (2007). Geoiris: Geospatial information retrieval and indexing system-content mining, semantics modelling, and complex queries. *IEEE TGRS*, 45(4), 839–852.

Stepinski, T., Netzel, P., Jasiewicz, J. (2014). Landex – A geoweb tool for query and retrieval of spatial patterns in land cover datasets. *IEEE JSTARS*, 7(1), 257–266.

TELEIOS Project (2013). Weltraumtourismus – Zukunft und Gegenwart [Online]. Available at: http://www.earthobservatory.eu/.

TerraSAR-X (2020). TerraSAR-X Science Service System [Online]. Available at: https://sss.terrasar-x.dlr.de/.

The CompLearn Toolkit (2003). CompLearn [Online]. Available at: http://complearn.sourceforge.net/.

Tomnod (2018). Tomnod [Online]. Available at: https://www.tomnod.com/.

Vaduva, C., Costachioiu, T., Patrascu, C., Gavat, I., Lazarescu, V., Datcu, M. (2013a). A latent analysis of earth surface dynamic evolution using change map time series. *IEEE Transactions on Geoscience and Remote Sensing*, 51(4), 2105–2118.

Vaduva, C., Gavat, I., Datcu, M. (2013b). Latent Dirichlet allocation for spatial analysis of satellite images. *IEEE Transactions on Geoscience and Remote Sensing*, 51(5), 2770–2786.

Viola, P. and Jones, M. (2004). Robust real-time face detection. *International Journal in Computer Vision*, 57, 1357–154.

Wu, J., Brubaker, S., Mullin, M., Rehg, J. (2008). Fast asymmetric learning for cascade face detection. *IEEE Transactions on Pattern Analysis and Machine Intelligence*, 30, 36–382.

Yao, W. (2019). Study cases on fast compression distance based data visualization. *IGARSS*, 5804–5807.

4

Optical Satellite Image Time Series Analysis for Environment Applications: From Classical Methods to Deep Learning and Beyond

Matthieu MOLINIER[1], Jukka MIETTINEN[1],
Dino IENCO[2], Shi QIU[3] and Zhe ZHU[3]

[1] *VTT Technical Research Centre of Finland Ltd, Espoo, Finland*
[2] *UMR TETIS Laboratory, INRAE, University of Montpellier, France*
[3] *University of Connecticut, Mansfield, USA*

4.1. Introduction

Satellite image time series (SITS) analysis is increasingly leveraged to address the needs related to environment monitoring, whether it is detecting *abrupt changes* like deforestation, forest fires or storm damages, *gradual environmental trends* like forest regrowth or similarly slow ecosystem changes, or both types of changes simultaneously.

Following the progressively increasing availability and acquisition frequency of open and free satellite imagery over the past decades, SITS methods have evolved

Change Detection and Image Time Series Analysis 2,
coordinated by Abdourrahmane M. ATTO, Francesca BOVOLO and Lorenzo BRUZZONE.
© ISTE Ltd 2021.

from earlier trivial "time series" of two images, to annual time series (one image per year, usually acquired at the most favorable time of the year, or through image compositing), up to the most recent dense time series approaches using all available data. The latter are particularly useful for timely detection and accurate evaluation of phenomena that may happen within a short period of time followed by a quick recovery, as well as accurately identifying drivers of changes, or performing online near-real-time monitoring for the most sensitive environmental ecosystems and resources.

Concurrently, growing data volumes and computing capabilities, coupled with recent advances in neural networks, have led to several breakthroughs in speech recognition, computer vision (CV) and other fields of applied sciences. Advances provided by deep learning (DL) methods in CV and large databases of natural images are progressively benefiting the field of remote sensing, as DL methods are being successfully adapted to the specificity of satellite images (spatial, spectral and temporal resolutions). Yet, relatively fewer works have focused so far on adapting or developing DL models for analyzing dense time series of satellite images, and margins for improvement remain.

The first objective of this chapter is to present an overview of the main time series analysis methods for environment monitoring with Earth Observation (EO), from classical methods to the recent DL methods. We will then demonstrate how the continuous cycle of alternate improvements between data availability (increased data frequency and harmonization between sensors) and methodological developments (dense time series analysis and DL) may lead to a convergence of these techniques with video processing and CV techniques.

Even though synthetic aperture radar (SAR) data can complement optical imagery, for example in forest monitoring, especially in tropical regions due to clouds, this chapter focuses solely on optical image time series, mainly at medium resolution (10–30 m) and considering very high resolution (VHR) imagery as well.

Chapter 4 is organized as follows. Section 4.2 briefly summarizes the main differences between bi-temporal change detection, annual time series and dense time series analyses, then presents the three main types of annual time series methods for environment monitoring – *thresholding*, *differencing* and *segmentation* – and details a few example algorithms for each type of method.

Section 4.3 focuses on dense time series methods using all available data, first presenting the main data preprocessing requirements, then an overview of the four main types of change detection methods based on dense time series analysis – *map classification*, *trajectory classification*, *statistical boundary* and *ensemble approaches* – including details about two of the most widely used algorithms.

After a brief overview of DL methods for remote sensing, section 4.4 details three kinds of network architectures suited for the analysis of SITS - recurrent neural networks (RNN), convolutional neural networks (CNN) and hybrid models combining both (ConvRNN), introducing the main algorithms each time, then identifies further tracks of research for DL in SITS analysis.

Finally, section 4.5 summarizes the key findings from the previous chapters, proposes a prospective reflection upon possible convergence at the crossroads between SITS analysis, video processing, CV and DL, and identifies gaps that need to be addressed further in the field of SITS analysis.

4.2. Annual time series

4.2.1. *Overview of annual time series methods*

The comparison of two images can be seen as the simplest form of change detection. Two observations over the area of interest contain more information than a single look, due to the additional temporal dimension they provide. This temporal dimension is most typically used for detecting changes in the area of interest, but it can also be useful, for example, for multitemporal land cover classification, helping to separate land cover classes with different seasonality characteristics. In their overview of the history and current status of change detection approaches, Hirschmugl *et al.* (2017) separate image-to-image change detection, where earlier and later images are used to detect changes, from more advanced time series analyses that use a sequence of images acquired over the period of interest. However, the frontier between image-to-image change detection and more elaborate time series analyses may sometimes be rather ambiguous. Using temporal transitivity, dual-change detection can be performed successively (i.e. "T0 to T1" and "T1 to T2", etc.), which may already be considered as time series analysis. Alternatively, the two images used in an image-to-image comparison may not always be single date images, but they may be multitemporal composite images, incorporating information from a long time series of images. These variations of approaches for deriving information from a time series of satellite images have been used in various ways in remote sensing-based environmental monitoring.

In this section, we focus on *time series approaches that involve more images than dual change detection*, and illustrate, through practical examples, the application possibilities of annual time series analyses for environmental monitoring. Approaches based on a comparison of two single date images are not discussed, due to the overwhelming number of such approaches used over the past few decades. Instead, we present selected methods that use multitemporal information derived from a series of images in various ways. The common feature to all of the applications presented in this section is that they are *mainly designed to produce annual products or detect changes in annual intervals from a set of images* containing the information. Another common aspect to the methods discussed in this section is that they all concentrate on the *analysis of historical datasets* (also known as *"offline methods"* (Zhu 2017)), as opposed to methods allowing the prediction of future observations, which can be used for rapid change detection (also known as *"online methods"*). The annual offline methods discussed in this section represent early time series analysis approaches, first developed at a time when image availability and data processing power were significantly lower than today. Nevertheless, these types of approaches are still used today for many environmental applications.

Most of the methods presented here use *multitemporal composite images as input data*. The composite images can be created with various compositing approaches and temporal frequencies, optimized depending on the purpose (e.g. land cover change detection, burnt area mapping, regeneration monitoring). Previously, high temporal resolution, but coarse spatial resolution satellite sensors (e.g. Moderate Resolution Imaging Spectroradiometer, MODIS) have been mainly used as input data. Since the opening of NASA Landsat archives (Woodcock *et al.* 2008) followed by the launches of ESA Sentinel-2, satellites have enabled the development of large-scale operational time series approaches at 10–30 m spatial resolution. These data allow the derivation of numerous indicators (e.g. spectral bands, indices, principal components) and annual or seasonal metrics (e.g. mean, maximum, range and selected percentile values) that can be used in environmental monitoring for various purposes, ranging from land cover classification to change detection and trend monitoring.

In the following, we will look at applications aiming to analyze the trajectories of a series of annual observations. The general objective of these types of analyses is to take advantage of the information provided by the temporal dimension of the dataset. Most typically, the temporal dimension is used to detect changes, including either gradual environmental trends (like ecosystem degradation due to air pollution) or abrupt changes (like deforestation, burnt area or windthrown trees), or both. From a technical point of view, time series analysis methods are often grouped into a few categories based on the main principles of the algorithm.

In this section, we follow the three categories defined by Zhu (2017), namely 1) *thresholding*, 2) *differencing* and 3) *segmentation*. Aiming to provide a larger context for the selected applications, the main features of each of the method categories are presented together with practical examples of applications for environmental monitoring.

4.2.2. *Examples of annual times series analysis applications for environmental monitoring*

The *thresholding methods* were among the earliest approaches developed for time series analysis, and are generally rather simple to implement. These methods are based on predefined thresholds of an indicator metric, which can be, for example, an index like the Normalized Difference Vegetation Index (NDVI) or some spectral band(s). The thresholds are used to identify specific interest classes (e.g. forest or grassland) or changes in these classes. Thresholding methods typically detect abrupt changes in the interest classes.

The Vegetation Change Tracker (VCT), developed by Huang *et al.* (2010a), is a thresholding method. It is designed to detect rapid changes in vegetation cover. It was originally developed using the Landsat time series stacks (LTSS) of the North American Forest Dynamics (NAFD) project, which provided biennial Landsat observations over study sites in North America between 1984 and 2006. The method is based on the creation of masks and indices for each observation, which are then analyzed in time series analysis, detecting drastic changes based on a set of thresholds. It uses a forest probability index called the "integrated forest z-score" as the change metric. The VCT has been used to detect stand-clearing disturbance events such as clearcuts, fire or deforestation (Novo-Fernández *et al.* 2018), but can also detect non-stand clearing events like selective logging.

Differencing methods offer another straightforward, but potentially effective way of deriving information from time series of observations. Differencing methods simply compare observations from different times and interpret large differences in the observations as changes. The approach is most reliable when spectral bands or indices are used as the indicator metric (Zhu 2017). But regardless of the indicator metric, it is essential that the observations are consistent between each other.

The Forest Canopy Disturbance Monitoring (FCDM) method (Langner *et al.* 2018) provides a good example of a recently developed annual change detection approach based on differencing (Figure 4.1). This approach is based on the creation (and subsequently comparison) of multitemporal composite images of self-referenced Normalized Burn Ratio (NBR) values for the period of interest. Maximum values of self-referenced NBR are retained in the composite image, indicating the most open forest canopy cover condition. Subsequently, the differences between the composite images are analyzed to derive information on inter-annual canopy cover changes. An essential feature of the method is the self-referencing of the NBR values, using the local statistics of a moving circular window. This self-referencing step ensures the consistency of the observations, which is often the weak point of methods based on differencing. The method was originally designed for deriving annual forest disturbance statistics in tropical evergreen forests, but it can also be used for shorter time periods, as long as a sufficient amount of image data is available to create cloud-free composite images. The method is implemented on top of the Google Earth Engine (GEE) processing platform and can use either Landsat or Sentinel-2 imagery.

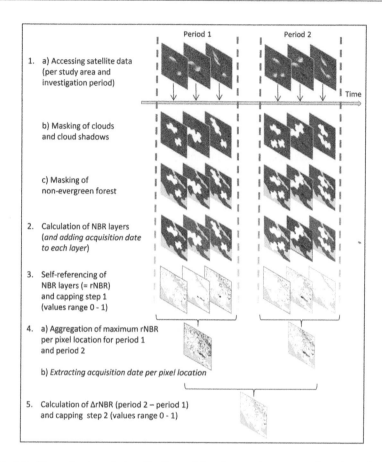

Figure 4.1. *Flow chart and visualization of the five major processing steps to derive canopy cover disturbance ($\Delta rNBR$) maps, based on differencing between two periods (Langner et al. 2018). Under CC BY 4.0 license. For a color version of this figure, see www.iste.co.uk/atto/change2.zip*

In a *segmentation method*, the entire time series under analysis is segmented into a series of straight line segments based on residual-error and angle criteria (Zhu 2017). The aim is to create temporal segmentation using straight line segments to model the important features of the trajectory, resulting in a simplified representation of the spectral trajectory. Segmentation methods are computationally significantly more demanding than the methods presented above, but the advantage is that these methods are capable of detecting both abrupt changes (like deforestation) and gradual changes/trends (like regrowth or ecosystem degradation due to air pollution).

A good example of a segmentation method in the field of environmental monitoring is LandTrendr (Kennedy *et al.* 2010), for Landsat-based Detection of

Trends in Disturbance and Recovery. It uses one observation per year, chosen as the closest cloud-free observation to the median Julian day of each year. Originally, it used NBR as the main change index to create maps of annual forest change. It has since been widely used for analyzing forest disturbances and recovery, as well as wider land cover changes. The development of the method has continued, with the most recent version using the random forest ensemble approach to combine the results of several spectral bands and indices into one result (Cohen *et al.* 2018). These types of ensemble approaches are discussed in more detail in the next section concentrating on dense time series analyses.

More recently, Hermosilla *et al.* (2018) developed the Virtual Land Cover Engine (VLCE), which was used to produce annual disturbance-informed land cover maps for Canada from 1984 to 2012. It relies on yearly best pixel composite images created by the Composite-2-Change (C2C) method (Hermosilla *et al.* 2016). The best pixels are determined by scoring functions that take into account the proximity to the mid-summer target date (Julian day 213 plus minus 30 days), clouds, atmospheric quality and acquisition sensor (White and Wulder 2014). The preliminary yearly composites are then refined by replacing noisy observations with synthetic values derived from a segmentation-based times series analysis applied to each pixel, resulting in seamless annual surface reflectance composites and the detection of change events. The resulting composites are classified into preliminary land cover classes using the random forest classification approach with seven metrics including, for example, the surface-reflectances of Landsat bands 4 and 7, Enhanced Vegetation Index (EVI) and elevation. As a final step, the multitemporal set of land cover maps is stabilized using a Hidden Markov Model (HMM) with land cover class transition probabilities on a given time series sequence, and by removing illogical land cover change candidates. The result is a consistent and logical land cover map time series from 1984 to 2012.

The series of VLCE maps was later analyzed to characterize forest fragmentation in Canada, attributing changes to different change types (e.g. fire, harvest) based on their spectral, temporal and geometrical characteristics (Hermosilla *et al.* 2019). The same underlying Composite-2-Change (C2C) compositing method was also used by White *et al.* (2018) to analyze the usability of NBR for forest recovery to Food and Agriculture Organization (FAO) defined forest definition (i.e. 10% canopy cover and 5 m height), using the yearly Landsat composite images from 1985–2012 from a study area in Finland. Overall, the C2C and VLCE approaches and their subsequent utilization for environmental monitoring highlight the power of combining annual time series analyses with more traditional image classification approaches well.

Other areas of environmental monitoring that benefit from yearly or seasonal time series analysis include the recovery of burnt areas (Chu *et al.* 2017; Morresi *et al.* 2019) and forest health monitoring. Particularly, coniferous defoliators cause long duration attacks that often last several years (Senf *et al.* 2017), and can be monitored in yearly intervals. Broadleaved defoliators, on the other hand, typically require denser time series analyses due to the short duration of the attacks.

Overall, the methods presented so far highlight the variety of options available for the utilization of annual time series data, whether the goal is to detect abrupt changes or long-term trends in annual intervals. The difficulty is often in attributing changes to various potential change agents (Senf *et al.* 2017). The challenge is even greater in the case of gradual changes, which may be caused by ecosystem degradation, increasing vegetation cover or a biotic attack on vegetation. Classifying these types of changes firstly requires a long time series to detect the change, and subsequently fine classification approaches to identify the driving forces behind the change. In this task, time series analyses need to be combined with traditional or novel classification approaches.

4.2.3. *Towards dense time series analysis*

Annual time series analyses can provide effective means for environmental monitoring. However, *all of the applications presented above rely on a single yearly observation* (although often created through the compositing of large multitemporal image datasets). *This limits the application possibilities to phenomena detectable in annual intervals.* Many environmental monitoring tasks may require shorter monitoring windows. For example, a broadleaved defoliator insect attack may be left entirely unnoticed in an annual time series analysis. Furthermore, annual observations cannot take full advantage of all of the information contained in the modern satellite datasets that provide high temporal frequency at a 10–30 m spatial resolution.

Some authors have also used the high number of observations when creating annual products by deriving the summary statistics of individual observations over the year. For example, Hansen *et al.* (2013) used a set of annual band-wise metrics (including, for example, minimum, maximum, mean) for several reflectance percentiles as inputs for their bagged decision trees designed to detect tree cover loss on global scale. Similarly, Pflugmacher *et al.* (2019) used annual and seasonal metrics, together with environmental features, to map 12 land cover and land use classes across Europe. They took three years (2014–2016) of Landsat 8 imagery and calculated numerous spectral temporal metrics for different seasons and annual periods, to be used as inputs for random forest-based classification. These types of approaches using dense time series enable the exploitation of the full temporal information contained in the time series, but they also require new methods to effectively handle large input datasets and extract the required information from the time series. Furthermore, due to the high number of individual input images in time series approaches using all available data, preprocessing aspects become crucially important in ensuring meaningful outputs where the effects of noise are minimized. In the next section, we will look into the requirements and approaches to use dense time series of satellite observations in environmental monitoring.

4.3. Dense time series analysis using all available data

Optical satellites with moderate spatial resolution (10–30 m), such as Landsat and Sentinel-2 have been widely used for understanding the Earth's surface change (Zhu 2017; Claverie *et al.* 2018; Wulder *et al.* 2019). Nevertheless, for a long time, most of their applications only required a few cloud-free satellite images collected at different dates (Singh 1989), mainly due to the high price of the image (Zhu *et al.* 2019). For instance, Landsat is one of the oldest continuous Earth observing satellites at moderate spatial resolution (30–60 meters), but in the 1980s, a Landsat image could cost $4,000 USD (Zhu *et al.* 2019). Since the United States Geological Survey (USGS) began to implement the *free and open policy of Landsat data in 2008* (Woodcock *et al.* 2008), Landsat data access has been much easier and its usage has increased. Launched in 2015, Sentinel-2 has also provided images free of charge (Drusch *et al.* 2012). This widely encouraged the use of time series analysis for change detection using dense time series of optical images at moderate resolution. In the past few decades, many research works using dense time series of Landsat and Sentinel-2 data have been published. According to Scopus, the peer-reviewed literature on "change detection", "time series" and "Landsat" has increased dramatically since the launch of Landsat data in 2008, and studies using Sentinel-2 began to appear and increase from 2016 (Figure 4.2), making change detection using dense time series data from Landsat and Sentinel-2 one of the hottest research topics in the remote sensing community (Woodcock *et al.* 2020).

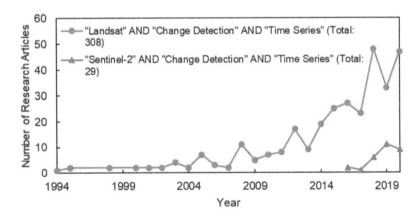

Figure 4.2. *Yearly research article publications from 1994 to 2020 indexed by Scopus. Besides the satellite name (e.g. "Landsat" and "Sentinel-2"), "Change Detection" and "Time Series" were considered in article titles, abstracts and keywords. The search was made on September 10, 2020, and the number in the bracket presents the total number of publications. For a color version of this figure, see www.iste.co.uk/atto/change2.zip*

The remainder of this section will present the usual technical requirements to perform dense satellite time series analysis, and a short overview of several key time series analysis algorithms using all available data.

4.3.1. *Making dense time series consistent*

A consistent dense time series of optical data is the precondition of good time series analyses (Qiu *et al.* 2019b). Up until now, Landsat and Sentinel-2 data are the most widely used data with moderate spatial resolution for time series-based change detection. One of the essential preconditions is to ensure that the time series images are geometrically aligned with high accuracy; otherwise, a serious mis-registration would cause unacceptable noise in the time series data, especially for the places with sharp discontinuities (e.g. field edges). For this purpose, USGS uses the Global Land Survey (GLS) ground control points and Global Positioning System (GPS) to geometrically correct each Landsat image to provide the standard Landsat Collection 1 product. Based on the geometric accuracy of each individual image, they are categorized into Tier 1 and Tier 2. The geometric accuracy of Tier 1 data is less than 12 m RMSE, and Tier 2 data is larger than 12 m RMSE (Wulder *et al.* 2019). The European Space Agency (ESA) also provide the Level 1 product for Sentinel-2, of which the overall geometric accuracy can reach 12.5 m with regard to their ground control points (Drusch *et al.* 2012). Though Landsat or Sentinel-2 data are geometrically consistent internally, the *mis-registration between Landsat and Sentinel-2 images* (sometimes more than 30 m) is still not acceptable for time series analysis (Storey *et al.* 2016). This inconsistency should be solved as *Landsat Collection 2 data* is released in mid-2021, by then Landsat data will be readjusted based on the Sentinel-2 Global Reference Image (Dechoz *et al.* 2015). Before this, any user who wants to combine the Landsat and Sentinel-2 to create a dense time series data is recommended to use automated image-to-image registration algorithms (Gao *et al.* 2009; Long *et al.* 2016; Yan *et al.* 2016). Besides, consistent time series will also need to consider atmospheric correction, cloud/cloud shadow detection and harmonization of multi-source images (Figure 4.3). In the harmonization process, the spatial co-registration, Bidirectional Reflectance Distribution Function (BRDF) correction and bandpass adjustment need to be considered (Claverie *et al.* 2018; Shang and Zhu 2019).

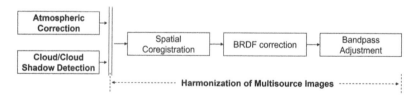

Figure 4.3. *Flowchart of generating consistent dense time series data*

4.3.1.1. *Atmospheric correction*

Atmospheric correction is a primary preprocessing step for a consistent dense time series. Generally, the atmospheric correction algorithms include the relative normalization of multi-date images (Song *et al.* 2001; Schroeder *et al.* 2006), empirical correction of single-date image like Dark-Object Subtraction (DOS) (Liang *et al.* 1997; Song and Woodcock 2003) and physical-based correction of single-date image, such as Atmospheric/Topographic CORrection (ATCOR) (Richter 1997), MODerate resolution atmospheric TRANsmission (MODTRAN) (Berk *et al.* 1998) and Second Simulation of the Satellite Signal in the Solar Spectrum (6S) code (Vermote *et al.* 1997). USGS adopted the 6S code as the fundamental approach and have used the Landsat Ecosystem Disturbance Adaptive Processing System (LEDAPS) (Masek *et al.* 2006) and the Landsat 8 Surface Reflectance Code (LaSRC) (Vermote *et al.* 2016) for the generation of Landsats 4–7 and Landsat 8 surface reflectance products since 2012. For Sentinel-2 data, ESA provides the Sen2Cor toolbox to produce surface reflectance, which integrates a semi-empirical correction algorithm based on the precomputed Look-up table (LUT) from libRadtran (Mayer and Kylling 2005; Louis *et al.* 2016). At the same time, ESA can also provide the preprocessed surface reflectance product to users. This free distribution of the surface reflectance products greatly benefits the use of dense time series observations combined from Landsat and Sentinel-2.

4.3.1.2. *Automated cloud and cloud shadow detection*

Clouds and cloud shadows cause the majority of noise in optical images, and their automated detection algorithms are required to process numerous images for time series analysis ahead of time (Zhu *et al.* 2018). The free and open policy of Landsat data in 2008 (Woodcock *et al.* 2008) has served as the catalyst for the creation of many automated cloud and cloud shadow detection algorithms.

Based on how many images are used, cloud detection methods can generally be classified into single-date and multitemporal algorithms. Until now, most of the algorithms are single-date, including physical-rule-based and machine learning (ML)-based approaches. The physical-rule-based algorithms usually consist of a set of constant or dynamic threshold filters in spectral/thermal bands, as well as the geometry properties of cloud and cloud shadow (Masek *et al.* 2006; Huang *et al.* 2010b; Oreopoulos *et al.* 2011; Wilson and Oreopoulos 2012; Zhu and Woodcock 2012; Zhu *et al.* 2015a; Louis *et al.* 2016; Vermote *et al.* 2016; Qiu *et al.* 2017; Frantz *et al.* 2018; Oishi *et al.* 2018; Qiu *et al.* 2019c). For example, clouds usually appear "bright", "white", "cold" and "high", while cloud shadows are "dark" and their locations can be determined by following the geometry between cloud, cloud shadow, sun and sensor (Zhu *et al.* 2018). Compared to the physical-rule-based algorithms, the machine leaning-based approaches are more straightforward, typically based on manually interpreted samples for training a classifier, such as decision trees (Roy *et al.* 2010; Potapov *et al.* 2011; Scaramuzza *et al.* 2012; Hollstein *et al.* 2016), support vector machines (SVM) (Zhou *et al.* 2016), fuzzy models (Melesse and Jordan 2002; Shao *et al.* 2017) and neural networks (Hughes and Hayes 2014; Zi *et al.* 2018; Chai *et al.* 2019; Shendryk *et al.* 2019; Segal-Rozenhaimer *et al.* 2020). Recently, algorithms using CNN can capture the spectral and contextual dimensions at the same time and achieve better results compared to the physical-result-based algorithms (Zi *et al.* 2018; Chai *et al.* 2019; Shendryk *et al.* 2019; Segal-Rozenhaimer *et al.* 2020), but they are often computationally expensive and require GPU computing. Besides, the performance of data-driven approaches will heavily rely on the quality of training data (Hughes and Hayes 2014). Even though several globally distributed cloud and cloud shadow assessment datasets have been created by careful manual interpretation, some errors remain in this data that may have a large impact on the training process of machine-leaning-based algorithms (Irish 2000; Hughes and Hayes 2014; Foga *et al.* 2017; Baetens *et al.* 2019).

The time series-based algorithms use information derived from images acquired on different dates. These kinds of algorithms usually require a real clear-sky image or a model predicted clear-sky image as reference to detect clouds and/or cloud shadows (Wang *et al.* 1999; Hagolle *et al.* 2010; Goodwin *et al.* 2013; Jin *et al.* 2013; Zhu and Woodcock 2014a; Chen *et al.* 2015; Zhu and Helmer 2018; Qiu *et al.* 2020). Those cloud (and cloud shadow) detection algorithms can make full use of the temporal dimension to detect clouds and cloud shadows, but they are more complicated to use and may be confused by various kinds of surface changes (Zhu and Woodcock 2014a).

Among such numerous cloud and cloud shadow detection algorithms, the single-date algorithm, especially for the physical-rule-based approaches, is most widely accepted by users, due to the simple implementation (White *et al.* 2014; Bolton *et al.* 2020; Yin *et al.* 2020). For instance, the Fmask (Function of mask) algorithm (Zhu and Woodcock 2012) has been integrated into the USGS data production system to provide the Quality Assessment (QA) band for Landsat 4-8 Collection 1-2 data (Foga *et al.* 2017). It is also being used to process the NASA Harmonized Landsat and Sentinel-2 product (HLS) (Claverie *et al.* 2018). As for the Sentinel-2 data, the Sen2Cor processor, officially provided by ESA, can also detect clouds and cloud shadows for each individual image based on several physical rules, but it still has lots of commission and omission errors that users should be aware of when using this tool (Baetens *et al.* 2019).

4.3.1.3. *Harmonization of multiple sensors*

An individual optical satellite with moderate resolution cannot often collect a very high frequency of time series data due to long interval revisits. For example, the revisit time of an individual Landsat satellite is 16 days, and even the combination of two Landsat satellites only improves the time by eight days. Sentinel-2 has two satellites (2A and 2B), and each of them can revisit a same location at the equator every 10 days. The presence of clouds may further reduce the revisit time. Since Landsat and Sentinel-2 share similar spectral bands, their harmonization provides a new insight to create more dense time series data (two to four days revisit time) (Li and Roy 2017).

Recently, NASA released Harmonized Landsat and Sentinel-2 (HLS) data with a 30-meter resolution, which was produced by a set of processes including the LaSRC atmospheric correction approach, Fmask cloud and cloud shadow detection, geometric resampling and geographic registration, BRDF normalization, and band pass adjustment (Claverie *et al.* 2018). However, this HLS product uses a global fixed linear model for adjusting the bandpass between Landsat 8 and Sentinel-2 sensors, and thus it may not be optimal locally. To reduce this effect, Shang and Zhu (2019) developed a Time Series-based Reflectance Adjustment (TRA) approach by selecting clear-sky observation pairs between Landsat 8 and Sentinel-2 on close dates, to build a new linear regression model for each individual pixel. This kind of approach harmonizing multiple sensors at pixel-level can provide more consistent dense time series observations.

4.3.2. *Change detection methods*

In this section, we focus on reviewing the change detection algorithms using dense time series of optical data from Landsat and Sentinel-2. These methods can be generally classified into three categories: *supervised, non-supervised and ensemble approaches* (Figure 4.4). The supervised algorithms often require a large amount of manually interpreted samples (including land cover type or change) to train a classification model for time series analysis. They can be subcategorized into map classification and trajectory classification, depending on the classification object. Most of the non-supervised algorithms do not need training data, but often predefined statistical boundaries to detect changes. The ensemble algorithms are a new "hybrid" time series analyses approach that are based on the change detection results from multiple algorithms. Note that some of the approaches mentioned here can be also used for the analysis of annual time series data (Section 4.2).

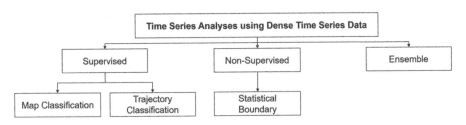

Figure 4.4. *Categories and subcategories of change detection algorithms using dense time series data*

4.3.2.1. *Map classification*

Usually, the map classification method (also called post-classification approach) is to *simply compare the land cover and land use classification maps on different dates*. Even though dense time series data would be used, most of them generate annual classification maps for multiple years by using the spectral or index metrics acquired from all available images within one year as inputs (Nutini *et al.* 2013; Tulbure and Broich 2013; Pardo-Pascual *et al.* 2014; Kontgis *et al.* 2015; Li *et al.* 2015; Potapov *et al.* 2015; Gong *et al.* 2019; Li *et al.* 2019). However, when the classification is based on the object shape features rather than the spectral characteristics, without the seasonal variations, each individual image could generate one classification map, and then the time series of the classification maps can be used to make the final analysis (Li and Narayanan 2003). The map classification algorithm is simple to implement and can also provide the land cover change information easily, but the quality of time series analysis highly depends on the accuracy of the classification map, since errors within each of the maps will be compounded into the final results. Even though they have been used for many applications, such as agriculture (Kontgis *et al.* 2015), hydrology (Li and Narayanan 2003; Tulbure and Broich 2013; Pardo-Pascual *et al.* 2014; Li *et al.* 2019), urban expansion (Li *et al.* 2015; Gong *et al.* 2019), change of different kinds of land cover and land use (Nutini *et al.* 2013), map classification algorithms are generally not recommended for change detection (Zhu 2017).

4.3.2.2. *Trajectory classification*

The trajectory classification method extracts the *temporal trajectory from the dense time series and then uses these trajectories to classify the time series stack pixel by pixel*. It often uses the time series of spectral bands and/or indices such as NDVI, and can be further grouped into empirical rules and temporal classification. The first trajectory approach often hypothesizes several sets of trajectory models for different kinds of changes (e.g. simple disturbance, reforestation, stable state, etc.) and then uses them to classify the time series (Kennedy *et al.* 2007). For example, Griffiths *et al.* (2020) detect grassland change caused by a mowing event according to the deviations from a given natural growing season trajectory. On the other hand, the temporal classification does not need to rely on any kind of known hypothesis ahead of time, only to train a "black box" classification model for identifying the changes (using training data of change pixels). For example, Hansen *et al.* (2014, 2016) manually interpreted a large amount of training data using Google Earth images, and extracted spectral metrics from the time series data as inputs to train a bagged decision tree model, which was used to classify forest cover loss and bare ground gain at national or global scales. A similar approach was also used to quantify forest cover loss in other regions like European Russia, the Democratic Republic of the Congo and Eastern Europe (Potapov *et al.* 2011, 2012, 2015). Hawbaker *et al.* (2017) used gradient boosted regression models to generate a burn probability layer based on many variables including change metrics from time series data, and then applied a simple threshold at pixel-level to map burned areas across the United States.

Roy *et al.* (2019) applied a random forest change regression, based on a spectral model of fire effects on reflectance, to map burned areas by combining Landsat 8 and Sentinel-2 time series data. Uhl and Leyk (2020) extracted time series descriptors, such as the mean variance for the annual time series of NDVI and the Normalized Difference Built-up Index (NDBI), as the inputs of SVM and K-means classification model to determine the changes in the built-up area. Additionally, some studies also combined the empirical rules and the classification approach together to better map land disturbances (Schroeder *et al.* 2017).

4.3.2.3. *Statistical boundary*

The statistical boundary algorithm calculates boundary statistics based on all of the time series data, and *when an observation significantly deviates from the statistical boundary, it is identified as a change*. Three components such as trend, seasonal change and noise are usually modeled to estimate the statistical boundary based on statistical quality control charts (Brooks *et al.* 2013), econometrics structural change monitoring (Verbesselt *et al.* 2010, 2012; DeVries *et al.* 2015; Dutrieux *et al.* 2015; Reiche *et al.* 2015; Hamunyela *et al.* 2016; Zhao *et al.* 2019) and model prediction (Zhu *et al.* 2012; Goodwin and Collett 2014; Zhu and Woodcock 2014b; Fu and Weng 2016; Vogelmann *et al.* 2016; Zhu *et al.* 2016a, 2020; Brown *et al.* 2020). Most of those algorithms use one or more indices, such as the NDVI (Dutrieux *et al.* 2015; Reiche *et al.* 2015; Hamunyela *et al.* 2016; Vogelmann *et al.* 2016; Zhao *et al.* 2019) and Normalized Difference Moisture Index (NDMI) (DeVries *et al.* 2015) to detect changes, but there are also some algorithms responding on the time series observations of the original spectral bands (Zhu *et al.* 2012, 2016a, 2020; Goodwin and Collett 2014; Zhu and Woodcock 2014b; Fu and Weng 2016; Deng and Zhu 2018). Besides, most of these algorithms are capable of detecting changes in near real-time (or continuously). At the same time, Hamunyela *et al.* (2016) used a spatially normalized NDVI (sNDVI) with a regular window to reduce the effects from phenological variations, and reported that including such a spatial feature could further improve the accuracy of change detection. The statistical boundary method can make full use of the temporal depth of dense time series data and tolerate the seasonal variations to identify change as new observations are collected, but they often require large data storage and high-performance computing.

4.3.2.4. *Ensemble approach*

The ensemble approach *combines the results of multiple change detection algorithms to track changes from time series data*. Earlier, the ensemble algorithm was often used for land cover classification (Woźniak *et al.* 2014), which applied voting, rule-based decision and classification approaches to compute an optimal result from different results that already existed. By comparing different forest disturbance algorithms, Cohen *et al.* (2017) found that there are large disagreements and each of them has some strengths and weaknesses. Recently, in order to improve the detection of forest disturbances, Cohen *et al.* (2018) explored different spectral bands and indices as inputs to run the LandTrendr algorithm to generate different outputs, and then the multiple ensembles were aligned into one using a random forest model calibrated with precollected reference data. Healey *et al.* (2018) combined the outputs derived from several change detection algorithms (e.g. CCDC, VCT, LandTrendr, etc.) and substantially increased change detection accuracy. Similarly, Bullock *et al.* (2020) proposed a new time series analysis algorithm in which there are sequential processes from the Continuous Change Detection and Classification (CCDC) algorithm, the CUSUM Test (Brown *et al.* 1975) and the Chow Test (Chow 1960). This kind of algorithm is a relatively new direction, which can accumulate advances from each individual algorithm to improve the overall performance, but it is extensively time-consuming since it depends on the results of the already existing algorithms and all of the different algorithms need to be run at least once.

4.3.2.5. *Two of the widely used algorithms*

Although there are many studies using dense time series data for change detection, in this section, we will take a closer look into two widely used change detection approaches based on dense time series data, including the Breaks for Additive Season and Trend (BFAST) (Verbesselt *et al.* 2010, 2012) and the Continuous Change Detection and Classification (CCDC) (Zhu and Woodcock 2014b). Figure 4.5 shows the citations of the two algorithms from 2010 to date (as of September 2020).

The *BFAST algorithm* detects changes (including seasonal, abrupt and gradual) by decomposing the entire time series into trend, season and noise components (Verbesselt *et al.* 2010). This was originally proposed for analyzing vegetation changes from the already existing MODIS time series (offline model), but in 2012, it was updated to a new version named BFAST-Monitor to detect drought-related disturbances in near real-time with an online model (Verbesselt *et al.* 2012). The NDVI or NDMI indices are often used as its input. Over the past few years, it also shows potential performance on the dense time series at moderate resolution (e.g. Landsat) for monitoring forest disturbances (DeVries *et al.* 2015, 2016; Dutrieux *et al.* 2015; Reiche *et al.* 2015; Hamunyela *et al.* 2016), agricultural cultivation (Dutrieux *et al.* 2016) and wetland dynamics (Chen *et al.* 2014).

The *CCDC algorithm* is an online algorithm derived from a Continuous Monitoring of Forest Disturbance Algorithm (CMFDA) (Zhu *et al.* 2012). It can detect many kinds of land cover changes continuously by using all of the spectral bands of Landsat data. It creates a harmonic model using all available time series data to predict the reflectance on any date, and continuously compares the model predictions and the satellite observations to detect changes. Later, the change detection component was improved by dynamically selecting time series model (Zhu *et al.* 2015b) and the classification component was improved by optimizing the strategy of training data selection and integrating new auxiliary data (Zhu *et al.* 2016b). Recently, the CCDC algorithm has been used as the core algorithm for the USGS Land Change Monitoring, Assessment and Projection (LCMAP) program for generating land change products for the United States (Pengra *et al.* 2016; Zhu *et al.* 2016b; Brown *et al.* 2020). The CCDC algorithm was originally developed to detect land cover and land use change that often has large change magnitude. This approach is less useful for detecting land disturbances (caused by stress, wind, hydrology, debris, harvest, mechanical and fire). Building upon the CCDC algorithm, Zhu *et al.* (2020) developed the COntinuous Land Disturbance (COLD) algorithm for monitoring all kinds of land disturbances continuously. The CCDC has been successfully used in many applications, such as urban expansion (Fu and Weng 2016; Deng and Zhu 2018), grassland change (Zhou *et al.* 2019), hydrology dynamics (Berhane *et al.* 2020), forest disturbance (Sulla-Menashe *et al.* 2016), insect breakout (Pasquarella *et al.* 2017) and multiple types of land conversions (Arévalo *et al.* 2020).

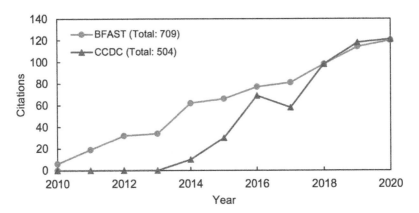

Figure 4.5. *Comparison of citations of the BFAST and CCDC algorithms from 2010 to date indexed by Scopus. The search only considered the first paper introducing the algorithm. The number in the bracket presents the total citations for each algorithm. Note that the search was made on September 10, 2020 and thus the numbers for 2020 are not fully representative. For a color version of this figure, see www.iste. co.uk/atto/change2.zip*

4.3.3. *Summary and future developments*

We have witnessed a rapid increase in the number of algorithms developed for change detection using dense time series observations, thanks to the free and open data policy. Among these algorithms, Landsat data are still one of the most widely used data, mainly due to the long-term records of the Earth's surface and the ready-to-use high-level data products.

The integration of Landsat and Sentinel-2 data can make time series observation even denser; however, their revisit time still cannot reach daily frequency (Claverie *et al.* 2018). Harmonizing the data from other multi-source platforms such as PlanetScope to consistent and denser time series data (real-time) will be a key step for the future (Houborg and McCabe 2018).

Additionally, until now, there are still very few studies that have considered spatio-temporal features for change detection using dense time series, which is difficult, but also potentially rewarding.

Finally, most of the applications are focusing on local and small areas, caused by the limitation of the storage and computing resources. The development of the computer technology and availability of cloud processing platforms will mitigate these issues, and more continental and even global products based on dense time series observation are expected in the near future.

In the meantime, ML-based approaches for dense time series analysis have a promising margin for improvement, propelled by the recent advances of DL methods.

4.4. Deep learning-based time series analysis approaches

Recently, DL approaches (Zhang *et al.* 2016b; Zhu *et al.* 2017) have emerged as a valuable tool to automatically manage and analyze signal data (LeCun *et al.* 2015). In domains such as CV, speech and audio recognition, text and language processing, DL frameworks, or more generally representational learning strategies (Bengio *et al.* 2013), have drastically advanced the state-of-the-art regarding the analysis and the understanding of such domains.

Unlike standard (supervised) ML approaches such as SVM and Random Forest (Inglada *et al.* 2017), where the learning process is mainly devoted to finding the best model to separate the examples according to their features, DL approaches simultaneously learn a new data representation with an associated classifier to deal with the discrimination task (Bengio *et al.* 2013). In more detail, the main characteristic associated with the DL model is their ability to extract a suitable representation of the input data, optimized for the particular task at hand, avoiding the tedious and costly manual feature engineering process as part of the learning process.

A DL model is generally associated with an architecture defined as a set of (processing) layers. We can distinguish three main layer categories: input, hidden and output layers. The new learnt representation is, generally, the outcome of multiple nonlinear transformations, where each nonlinear transformation is associated with a particular hidden layer.

By considering the general DL field, we can roughly organize the approaches according to their topology, as well as the type of information they are working on.

By considering the topology, we can distinguish two main families: *feed-forward and RNN*. While the former is characterized by the fact that information flows in the model from the input layers to the output layers, the latter allows a self-loop associated with the nonlinear transformation (hidden) layers.

Regarding the type of information, we can point out several types of models. When working with vectors or attribute-relational data, we can employ Fully-Connected (FCN) or Multi-layer Perceptron (MLP) architecture (Jiang *et al.* 2018). If the incoming input information has a *one-dimensional, two-dimensional or multi-dimensional structure*, CNN are commonly employed (He *et al.* 2016). While the former makes no assumption on the structure of the data and considers the input information as a flat (ordered) set of features, CNN techniques leverage convolutional operations (LeCun *et al.* 2015) to deal with local data dependencies. CNNs are therefore well suited to manage and exploit spatial auto-correlations in image data. Commonly, both kinds of DL methods are categorized as feed-forward neural networks. Conversely, if the *input signal can be structured as a time series or a sequence of events,* RNN are well adapted. More specifically, models like Long–Short-Term Memory (LSTM) (Greff *et al.* 2017) or Gated Recurrent Unit (GRU) (Cho *et al.* 2014) are the standard RNN units that are commonly adopted by the Signal Processing and Natural Language Processing community.

For more technical details about DL model architectures and topologies typically used in SITS analysis, we advise the reader to refer to Chapter 2 of this book.

Despite the fact that most of the DL literature is focused on supervised learning problems where class or label information is available to build discriminative models, many DL frameworks were also proposed to tackle *semi-supervised* (Kipf and Welling 2017) or *unsupervised* (Xie *et al.* 2016) tasks, in which partial or no supervision is available to guide the learning process. In these cases, all of the previous mentioned DL models can be employed.

Considering the *remote sensing domain*, DL techniques are getting more and more attention (Zhang *et al.* 2016b; Zhu *et al.* 2017) due to their ability to manage and analyze large amounts of imagery information. In the beginning, most of the efforts were devoted to simply applying DL models developed in the CV field to remote sensing data, without modifications to account for the specificity of remote sensing imagery. Recently, the remote sensing community has gained experience in deploying DL approaches on EO data characterized by multi-scale resolution, multi-sensor information, as well as multitemporal acquisitions (Zhu *et al.* 2017). The latter point results in the exploitation and analysis of SITS information.

In the *active field of research related to SITS analysis*, DL strategies are emerging due to their ability to leverage the sequential nature that is intrinsic to such rich sources of information. Most of the DL approaches in the field of SITS analysis are dedicated to Land Use Land Cover (LULC) mapping, exploiting the information associated with the evolution of the radiometric information to discriminate among several LULC classes to deal with, for example, agricultural mapping (Interdonato *et al.* 2019), land management planning (Qiu *et al.* 2019a), forest monitoring (Du *et al.* 2020) and yield estimation and natural resource mapping (Mu *et al.* 2019). In the *context of DL-based SITS classification*, two different levels of spatial granularity are commonly employed: pixel or object (Blaschke 2010). While in the pixel-based analysis, the basic unit is the pixel, in object-based image analysis (OBIA), the images are first segmented obtaining groups of radiometrically homogeneous pixels (objects), which become the basic units in any further analysis.

From a more methodological point of view, Ienco *et al.* (2017) evaluates the use of RNN (GRU) to cope with LULC mapping considering both pixel-level and object-level optical SITS data. They demonstrate that GRU models were able to gain in performance regarding both levels of spatial granularity, with respect to previous state-of-the-art ML models. Pelletier *et al.* (2019) proposes to work at the pixel-level to perform LULC mapping via CNNs applied on the temporal domain, to explicitly consider the temporal dynamic associated with the pixel time series. The proposed study reports an in-depth evaluation of CNN models for optical SITS data and highlights the quality of such models to manage the temporal information characterizing EO data.

Beyond the use of a single RNN or CNN model to deal with a Satellite Image Time Series classifier, (Rußwurm and Körner 2018; Interdonato *et al.* 2019; Qiu *et al.* 2019a) leverage *more sophisticated frameworks that combine both RNN and CNN* to get the most out of the two types of models. All such models work at the pixel-level and are devoted to LULC mapping for different applications: urban, agricultural or general land cover classification.

The first two approaches combine the CNN and RNN models sequentially (Rußwurm and Körner 2018; Qiu *et al.* 2019a). Firstly, a CNN is applied considering a pixel with its spatial context, at each time stamp and, in a second stage, the output of the CNN is fed into the RNN model to take into account temporal dynamics. Both approaches take inspiration from the ConvLSTM (Convolutional Long–Short-Term Memory) recently proposed in Shi *et al.* (2015) for spatio-temporal time series forecasting. Conversely, the DL methodology introduced in Interdonato *et al.* (2019) combines the RNN and CNN models with the aim of getting a different representation of the same SITS data leveraging the complimentarity of the information extracted by the two DL models.

All of the *previous examples address the supervised analysis of optical SITS data while*, in the literature, approaches that cope with *unsupervised analysis* are recently being considered.

A bi-temporal unsupervised change detection approach based on DL strategy is proposed in Kalinicheva *et al.* (2019). The authors study the temporal evolution around the city of Montpellier (South of France) between 2002 and 2008 using SPOT-5 satellite images. The goal of the proposed framework is to distinguish between trivial and non-trivial changes, with the latter representing rare events that happen during the considered time period.

Sanchez *et al.* (2019) introduced a more methodological work with the objective of learning totally unsupervised representations of optical SITS data leveraging the large amounts of unlabeled data now available from open satellite image archives. Due to the methodological nature of the work, the evaluation is carried out considering different and uncorrelated geographical areas and Sentinel-2 SITS spanning from March 2016 to May 2018.

Overall, DL approaches are demonstrating their ability and their adequateness to deal with the massive amounts of SITS provided by modern EO systems. Notwithstanding the fact that we are still at the early adoption phase considering such methodologies, the first results considering land cover mapping tasks are promising.

The remainder of this section will focus on the three main types of DL models used so far for SITS analysis.

4.4.1. *Recurrent Neural Network (RNN) for Satellite Image Time Series*

A family of DL methods, especially tailored to cope with temporal correlations, are RNN (Bengio *et al.* 2013) and, in particular, LSTM networks (Greff *et al.* 2017) and GRU (Cho *et al.* 2014). Such models explicitly capture temporal correlations by recursion and have already proved their quality in different domains, such as speech recognition (Graves *et al.* 2013), natural language processing (Linzen *et al.* 2016) and image completion (van den Oord *et al.* 2016).

Thanks to their *ability to consider time-dependent information,* RNN seems to be a well-suited tool to deal with SITS. In the remote sensing field, the work proposed in Lyu *et al.* (2016) performed preliminary experiments with an LSTM model on a multitemporal Landsat-7 dataset (only two dates), to perform supervised binary change detection (changed vs. no-changed) on urban areas. This work underlines the appropriateness of RNN models to deal with optical SITS data. Figure 4.6 depicts the LSTM model with the corresponding gating structure (Figure 4.6(a)) and the model employed to perform bi-temporal land cover change detection in Lyu *et al.* (2016) (Figure 4.6(b)).

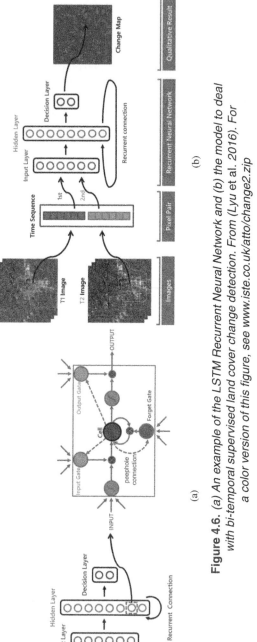

Figure 4.6. *(a) An example of the LSTM Recurrent Neural Network and (b) the model to deal with bi-temporal supervised land cover change detection. From (Lyu et al. 2016). For a color version of this figure, see www.iste.co.uk/atto/change2.zip*

In Ienco *et al.* (2017), an LSTM model is employed to deal with general LULC mapping considering both pixel-level and object-level scale of analyses. Considering the pixel-level analysis, SITS are derived by a sequence of 23 Landsat 8 images, while the object-based analysis is performed considering a sequence of 3 Pleiades images at a 2 m spatial resolution. In addition, the same work evaluates the quality of the representation learned via the neural network approach as input features to feed standard classification algorithms (i.e. SVM or Random Forest). The reported tests show that such standard classification algorithms benefit from the new representation induced by the RNN model.

Jia *et al.* (2017) proposes a modification of the basic LSTM to tackle oil palm plantation detection and the identification of burned areas exploiting both long-term and short-term temporal variation patterns. The proposed framework considers a multi-annual SITS of MODIS images from 2001 to 2009. As with previous similar works dealing with class imbalance or class representativity, the proposed research tackles the issues related to misaligned land cover classes between training and test data, i.e. classes that are available on the test data, but are not represented in the training set.

An experimental evaluation of different DL approaches was recently reported in Garnot *et al.* (2019). The authors investigated several structured DL models for crop-type classification on Sentinel-2 imagery. One of the main objectives related to this work is the assessment of the respective importance of spatial and temporal structures in Sentinel-2 data.

4.4.2. *Convolutional Neural Networks (CNN) for Satellite Image Time Series*

CNN are the most popular DL methods (LeCun *et al.* 2015) adopted to *cope with multi-dimensional correlations*. In the Remote Sensing community, this approach is usually employed to deal with scene classification (de Lima and Marfurt 2020), semantic segmentation (Volpi and Tuia 2017), hyperspectral categorization (Chen *et al.* 2016) and multi-source data fusion (Kampffmeyer *et al.* 2018), considering 1D (Pelletier *et al.* 2019), 2D (Gaetano *et al.* 2018) and 3D (Ji *et al.* 2018) signal information.

Regarding the analysis of SITS imagery, several research works leveraged the CNN model to deal with SITS analysis.

The first work that considers CNN models for land cover and crop-type classification for multitemporal data is introduced in Kussul *et al.* (2017). The authors considered optical SITS acquired via Landsat 8, as well as Sentinel-1 radar images acquired over the same area. Two types of CNN models were evaluated: the first one performed convolution on the time domain (1D), while the second one performed two-dimensional (2D) convolution on the spatial domain, working on the whole set of data. Both models achieved better performances than baseline methods, with a slightly better performance obtained by the 2D CNN. The best gains for the CNN models were reached on agricultural crops, for which the time dimension plays a major role since it captures the cultural cycle information.

Recently, Pelletier *et al.* (2019) proposed a comprehensive study of the 1D CNN model named Temporal Convolutional Neural Networks (TempCNNs), a DL approach which applies convolutions in the temporal dimension, in order to automatically learn temporal (and spectral) features. The evaluation still consider the task of land cover mapping via multitemporal information. The evaluation is carried out on Formosat-2 images with a SITS composed of 46 scenes and involving around one million labeled pixel-wise time series. Figure 4.7(a) depicts the 1D CNN architecture proposed in this work, while Figure 4.7(b) shows one reference image, the land cover maps generated considering a Random Forest, as well as the proposed 1D CNN and, finally, the difference map between the prediction of the two models.

Another example of agricultural land cover mapping for summer crops is presented in Zhong *et al.* (2019). Also, in this case, the authors experiment a 1D CNN considering information coming from the Landsat Enhanced Vegetation Index (EVI) time series. Despite the fact that the proposed method improves the discrimination performance, the research introduces an extensive study related to the interpretation of the features extracted by the DL model and their connection with agronomic information. In particular, the authors underline that lower convolutional hidden layers capture small-scale temporal variations, while upper hidden layers focus more on the global seasonal patterns.

A different use of SITS is presented in Mu *et al.* (2019), where the objective is to perform winter wheat yield estimation from multitemporal data. While all of the other works listed above are devoted to classification mapping tasks, here, the CNN model is employed to predict a continuous quantity (regression). The approach is deployed considering MODIS SITS spanning over more than 10 years (2006–2016) acquired over the North of China. The research work concludes that the CNN model can effectively predict future winter wheat yield in real-time, overcoming the constraints of the traditional statistical model on the fitting of complex relationships.

Overall, CNN are getting more and more attention in the remote sensing community and, when related to the analysis and exploitation of optical SITS, such models are proving their ability to get the most out of the temporal dynamics characterizing such data. In addition to their capacity to deal with land cover mapping tasks, they are also demonstrating their value to cope with yield estimation for agricultural monitoring.

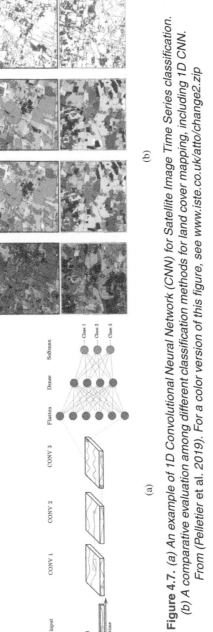

Figure 4.7. (a) An example of 1D Convolutional Neural Network (CNN) for Satellite Image Time Series classification. (b) A comparative evaluation among different classification methods for land cover mapping, including 1D CNN. From (Pelletier et al. 2019). For a color version of this figure, see www.iste.co.uk/atto/change2.zip

4.4.3. *Hybrid models: Convolutional Recurrent Neural Network (ConvRNN) models for Satellite Image Time Series*

The previous approaches introduce and analyze the behavior of single models (or components) like RNN or CNN. Recently, hybrid neural networks combining both kinds of models appeared in the ML literature (Shi *et al.* 2015) under the name Convolutional Recurrent Neural Networks (ConvRNN). The objective of such approaches is to *directly deal with spatio-spectral–temporal information*, leveraging the ability of RNN to cope with temporal or sequential information, as well as the capacity of CNN to extract and characterize local spatial correlations. While the first DL models took some time to percolate from the general domains of signal processing and ML to the remote sensing field, nowadays, new proposed frameworks (i.e. ConvRNN) are transferred more quickly from a domain to another. In particular, due to the appealing features ConvRNN (or any other combination of CNN and RNN models) incorporate, studies involving such models are being released in the remote sensing field, with particular emphasis on the analysis of SITS.

A first application of the Convolutional Recurrent Neural Network is presented in Rußwurm and Körner (2018), with a Convolutional Long–Short-Term Memory (ConvLSTM) network developed for agricultural land cover mapping in Germany. The model combines two ConvLSTM networks, the first to process data in chronological order and the second to analyze data in reverse order with respect to the time. The data comes from Sentinel-2 sensors acquired from January 2016 to November 2017. Differently from previous works, the authors set up a semantic segmentation task where the major constraint is related to the availability of densely annotated reference data (Volpi and Tuia 2017) to train the DL model. On the other hand, if the ground truth constraint is met, the obtained model has the advantage of encapsulating spatial correlation among the pixels belonging to the same prediction. Figure 4.8 depicts the general overview of the ConvLSTM framework introduced to deal with Sentinel-2 SITS.

Convolutional Long–Short-Term Memory networks have also recently been employed in Qiu *et al.* (2019a) to deal with the local climate zone mapping of urban areas. The study presents the analysis of nine different European urban areas with a seasonal time series and a coarse land cover categorization (six classes) with respect to the standard 17 class nomenclature. The considered time series were acquired between winter 2016/2017 and autumn 2017 via Sentinel-2 mission. Despite the short analyzed time series (only four images, one for each season), the LSTM network on top of the convolutional analysis still supplies an effective way to get the most out of the sequential information contained in the time series. In addition, when spatial, as well as temporal information needs to be exploited (e.g. to detect classes like *Compact built-up area* or *Open built-up area* for the local climate zone mapping), Convolutional Recurrent Neural Networks constitute a powerful and adequate tool.

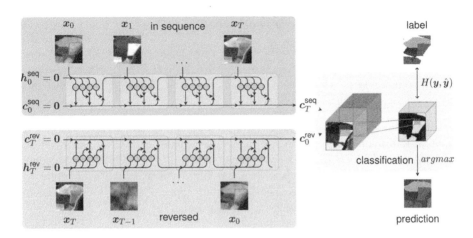

Figure 4.8. *Overview of the framework proposed in Rußwurm and Körner (2018). Two ConvLSTM units are deployed to analyze the data considering two possible directions. The neural frameworks provide a dense output where it predicts the labels not only for one pixel, but for the whole spatial patch at once. For a color version of this figure, see www.iste.co.uk/atto/change2.zip*

A different way of combining Convolutional and Recurrent DL approaches to deal with optical SITS was introduced in Interdonato *et al.* (2019) under the name DUPLO (A DUal view Point deep Learning architecture for time series classificatiOn). While all of the previous strategies sequentially combine the two models (the feature extracted from spatial convolutions are, generally, the inputs of the recurrent process), *DUPLO* suggests leveraging CNN and RNN as two possible views of the same information. In particular, the representations extracted by the two models are combined together (in parallel), with the aim of learning complementary representations of the same input information. The framework is deployed to perform general land cover mapping (urban and agricultural), at regional scale, over two different study areas under operational settings (sparse and limited annotated data). The time series of Sentinel-2 imagery spans over more than a year, between 20 and 35 images per time series.

Overall, the combinations of CNN and RNN are not yet extensively studied in the remote sensing community since only a few studies have been published, compared to the many works (e.g.) devoted to exploring CNN. Such hybrid CNN/RNN models, thanks to their abilities to capture and leverage spatio-spectral–temporal information at the same time, constitute an attractive research track for further studies on SITS analysis.

4.4.4. *Synthesis and future developments*

Nowadays, we are gradually shifting from a first stage, in which DL frameworks developed in the CV field were used *as they are*, to a second stage in which the remote sensing community is starting to develop *ad hoc* solutions, especially tailored for specific challenges such as the analysis of SITS.

Due to the ability of such models to deal with spatial and spectral, as well as temporal information at once, hybrid models leveraging both CNN and RNN are emerging as useful tools for SITS analysis and they constitute an interesting research direction to pursuit. There is also room for improvement in the near future for unsupervised analysis, as well as change detection approaches that, for the moment, are not yet well investigated considering DL approaches for SITS.

Another promising direction is related to the combination of optical SITS with other sensors or information (i.e. Very High Spatial imagery, Volunteer Geographical Information, radar satellite image data, etc.) due to the increasing volume and diversity of available EO data. Also, in this case, DL methods can support the fusion of different data sensors with optical SITS to perform fusion at the decision level (Schmitt and Zhu 2016), avoiding the generation of intermediate products that can inject noisy and bias in the analysis.

Temporal and spatial transfer will be another possible research direction that can be addressed via deep neural network processing. How to transfer the model learned on a study area to a different study area or how to reuse or transfer a classification model learnt on a SITS associated with a particular period to a SITS spanning another period can also be explored. Techniques related to transfer learning and domain adaptation exist in the general CV field, but none of them can be directly used to deal with SITS data. This is an exemplar scenario in which techniques and frameworks particularly tailored for SITS data need to be developed.

Last but not least, understanding why and how the DL models are working is crucial to make connections with background and thematic knowledge. In the particular case of SITS data, side information extracted from DL models can support the comprehension of the process but, in the near future, the model itself should be designed considering its explanation as one of the direct outcomes of the analysis. Model explainability should be especially important in the analysis of SITS data, since a first explanation that can be supplied should be related to the important time intervals that support the discrimination among several land cover or land use classes.

4.5. Beyond satellite image time series and deep learning: convergence between time series and video approaches

It is expected that successive improvements in data acquisition frequencies and time series processing capabilities, driven by dense time series analysis and DL methods, will fuel a virtuous cycle of improvements in these technologies applied to environment monitoring. In this section, we examine prospective joint evolutions and convergences between the fields of SITS analysis, CV techniques, video processing and DL.

4.5.1. *Increased image acquisition frequency: from time series to spaceborne time-lapse and videos*

Over the past few decades, there has been a *continuous trend of increasing the revisit frequency* from national EO missions at moderate to high resolution: from a 16 day revisit time with single mission Landsat to eight days with two satellites, three to five days revisit frequency for Sentinel-2A and 2B, and up to 2.9 days global median average revisit interval by harmonizing and combining Landsat and Sentinel time series (Li and Roy 2017). This increased temporal resolution, coupled with open data policies, allowed dense time series analysis approaches to emerge over the past few years (as shown in sections 4.2 and 4.3), but dense time series approaches come at the cost of a vast increase in data storage and processing demands.

Several services make use of this increased data density to demonstrate spaceborne time-lapse imaging capabilities to a wider audience, in a free or easy-to-use manner, which also removes or alleviates the technical hurdles related to data storage, management and processing. To this end, the *Google Earth Engine* (GEE) was the first service to showcase several use cases of SITS analysis, for example, for visualizing and monitoring deforestation based on Landsat image time series, with Google Earth Engine Timelapse or Global Forest Watch and its annual Tree Cover Loss maps. GEE also offers the possibility for researchers and developers to implement their own algorithms and deploy multitemporal map products on top of the GEE, such as FCDM (section 4.2.2), BFAST-Monitor and CCDC algorithms (section 4.3). The recently developed package for Python programming language, *geemap* (Wu 2020), provides interactive mapping capability with GEE, coupled with an easy-to-use time-lapse production online tool. A similar cloud processing and time-lapse production capability was specifically developed for ESA Sentinel imagery, with Sinergise's *Sentinel-Hub* and *EO Browser* platforms. Both GEE and Sentinel-Hub now host Landsat and Sentinel data archives and offer time series processing capabilities for both image sources.

Commercial imaging satellite constellations will complement national missions with very-high-resolution images at increased temporal resolution. In September 2019, Planet Labs was the first commercial satellite provider to reach *intra-day revisit*, announcing revisits up to 12 times a day for its SkySat constellation. MAXAR's WorldView Legion constellation will provide up to 15 revisit per day at a 30 cm resolution, with an expected launch in 2021.

The *increased temporal resolution of VHR imaging satellites* on lower Earth orbits (LEO) will consolidate the capacity to fulfill the currently most demanding monitoring applications for natural disaster relief, emergency response or maritime surveillance. It will also enable novel applications such as finely monitoring fast changing natural or human-made events, and infrastructures (e.g. active construction sites and mining operations for business intelligence), several times a day. However, due to the physical limitations imposed by gravitational laws and the occupational limits on lower orbits, LEO single imaging constellations may not reach the same temporal resolution or consistency as geostationary satellites dedicated, for example, to weather monitoring and forecasts. There will still remain a gap in temporal resolution between the most dense SITS that will reach 10–15 revisits per day, and true videos which allow, for example, real-time tracking of fast moving objects.

The first commercial *spaceborne VHR videos* were provided in late 2013 by SkyBox Imaging (later bought by Planet). The current Planet's SkySat satellites can capture videos at 30 frames per second for up to 90 seconds, and several other players are emerging on the segment of spaceborne video acquisition, such as Sen EarthTV. In-orbit very-high-resolution SAR video has also been demonstrated in March 2020 by ICEYE. Unique applications of VHR spaceborne videos include analyzing traffic patterns for road network planning, logistic and supply chain analysis, live monitoring of humanitarian crises for emergency response, monitoring movements of large groups of people, or analyzing plume activity to estimate power plant production. Although LEO video acquisitions are limited to a few seconds or a couple of minutes due to orbital constraints, spaceborne VHR video capability may raise concerns about privacy issues (Beam 2019).

With the emergence of fast revisit imaging satellites, intra-day time-lapse capability and VHR spaceborne videos, EO has become increasingly relevant and attractive for approaches that have so far been specific to CV.

4.5.2. *Deep learning and computer vision as technology enablers*

Using *CV techniques to analyze spaceborne timelapses and videos* has now become a possibility. Theoretically, the significant increase in EO data density allows approaches similar to video processing, for example, gap filling or cloud detection in a similar way to how background subtraction is used in CV to identify moving targets. Some published works already address processing SITS as videos (Alfergani *et al.* 2020), using background subtraction or object tracking techniques. Current spaceborne videos, even though shorter in duration, can be processed using similar methods as for airborne drone or ground-based videos, for example, traffic monitoring (Ali Ahmadi *et al.* 2019).

Concurrently, *synergies and convergences have strengthened between CV, ML and EO* research fields and communities, with the *DL method as one of the technology enablers*. ML methods have long been used in CV and EO fields, mostly independently. Recently, the CV community has been increasingly active within the EO field, not only for time series analysis, but as a whole, through:

– joint workshops at high profile CV and EO conferences, such as EO workshops at CVPR (Conference on Computer Vision and Pattern Recognition), which also attract researchers from the remote sensing community towards top CV conferences;

– publications in remote sensing journals and conferences, adapting the CV point of view and techniques into EO data and research;

– the organization of several challenges on EO datasets, notably several SpaceNet challenges (including SpaceNet 7 on Multitemporal Urban Development Challenge) and Kaggle competitions (e.g. Planet's "Understanding the Amazon from Space - Using satellite data to track the human footprint in the Amazon rainforest");

– establishing EO benchmark datasets for large-scale processing, recently also for SITS. Datasets for most challenges mentioned above are now available as benchmark datasets.

It is to be noted that the *culture of benchmark datasets is much stronger in the field of CV* than in EO, with a longer history of using benchmarks, more datasets being used as public benchmarks, and including significantly more images (tens of thousands) than the typical EO benchmark datasets (few dozens, rarely more than a hundred). Many of the DL breakthroughs in CV were highlighted on a very large scale and challenging benchmarks, such as ImageNet. The very fact that DL methods could significantly improve upon a long-lasting large-scale benchmark was in itself a remarkable achievement which contributed to its rise in popularity.

There has been a *need for standardized benchmark datasets in several fields of remote sensing, especially change detection and time series*, that is currently beginning to be addressed. For example, the Onera Satellite Change Detection Dataset (Caye Daudt *et al.* 2018) provides 24 pairs of multispectral Sentinel-2 images between 2015 and 2018 in urban areas, and the TiSeLaC Time Series Land Cover Classification Challenge includes 23 Landsat 8 images acquired in 2014 above Reunion Island[1]. This on-going shift of attitude towards benchmarks in the EO field could be partly attributed to the growing interactions between the CV and EO fields.

4.5.3. *Future steps*

DL methods have brought significant breakthroughs in CV, and to some extent also in EO. Still, *gaps remain to be addressed between the increased EO data temporal resolution and DL capabilities already demonstrated in CV.*

---

1. See: https://sites.google.com/site/dinoienco/tiselc Accessed 12/09/2020.

DL is increasingly applied to SITS, but some limitations remain. So far, most DL time series analysis methods are concerned with map classification, as defined in section 4.3.2. More efforts should be put on *deep leaning methods for dense time series analysis using all available data, especially trajectory classification and online methods*. DL methods for SITS should be more systematically compared to classical dense time series approaches, and perhaps even the hybridization between the two types of methods should be investigated.

To that end, a *benchmark for dense SITS analysis*, using all available Landsat and/or Sentinel-2 imagery and with proper labeling, would be desirable. Work is also ongoing in the field of unsupervised SITS analysis, which, when successful, could be a breakthrough compared to classical SITS analysis methods.

It can be foreseen that, as satellite image data density keeps on increasing and the EO field further benefits from CV expertise, those gaps would be reduced.

4.6. References

Alfergani, H., Bouaynaya, N., Nazari, R. (2020). Spatio-temporal statistical sequential analysis for temperature change detection in satellite imagery. *IEEE International Geoscience and Remote Sensing Symposium (IGARSS)*.

Ali Ahmadi, S., Ghorbanian, A., Mohammadzadeh, A. (2019). Moving vehicle detection, tracking and traffic parameter estimation from a satellite video: A perspective on a smarter city. *International Journal of Remote Sensing*, 40(22), 8379–8394.

Arévalo, P., Olofsson, P., Woodcock, C.E. (2020). Continuous monitoring of land change activities and post-disturbance dynamics from Landsat time series: A test methodology for REDD+ reporting. *Remote Sensing of Environment*, 238, 111051.

Baetens, L., Desjardins, C., Hagolle, O. (2019). Validation of copernicus Sentinel-2 cloud masks obtained from maja, Sen2Cor, and Fmask processors using reference cloud masks generated with a supervised active learning procedure. *Remote Sensing*, 11(4), 433.

Beam, C. (2019). Soon, satellites will be able to watch you everywhere all the time. *MIT Technology Review* [Online]. Available at: https://www.technologyreview.com/ 2019/06/26/102931/satellites-threaten-privacy/ [Accessed 12 September 2020].

Bengio, Y., Courville, A.C., Vincent, P. (2013). Representation learning: A review and new perspectives. *IEEE TPAMI*, 35(8), 1798–1828.

Berhane, T.M., Lane, C.R., Mengistu, S., Christensen, J., Golden, H.E., Qiu, S., Zhu, Z., Wu, Q. (2020). Land-cover changes to surface-water buffers in the midwestern USA: 25 years of Landsat data analyses (1993–2017). *Remote Sensing*, 12(5), 754.

Berk, A., Bernstein, L., Anderson, G., Acharya, P., Robertson, D., Chetwynd, J., Adler-Golden, S. (1998). Modtran cloud and multiple scattering upgrades with application to aviris. *Remote Sensing of Environment*, 65(3), 367–375.

Blaschke, T. (2010). Object based image analysis for remote sensing. *ISPRS Journal of Photogrammetry and Remote Sensing*, 65(1), 2–16.

Bolton, D.K., Gray, J.M., Melaas, E.K., Moon, M., Eklundh, L., Friedl, M.A. (2020). Continental-scale land surface phenology from harmonized Landsat 8 and Sentinel-2 imagery. *Remote Sensing of Environment*, 240, 111685.

Brooks, E.B., Wynne, R.H., Thomas, V.A., Blinn, C.E., Coulston, J.W. (2013). On-the-fly massively multitemporal change detection using statistical quality control charts and Landsat data. *IEEE Transactions on Geoscience and Remote Sensing*, 52(6), 3316–3332.

Brown, R.L., Durbin, J., Evans, J.M. (1975). Techniques for testing the constancy of regression relationships over time. *Journal of the Royal Statistical Society: Series B (Methodological)*, 37(2), 149–163.

Brown, J.F., Tollerud, H.J., Barber, C.P., Zhou, Q., Dwyer, J.L., Vogelmann, J.E., Loveland, T.R., Woodcock, C.E., Stehman, S.V., Zhu, Z., Smith, K., Horton, J.A., Xian, G., Auch, R.F., Sohl, T.L., Sayler, K.L., Gallant, A.L., Zelenak, D., Reker, R.R., Rover, J. (2020). Lessons learned implementing an operational continuous United States national land change monitoring capability: The Land Change Monitoring, Assessment, and Projection (LCMAP) approach. *Remote Sensing of Environment*, 238, 111356.

Bullock, E.L., Woodcock, C.E., Holden, C.E. (2020). Improved change monitoring using an ensemble of time series algorithms. *Remote Sensing of Environment*, 238, 111165.

Caye Daudt, R., Le Saux, B., Boulch, A., Gousseau, Y. (2018). Urban change detection for multispectral earth observation using convolutional neural networks. *IEEE International Geoscience and Remote Sensing Symposium (IGARSS)*.

Chai, D., Newsam, S., Zhang, H.K., Qiu, Y., Huang, J. (2019). Cloud and cloud shadow detection in Landsat imagery based on deep convolutional neural networks. *Remote Sensing of Environment*, 225, 307–316.

Chen, L., Michishita, R., Xu, B. (2014). Abrupt spatiotemporal land and water changes and their potential drivers in Poyang Lake, 2000–2012. *ISPRS Journal of Photogrammetry and Remote Sensing*, 98, 85–93.

Chen, S., Chen, X., Chen, J., Jia, P., Cao, X., Liu, C. (2015). An iterative haze optimized transformation for automatic cloud/haze detection of Landsat imagery. *IEEE Transactions on Geoscience and Remote Sensing*, 54(5), 2682–2694.

Chen, Y., Jiang, H., Li, C., Jia, X., Ghamisi, P. (2016). Deep feature extraction and classification of hyperspectral images based on convolutional neural networks. *IEEE Transactions on Geoscience and Remote Sensing*, 54(10), 6232–6251.

Cho, K., van Merrienboer, B., Gülçehre, Ç., Bahdanau, D., Bougares, F., Schwenk, H., Bengio, Y. (2014). Learning phrase representations using RNN encoder-decoder for statistical machine translation. *EMNLP*, pp. 1724–1734.

Chow, G.C. (1960). Tests of equality between sets of coefficients in two linear regressions. *Econometrica: Journal of the Econometric Society*, pp. 591–605.

Chu, T., Guo, X., Takeda, K. (2017). Effects of burn severity and environmental conditions on post-fire regeneration in Siberian larch forest. *Forests*, 8(3), 76.

Claverie, M., Ju, J., Masek, J.G., Dungan, J.L., Vermote, E.F., Roger, J.-C., Skakun, S.V., Justice, C. (2018). The harmonized Landsat and Sentinel-2 surface reflectance data set. *Remote Sensing of Environment*, 219, 145–161.

Cohen, W.B., Healey, S.P., Yang, Z., Stehman, S.V., Brewer, C.K., Brooks, E.B., Gorelick, N., Huang, C., Hughes, M.J., Kennedy, R.E., Loveland, T.R., Moisen, G.G., Schroeder, T.A., Vogelmann, J.E., Woodcock, C.E., Yang, L., Zhu, Z. (2017). How similar are forest disturbance maps derived from different Landsat time series algorithms? *Forests*, 8(4), 98.

Cohen, W.B., Yang, Z., Healey, S.P., Kennedy, R.E., Gorelick, N. (2018). A LandTrendr multispectral ensemble for forest disturbance detection. *Remote Sensing of Environment*, 205, 131–140.

Dechoz, C., Poulain, V., Massera, S., Languille, F., Greslou, D., de Lussy, F., Gaudel, A., L'Helguen, C., Picard, C., Trémas, T. (2015). Sentinel 2 global reference image. *Image and Signal Processing for Remote Sensing XXI*, International Society for Optics and Photonics, 9643, 96430A.

Deng, C. and Zhu, Z. (2018). Continuous subpixel monitoring of urban impervious surface using Landsat time series. *Remote Sensing of Environment*, p. 110929.

DeVries, B., Decuyper, M., Verbesselt, J., Zeileis, A., Herold, M., Joseph, S. (2015). Tracking disturbance-regrowth dynamics in tropical forests using structural change detection and Landsat time series. *Remote Sensing of Environment*, 169, 320–334.

DeVries, B., Pratihast, A.K., Verbesselt, J., Kooistra, L., Herold, M. (2016). Characterizing forest change using community-based monitoring data and Landsat time series. *PloS One*, 11(3), 1–25.

Drusch, M., Del Bello, U., Carlier, S., Colin, O., Fernandez, V., Gascon, F., Hoersch, B., Isola, C., Laberinti, P., Martimort, P., Meygret, A., Spoto, F., Sy, O., Marchese, F., Bargellini, P. (2012). Sentinel-2: ESA's optical high-resolution mission for GMES operational services. *Remote Sensing of Environment*, 120, 25–36.

Du, L., McCarty, G.W., Zhang, X., Lang, M.W., Vanderhoof, M.K., Li, X., Huang, C., Lee, S., Zou, Z. (2020). Mapping forested wetland inundation in the Delmarva Peninsula, USA using deep convolutional neural networks. *Remote Sensing*, 12(4), 644.

Dutrieux, L.P., Verbesselt, J., Kooistra, L., Herold, M. (2015). Monitoring forest cover loss using multiple data streams, a case study of a tropical dry forest in Bolivia. *ISPRS Journal of Photogrammetry and Remote Sensing*, 107, 112–125.

Dutrieux, L.P., Jakovac, C.C., Latifah, S.H., Kooistra, L. (2016). Reconstructing land use history from Landsat time series: Case study of a swidden agriculture system in Brazil. *International Journal of Applied Earth Observation and Geoinformation*, 47, 112–124.

Foga, S., Scaramuzza, P.L., Guo, S., Zhu, Z., Dilley Jr., R.D., Beckmann, T., Schmidt, G.L., Dwyer, J.L., Hughes, M.J., Laue, B. (2017). Cloud detection algorithm comparison and validation for operational Landsat data products. *Remote Sensing of Environment*, 194, 379–390.

Frantz, D., Haß, E., Uhl, A., Stoffels, J., Hill, J. (2018). Improvement of the Fmask algorithm for Sentinel-2 images: Separating clouds from bright surfaces based on parallax effects. *Remote Sensing of Environment*, 215, 471–481.

Fu, P. and Weng, Q. (2016). A time series analysis of urbanization induced land use and land cover change and its impact on land surface temperature with Landsat imagery. *Remote Sensing of Environment*, 175, 205–214.

Gaetano, R., Ienco, D., Ose, K., Cresson, R. (2018). A two-branch CNN architecture for land cover classification of PAN and MS imagery. *Remote Sensing*, 10(11), 1746.

Gao, F., Masek, J.G., Wolfe, R.E. (2009). Automated registration and orthorectification package for Landsat and Landsat-like data processing. *Journal of Applied Remote Sensing*, 3(1), 033515.

Garnot, V.S.F., Landrieu, L., Giordano, S., Chehata, N. (2019). Time-space tradeoff in deep learning models for crop classification on satellite multi-spectral image time series. *IEEE International Geoscience and Remote Sensing Symposium (IGARSS)*, pp. 6247–6250.

Gong, P., Li, X., Zhang, W. (2019). 40-year (1978–2017) human settlement changes in China reflected by impervious surfaces from satellite remote sensing. *Science Bulletin*, 64(11), 756–763.

Goodwin, N.R. and Collett, L.J. (2014). Development of an automated method for mapping fire history captured in Landsat TM and ETM+ time series across Queensland, Australia. *Remote Sensing of Environment*, 148, 206–221.

Goodwin, N.R., Collett, L.J., Denham, R.J., Flood, N., Tindall, D. (2013). Cloud and cloud shadow screening across Queensland, Australia: An automated method for Landsat TM/ETM+ time series. *Remote Sensing of Environment*, 134, 50–65.

Graves, A., Mohamed, A., Hinton, G.E. (2013). Speech recognition with deep recurrent neural networks. *ICASSP*, pp. 6645–6649.

Greff, K., Srivastava, R.K., Koutník, J., Steunebrink, B.R., Schmidhuber, J. (2017). LSTM: A search space odyssey. *IEEE Transactions on Neural Networks and Learning Systems*, 28(10), 2222–2232.

Griffiths, P., Nendel, C., Pickert, J., Hostert, P. (2020). Towards national-scale characterization of grassland use intensity from integrated Sentinel-2 and Landsat time series. *Remote Sensing of Environment*, 238, 111124.

Hagolle, O., Huc, M., Pascual, D.V., Dedieu, G. (2010). A multi-temporal method for cloud detection, applied to FORMOSAT-2, venμs, Landsat and Sentinel-2 images. *Remote Sensing of Environment*, 114(8), 1747–1755.

Hamunyela, E., Verbesselt, J., Herold, M. (2016). Using spatial context to improve early detection of deforestation from Landsat time series. *Remote Sensing of Environment*, 172, 126–138.

Hansen, M.C., Potapov, P.V., Moore, R., Hancher, M., Turubanova, S.A., Tyukavina, A., Thau, D., Stehman, S.V., Goetz, S.J., Loveland, T.R., Kommareddy, A., Egorov, A., Chini, L., Justice, C.O., Townshend, J.R.G. (2013). High-resolution global maps of 21st-century forest cover change. *Science*, 342(6160), 850–853.

Hansen, M.C., Egorov, A., Potapov, P.V., Stehman, S., Tyukavina, A., Turubanova, S., Roy, D.P., Goetz, S., Loveland, T.R., Ju, J., Kommareddy, A., Kovalskyy, V., Forsyth, C., Bents, T. (2014). Monitoring conterminous United States (conus) land cover change with web-enabled Landsat data (weld). *Remote Sensing of Environment*, 140, 466–484.

Hansen, M.C., Krylov, A., Tyukavina, A., Potapov, P.V., Turubanova, S., Zutta, B., Ifo, S., Margono, B., Stolle, F., Moore, R. (2016). Humid tropical forest disturbance alerts using Landsat data. *Environmental Research Letters*, 11(3), 034008.

Hawbaker, T.J., Vanderhoof, M.K., Beal, Y.-J., Takacs, J.D., Schmidt, G.L., Falgout, J.T., Williams, B., Fairaux, N.M., Caldwell, M.K., Picotte, J.J., Howard, S.M., Stitt, S., Dwyer, J.L. (2017). Mapping burned areas using dense time series of Landsat data. *Remote Sensing of Environment*, 198, 504–522.

He, K., Zhang, X., Ren, S., Sun, J. (2016). Deep residual learning for image recognition. *CVPR*, pp. 770–778.

Healey, S.P., Cohen, W.B., Yang, Z., Brewer, C.K., Brooks, E.B., Gorelick, N., Hernandez, A.J., Huang, C., Hughes, M.J., Kennedy, R.E., Loveland, T.R., Moisen, G.G., Schroeder, T.A., Stehman, S.V., Vogelmann, J.E., Woodcock, C.E., Yang, L., Zhu, Z. (2018). Mapping forest change using stacked generalization: An ensemble approach. *Remote Sensing of Environment*, 204, 717–728.

Hermosilla, T., Wulder, M.A., White, J.C., Coops, N.C., Hobart, G.W., Campbell, L.B. (2016). Mass data processing of time series Landsat imagery: Pixels to data products for forest monitoring. *International Journal of Digital Earth*, 9(11), 1035–1054.

Hermosilla, T., Wulder, M.A., White, J.C., Coops, N.C., Hobart, G.W. (2018). Disturbance-informed annual land cover classification maps of Canada's forested ecosystems for a 29-year Landsat time series. *Canadian Journal of Remote Sensing*, 44(1), 67–87.

Hermosilla, T., Wulder, M.A., White, J.C., Coops, N.C., Pickell, P.D., Bolton, D.K. (2019). Impact of time on interpretations of forest fragmentation: Three-decades of fragmentation dynamics over Canada. *Remote Sensing of Environment*, 222, 65–77.

Hirschmugl, M., Gallaun, H., Dees, M., Datta, P., Deutscher, J., Koutsias, N., Schardt, M. (2017). Methods for mapping forest disturbance and degradation from optical earth observation data: A review. *Current Forestry Reports*, 3(1), 32–45.

Hollstein, A., Segl, K., Guanter, L., Brell, M., Enesco, M. (2016). Ready-to-use methods for the detection of clouds, cirrus, snow, shadow, water and clear sky pixels in Sentinel-2 MSI images. *Remote Sensing*, 8(8), 666.

Houborg, R. and McCabe, M.F. (2018). A cubesat enabled spatio-temporal enhancement method (CESTEM) utilizing planet, Landsat and modis data. *Remote Sensing of Environment*, 209, 211–226.

Huang, C., Goward, S.N., Masek, J.G., Thomas, N., Zhu, Z., Vogelmann, J.E. (2010a). An automated approach for reconstructing recent forest disturbance history using dense Landsat time series stacks. *Remote Sensing of Environment*, 114(1), 183–198.

Huang, C., Thomas, N., Goward, S.N., Masek, J.G., Zhu, Z., Townshend, J.R., Vogelmann, J.E. (2010b). Automated masking of cloud and cloud shadow for forest change analysis using Landsat images. *International Journal of Remote Sensing*, 31(20), 5449–5464.

Hughes, M.J. and Hayes, D.J. (2014). Automated detection of cloud and cloud shadow in single-date Landsat imagery using neural networks and spatial post-processing. *Remote Sensing*, 6(6), 4907–4926.

Ienco, D., Gaetano, R., Dupaquier, C., Maurel, P. (2017). Land cover classification via multitemporal spatial data by deep recurrent neural networks. *IEEE Geoscience and Remote Sensing Letters*, 14(10), 1685–1689.

Inglada, J., Vincent, A., Arias, M., Tardy, B., Morin, D., Rodes, I. (2017). Operational high resolution land cover map production at the country scale using satellite image time series. *Remote Sensing*, 9(1), 95.

Interdonato, R., Ienco, D., Gaetano, R., Ose, K. (2019). Duplo: A dual view point deep learning architecture for time series classification. *ISPRS Journal of Photogrammetry and Remote Sensing*, 149, 91–104.

Irish, R.R. (2000). Landsat 7 automatic cloud cover assessment. *Algorithms for Multispectral, Hyperspectral, and Ultraspectral Imagery VI*, International Society for Optics and Photonics, 4049, 348–355.

Ji, S., Zhang, C., Xu, A., Shi, Y., Duan, Y. (2018). 3D convolutional neural networks for crop classification with multi-temporal remote sensing images. *Remote Sensing*, 10(1), 75.

Jia, X., Khandelwal, A., Nayak, G., Gerber, J., Carlson, K., West, P.C., Kumar, V. (2017). Incremental dual-memory LSTM in land cover prediction. *KDD*, pp. 867–876.

Jiang, W., He, G., Long, T., Ni, Y., Liu, H., Peng, Y., Lv, K., Wang, G. (2018). Multilayer perceptron neural network for surface water extraction in Landsat 8 OLI satellite images. *Remote Sensing*, 10(5), 755.

Jin, S., Homer, C., Yang, L., Xian, G., Fry, J., Danielson, P., Townsend, P.A. (2013). Automated cloud and shadow detection and filling using two-date Landsat imagery in the USA. *International Journal of Remote Sensing*, 34(5), 1540–1560.

Kalinicheva, E., Sublime, J., Trocan, M. (2019). Change detection in satellite images using reconstruction errors of joint autoencoders. *ICANN*, pp. 637–648.

Kampffmeyer, M., Salberg, A., Jenssen, R. (2018). Urban land cover classification with missing data modalities using deep convolutional neural networks. *IEEE Journal of Selected Topics in Applied Earth Observations and Remote Sensing*, 11(6), 1758–1768.

Kennedy, R.E., Cohen, W.B., Schroeder, T.A. (2007). Trajectory-based change detection for automated characterization of forest disturbance dynamics. *Remote Sensing of Environment*, 110(3), 370–386.

Kennedy, R.E., Yang, Z., Cohen, W.B. (2010). Detecting trends in forest disturbance and recovery using yearly Landsat time series 1: LandTrendr – Temporal segmentation algorithms. *Remote Sensing of Environment*, 114(12), 2897–2910.

Kipf, T.N. and Welling, M. (2017). Semi-supervised classification with graph convolutional networks. *ICLR*.

Kontgis, C., Schneider, A., Ozdogan, M. (2015). Mapping rice paddy extent and intensification in the Vietnamese Mekong River Delta with dense time stacks of Landsat data. *Remote Sensing of Environment*, 169, 255–269.

Kussul, N., Lavreniuk, M., Skakun, S., Shelestov, A. (2017). Deep learning classification of land cover and crop types using remote sensing data. *IEEE Geoscience and Remote Sensing Letters*, 14(5), 778–782.

Langner, A., Miettinen, J., Kukkonen, M., Vancutsem, C., Simonetti, D., Vieilledent, G., Verhegghen, A., Gallego, J., Stibig, H.-J. (2018). Towards operational monitoring of forest canopy disturbance in evergreen rain forests: A test case in continental Southeast Asia. *Remote Sensing*, 10(4), 544.

LeCun, Y., Bengio, Y., Hinton, G. (2015). Deep learning. *Nature*, 521(7553), 436–444.

Li, J. and Narayanan, R.M. (2003). A shape-based approach to change detection of lakes using time series remote sensing images. *IEEE Transactions on Geoscience and Remote Sensing*, 41(11), 2466–2477.

Li, J. and Roy, D.P. (2017). A global analysis of Sentinel-2A, Sentinel-2B and Landsat-8 data revisit intervals and implications for terrestrial monitoring. *Remote Sensing*, 9(9), 902.

Li, X., Gong, P., Liang, L. (2015). A 30-year (1984–2013) record of annual urban dynamics of Beijing city derived from Landsat data. *Remote Sensing of Environment*, 166, 78–90.

Li, Z., Feng, Y., Gurgel, H., Xu, L., Dessay, N., Gong, P. (2019). Use of spatial autocorrelation and time series Landsat images for long-term monitoring of surface water shrinkage and expansion in Guanting Reservoir, China. *Remote Sensing Letters*, 10(12), 1192–1200.

Liang, S., Fallah-Adl, H., Kalluri, S., JáJá, J., Kaufman, Y.J., Townshend, J.R. (1997). An operational atmospheric correction algorithm for Landsat thematic mapper imagery over the land. *Journal of Geophysical Research: Atmospheres*, 102(D14), 17173–17186.

de Lima, R.P. and Marfurt, K. (2020). Convolutional neural network for remote-sensing scene classification: Transfer learning analysis. *Remote Sensing*, 12(1), 86.

Linzen, T., Dupoux, E., Goldberg, Y. (2016). Assessing the ability of LSTMS to learn syntax-sensitive dependencies. *TACL*, 4, 521–535.

Long, T., Jiao, W., He, G., Zhang, Z. (2016). A fast and reliable matching method for automated georeferencing of remotely-sensed imagery. *Remote Sensing*, 8(1), 56.

Louis, J., Debaecker, V., Pflug, B., Main-Knorn, M., Bieniarz, J., Mueller-Wilm, U., Cadau, E., Gascon, F. (2016). Sentinel-2 Sen2Cor: L2A processor for users. *Proceedings Living Planet Symposium*, Spacebooks Online, pp. 1–8.

Lyu, H., Lu, H., Mou, L. (2016). Learning a transferable change rule from a recurrent neural network for land cover change detection. *Remote Sensing*, 8(6), 506.

Masek, J.G., Vermote, E.F., Saleous, N.E., Wolfe, R., Hall, F.G., Huemmrich, K.F., Gao, F., Kutler, J., Lim, T.-K. (2006). A Landsat surface reflectance dataset for North America, 1990–2000. *IEEE Geoscience and Remote Sensing Letters*, 3(1), 68–72.

Mayer, B. and Kylling, A. (2005). Technical note: The libradtran software package for radiative transfer calculations – Description and examples of use. *Atmospheric Chemistry and Physics*, 5(7), 1855–1877 [Online]. Available at: https://www. atmos-chem-phys.net/5/1855/2005/.

Melesse, A.M. and Jordan, J.D. (2002). A comparison of fuzzy vs. augmented-isodata classification algorithms for cloud-shadow discrimination from Landsat images. *Photogrammetric Engineering and Remote Sensing*, 68(9), 905–912.

Morresi, D., Vitali, A., Urbinati, C., Garbarino, M. (2019). Forest spectral recovery and regeneration dynamics in stand-replacing wildfires of Central Apennines derived from Landsat time series. *Remote Sensing*, 11(3), 308.

Mu, H., Zhou, L., Dang, X., Yuan, B. (2019). Winter wheat yield estimation from multitemporal remote sensing images based on convolutional neural networks. *MultiTemp*, pp. 1–4.

Novo-Fernández, A., Franks, S., Wehenkel, C., López-Serrano, P.M., Molinier, M., López-Sánchez, C.A. (2018). Landsat time series analysis for temperate forest cover change detection in the Sierra Madre Occidental, Durango, Mexico. *International Journal of Applied Earth Observation and Geoinformation*, 73, 230–244 [Online]. Available at: http://www.sciencedirect.com/science/article/pii/S0303243418302812.

Nutini, F., Boschetti, M., Brivio, P., Bocchi, S., Antoninetti, M. (2013). Land-use and land-cover change detection in a semi-arid area of Niger using multi-temporal analysis of Landsat images. *International Journal of Remote Sensing*, 34(13), 4769–4790.

Oishi, Y., Ishida, H., Nakamura, R. (2018). A new Landsat 8 cloud discrimination algorithm using thresholding tests. *International Journal of Remote Sensing*, 39(23), 9113–9133.

van den Oord, A., Kalchbrenner, N., Espeholt, L., Kavukcuoglu, K., Vinyals, O., Graves, A. (2016). Conditional image generation with pixelcnn decoders. *NIPS*, pp. 4790–4798.

Oreopoulos, L., Wilson, M.J., Várnai, T. (2011). Implementation on Landsat data of a simple cloud-mask algorithm developed for MODIS land bands. *IEEE Geoscience and Remote Sensing Letters*, 8(4), 597–601.

Pardo-Pascual, J.E., Almonacid-Caballer, J., Ruiz, L.A., Palomar-Vázquez, J., Rodrigo-Alemany, R. (2014). Evaluation of storm impact on sandy beaches of the Gulf of Valencia using Landsat imagery series. *Geomorphology*, 214, 388–401.

Pasquarella, V.J., Bradley, B.A., Woodcock, C.E. (2017). Near-real-time monitoring of insect defoliation using Landsat time series. *Forests*, 8(8), 275.

Pelletier, C., Webb, G.I., Petitjean, F. (2019). Temporal convolutional neural network for the classification of satellite image time series. *Remote Sensing*, 11(5), 523.

Pengra, B., Gallant, A.L., Zhu, Z., Dahal, D. (2016). Evaluation of the initial thematic output from a continuous change-detection algorithm for use in automated operational land-change mapping by the U.S. geological survey. *Remote Sensing*, 8(10), 811.

Pflugmacher, D., Rabe, A., Peters, M., Hostert, P. (2019). Mapping Pan-European land cover using Landsat spectral-temporal metrics and the European LUCAS survey. *Remote Sensing of Environment*, 221, 583–595.

Potapov, P.V., Turubanova, S., Hansen, M.C. (2011). Regional-scale boreal forest cover and change mapping using Landsat data composites for European Russia. *Remote Sensing of Environment*, 115(2), 548–561.

Potapov, P.V., Turubanova, S.A., Hansen, M.C., Adusei, B., Broich, M., Altstatt, A., Mane, L., Justice, C.O. (2012). Quantifying forest cover loss in Democratic Republic of the Congo, 2000–2010, with Landsat ETM+ data. *Remote Sensing of Environment*, 122, 106–116.

Potapov, P.V., Turubanova, S., Tyukavina, A., Krylov, A., McCarty, J., Radeloff, V., Hansen, M.C. (2015). Eastern Europe's forest cover dynamics from 1985 to 2012 quantified from the full Landsat archive. *Remote Sensing of Environment*, 159, 28–43.

Qiu, S., He, B., Zhu, Z., Liao, Z., Quan, X. (2017). Improving Fmask cloud and cloud shadow detection in mountainous area for Landsats 4–8 images. *Remote Sensing of Environment*, 199, 107–119.

Qiu, C., Mou, L., Schmitt, M., Zhu, X. (2019a). Local climate zone-based urban land cover classification from multi-seasonal Sentinel-2 images with a recurrent residual network. *ISPRS Journal of Photogrammetry and Remote Sensing*, 154, 151–162.

Qiu, S., Lin, Y., Shang, R., Zhang, J., Ma, L., Zhu, Z. (2019b). Making Landsat time series consistent: Evaluating and improving Landsat analysis ready data. *Remote Sensing*, 11(1), 51.

Qiu, S., Zhu, Z., He, B. (2019c). Fmask 4.0: Improved cloud and cloud shadow detection in Landsats 4–8 and Sentinel-2 imagery. *Remote Sensing of Environment*, 231, 111205.

Qiu, Q., Zhu, Z., Woodcock, C.E. (2020). Cirrus clouds that adversely affect Landsat 8 images: What are they and how to detect them? *Remote Sensing of Environment*. Elsevier, 246, 111884.

Reiche, J., Verbesselt, J., Hoekman, D., Herold, M. (2015). Fusing Landsat and SAR time series to detect deforestation in the tropics. *Remote Sensing of Environment*, 156, 276–293.

Richter, R. (1997). Correction of atmospheric and topographic effects for high spatial resolution satellite imagery. *International Journal of Remote Sensing*, 18(5), 1099–1111.

Roy, D.P., Ju, J., Kline, K., Scaramuzza, P.L., Kovalskyy, V., Hansen, M.C., Loveland, T.R., Vermote, E.F., Zhang, C. (2010). Web-enabled Landsat data (weld): Landsat ETM+ composited mosaics of the conterminous united states. *Remote Sensing of Environment*, 114(1), 35–49.

Roy, D.P., Huang, H., Boschetti, L., Giglio, L., Yan, L., Zhang, H.H., Li, Z. (2019). Landsat-8 and Sentinel-2 burned area mapping – A combined sensor multi-temporal change detection approach. *Remote Sensing of Environment*, 231, 111254.

Rußwurm, M. and Körner, M. (2018). Multi-temporal land cover classification with sequential recurrent encoders. *ISPRS International Journal of Geo-Information*, 7(4), 129.

Sanchez, E.H., Serrurier, M., Ortner, M. (2019). Learning disentangled representations of satellite image time series. *ECML/PKDD*.

Scaramuzza, P.L., Bouchard, M.A., Dwyer, J.L. (2012). Development of the Landsat data continuity mission cloud-cover assessment algorithms. *IEEE Transactions on Geoscience and Remote Sensing*, 50(4), 1140–1154.

Schmitt, M. and Zhu, X.X. (2016). Data fusion and remote sensing: An ever-growing relationship. *IEEE Geoscience and Remote Sensing Magazine*, 4(4), 6–23.

Schroeder, T.A., Cohen, W.B., Song, C., Canty, M.J., Yang, Z. (2006). Radiometric correction of multi-temporal Landsat data for characterization of early successional forest patterns in western Oregon. *Remote Sensing of Environment*, 103(1), 16–26.

Schroeder, T.A., Schleeweis, K.G., Moisen, G.G., Toney, C., Cohen, W.B., Freeman, E.A., Yang, Z., Huang, C. (2017). Testing a Landsat-based approach for mapping disturbance causality in U.S. forests. *Remote Sensing of Environment*, 195, 230–243.

Segal-Rozenhaimer, M., Li, A., Das, K., Chirayath, V. (2020). Cloud detection algorithm for multi-modal satellite imagery using convolutional neural-networks (CNN). *Remote Sensing of Environment*, 237, 111446.

Senf, C., Pflugmacher, D., Hostert, P., Seidl, R. (2017a). Using Landsat time series for characterizing forest disturbance dynamics in the coupled human and natural systems of Central Europe. *ISPRS Journal of Photogrammetry and Remote Sensing*, 130, 453–463.

Senf, C., Seidl, R., Hostert, P. (2017b). Remote sensing of forest insect disturbances: Current state and future directions. *International Journal of Applied Earth Observation and Geoinformation*, 60, 49–60.

Shang, R. and Zhu, Z. (2019). Harmonizing Landsat 8 and Sentinel-2: A time series-based reflectance adjustment approach. *Remote Sensing of Environment*, 235, 111439.

Shao, Z., Deng, J., Wang, L., Fan, Y., Sumari, N.S., Cheng, Q. (2017). Fuzzy autoencode based cloud detection for remote sensing imagery. *Remote Sensing*, 9(4), 311.

Shendryk, Y., Rist, Y., Ticehurst, C., Thorburn, P. (2019). Deep learning for multi-modal classification of cloud, shadow and land cover scenes in PlanetScope and Sentinel-2 imagery. *ISPRS Journal of Photogrammetry and Remote Sensing*, 157, 124–136.

Shi, X., Chen, Z., Wang, H., Yeung, D., Wong, W., Woo, W. (2015). Convolutional LSTM network: A machine learning approach for precipitation nowcasting. *NIPS*, pp. 802–810.

Singh, A. (1989). Digital change detection techniques using remotely-sensed data. *International Journal of Remote Sensing*, 10(6), 989–1003.

Song, C. and Woodcock, C.E. (2003). Monitoring forest succession with multitemporal Landsat images: Factors of uncertainty. *IEEE Transactions on Geoscience and Remote Sensing*, 41(11), 2557–2567.

Song, C., Woodcock, C.E., Seto, K.C., Lenney, M.P., Macomber, S.A. (2001). Classification and change detection using Landsat TM data: When and how to correct atmospheric effects? *Remote Sensing of Environment*, 75(2), 230–244.

Storey, J., Roy, D.P., Masek, J., Gascon, F., Dwyer, J., Choate, M. (2016). A note on the temporary misregistration of Landsat-8 operational land imager (OLI) and Sentinel-2 multi spectral instrument (MSI) imagery. *Remote Sensing of Environment*, 186, 121–122.

Sulla-Menashe, D., Friedl, M.A., Woodcock, C.E. (2016). Sources of bias and variability in long-term Landsat time series over Canadian boreal forests. *Remote Sensing of Environment*, 177, 206–219.

Tulbure, M.G. and Broich, M. (2013). Spatiotemporal dynamic of surface water bodies using Landsat time series data from 1999 to 2011. *ISPRS Journal of Photogrammetry and Remote Sensing*, 79, 44–52.

Uhl, J.H. and Leyk, S. (2020). Towards a novel backdating strategy for creating built-up land time series data using contemporary spatial constraints. *Remote Sensing of Environment*, 238, 111197.

Verbesselt, J., Hyndman, R., Newnham, G., Culvenor, D. (2010). Detecting trend and seasonal changes in satellite image time series. *Remote Sensing of Environment*, 114(1), 106–115.

Verbesselt, J., Zeileis, A., Herold, M. (2012). Near real-time disturbance detection using satellite image time series. *Remote Sensing of Environment*, 123, 98–108.

Vermote, E.F., Tanré, D., Deuze, J.L., Herman, M., Morcette, J.-J. (1997). Second simulation of the satellite signal in the solar spectrum, 6S: An overview. *IEEE Transactions on Geoscience and Remote Sensing*, 35(3), 675–686.

Vermote, E.F., Justice, C., Claverie, M., Franch, B. (2016). Preliminary analysis of the performance of the Landsat 8/OLI land surface reflectance product. *Remote Sensing of Environment*, 185, 46–56.

Vogelmann, J.E., Gallant, A.L., Shi, H., Zhu, Z. (2016). Perspectives on monitoring gradual change across the continuity of Landsat sensors using time series data. *Remote Sensing of Environment*, 185, 258–270.

Volpi, M. and Tuia, D. (2017). Dense semantic labeling of subdecimeter resolution images with convolutional neural networks. *IEEE Transactions on Geoscience and Remote Sensing*, 55(2), 881–893.

Wang, B., Ono, A., Muramatsu, K., Fujiwara, N. (1999). Automated detection and removal of clouds and their shadows from Landsat TM images. *IEICE Transactions on Information and Systems*, 82(2), 453–460.

White, J.C. and Wulder, M.A. (2014). The Landsat observation record of Canada: 1972–2012. *Canadian Journal of Remote Sensing*, 39(6), 455–467.

White, J., Wulder, M., Hobart, G., Luther, J., Hermosilla, T., Griffiths, P., Coops, N., Hall, R., Hostert, P., Dyk, A., Guindon, L. (2014). Pixel-based image compositing for large-area dense time series applications and science. *Canadian Journal of Remote Sensing*, 40(3), 192–212.

White, J.C., Saarinen, N., Kankare, V., Wulder, M.A., Hermosilla, T., Coops, N.C., Pickell, P.D., Holopainen, M., Hyyppä, J., Vastaranta, M. (2018). Confirmation of post-harvest spectral recovery from Landsat time series using measures of forest cover and height derived from airborne laser scanning data. *Remote Sensing of Environment*, 216, 262–275.

Wilson, M.J. and Oreopoulos, L. (2012). Enhancing a simple modis cloud mask algorithm for the Landsat data continuity mission. *IEEE Transactions on Geoscience and Remote Sensing*, 51(2), 723–731.

Woodcock, C.E., Allen, R., Anderson, M., Belward, A., Bindschadler, R., Cohen, W., Gao, F., Goward, S.N., Helder, D., Helmer, E., Nemani, R., Oreopoulos, L., Schott, J., Thenkabail, P.S., Vermote, E.F., Vogelmann, J., Wulder, M.A., Wynne, R. (2008). Free access to Landsat imagery. *Science*, 320(5879). 1011–1011.

Woodcock, C.E., Loveland, T.R., Herold, M., Bauer, M.E. (2020). Transitioning from change detection to monitoring with remote sensing: A paradigm shift. *Remote Sensing of Environment*, 238, 111558.

Woźniak, M., Graña, M., Corchado, E. (2014). A survey of multiple classifier systems as hybrid systems. *Information Fusion*, 16, 3–17.

Wu, Q. (2020). geemap: A Python package for interactive mapping with Google Earth Engine. *Journal of Open Source Software*, 5(51), 2305 [Online]. Available at: https://doi.org/10.21105/joss.02305.

Wulder, M.A., Loveland, T.R., Roy, D.P., Crawford, C.J., Masek, J.G., Woodcock, C.E., Allen, R.G., Anderson, M.C., Belward, A.S., Cohen, W.B. *et al.* (2019). Current status of Landsat program, science, and applications. *Remote Sensing of Environment*, 225, 127–147.

Xie, J., Girshick, R.B., Farhadi, A. (2016). Unsupervised deep embedding for clustering analysis. *ICML*, pp. 478–487.

Yan, L., Roy, D.P., Zhang, H., Li, J., Huang, H. (2016). An automated approach for sub-pixel registration of Landsat-8 operational land imager (OLI) and Sentinel-2 multi spectral instrument (MSI) imagery. *Remote Sensing*, 8(6), 520.

Yin, C., He, B., Yebra, M., Quan, X., Edwards, A.C., Liu, X., Liao, Z. (2020). Improving burn severity retrieval by integrating tree canopy cover into radiative transfer model simulation. *Remote Sensing of Environment*, 236, 111454.

Zhang, L., Zhang, L., Du, B. (2016). Deep learning for remote sensing data: A technical tutorial on the state of the art. *IEEE Geoscience and Remote Sensing Magazine*, 4(2), 22–40.

Zhao, K., Wulder, M.A., Hu, T., Bright, R., Wu, Q., Qin, H., Li, Y., Toman, E., Mallick, B., Zhang, X., Brown, M. (2019). Detecting change-point, trend, and seasonality in satellite time series data to track abrupt changes and nonlinear dynamics: A Bayesian ensemble algorithm. *Remote Sensing of Environment*, 232, 111181.

Zhong, L., Hu, L., Zhou, H. (2019). Deep learning based multi-temporal crop classification. *Remote Sensing of Environment*, 221, 430–443.

Zhou, G., Zhou, X., Yue, T., Liu, Y. (2016). An optional threshold with SVM cloud detection algorithm and DSP implementation. *International Archives of the Photogrammetry, Remote Sensing & Spatial Information Sciences*, 41.

Zhou, Q., Rover, J., Brown, J., Worstell, B., Howard, D., Wu, Z., Gallant, A.L., Rundquist, B., Burke, M. (2019). Monitoring landscape dynamics in central US grasslands with harmonized Landsat-8 and Sentinel-2 time series data. *Remote Sensing*, 11(3), 328.

Zhu, Z. (2017). Change detection using Landsat time series: A review of frequencies, preprocessing, algorithms, and applications. *ISPRS Journal of Photogrammetry and Remote Sensing*, 130, 370–384.

Zhu, X. and Helmer, E.H. (2018). An automatic method for screening clouds and cloud shadows in optical satellite image time series in cloudy regions. *Remote Sensing of Environment*, 214, 135–153.

Zhu, Z. and Woodcock, C.E. (2012). Object-based cloud and cloud shadow detection in Landsat imagery. *Remote Sensing of Environment*, 118, 83–94.

Zhu, Z. and Woodcock, C.E. (2014a). Automated cloud, cloud shadow, and snow detection in multitemporal Landsat data: An algorithm designed specifically for monitoring land cover change. *Remote Sensing of Environment*, 152, 217–234.

Zhu, Z. and Woodcock, C.E. (2014b). Continuous change detection and classification of land cover using all available Landsat data. *Remote Sensing of Environment*, 144, 152–171.

Zhu, Z., Woodcock, C.E., Olofsson, P. (2012). Continuous monitoring of forest disturbance using all available Landsat imagery. *Remote Sensing of Environment*, 122, 75–91.

Zhu, Z., Wang, S., Woodcock, C.E. (2015a). Improvement and expansion of the Fmask algorithm: Cloud, cloud shadow, and snow detection for Landsats 4–7, 8, and Sentinel 2 images. *Remote Sensing of Environment*, 159, 269–277.

Zhu, Z., Woodcock, C.E., Holden, C., Yang, Z. (2015b). Generating synthetic Landsat images based on all available Landsat data: Predicting Landsat surface reflectance at any given time. *Remote Sensing of Environment*, 162, 67–83.

Zhu, Z., Fu, Y., Woodcock, C.E., Olofsson, P., Vogelmann, J.E., Holden, C., Wang, M., Dai, S., Yu, Y. (2016a). Including land cover change in analysis of greenness trends using all available Landsat 5, 7, and 8 images: A case study from Guangzhou, China (2000–2014). *Remote Sensing of Environment*, 185, 243–257.

Zhu, Z., Gallant, A.L., Woodcock, C.E., Pengra, B., Olofsson, P., Loveland, T.R., Jin, S., Dahal, D., Yang, L., Auch, R.F. (2016b). Optimizing selection of training and auxiliary data for operational land cover classification for the LCMAP initiative. *ISPRS Journal of Photogrammetry and Remote Sensing*, 122, 206–221.

Zhu, X.X., Tuia, D., Mou, L., Xia, G., Zhang, L., Xu, F., Fraundorfer, F. (2017). Deep learning in remote sensing: A comprehensive review and list of resources. *IEEE Geoscience and Remote Sensing Magazine*, 5(4), 8–36.

Zhu, Z., Qiu, S., He, B., Deng, C. (2018). Cloud and cloud shadow detection for Landsat images: The fundamental basis for analyzing Landsat time series. *Remote Sensing Time Series Image Processing*, CRC Press, Boca Raton, FL, pp. 25–46.

Zhu, Z., Wulder, M.A., Roy, D.P., Woodcock, C.E., Hansen, M.C., Radeloff, V.C., Healey, S.P., Schaaf, C., Hostert, P., Strobl, P. *et al.* (2019). Benefits of the free and open Landsat data policy. *Remote Sensing of Environment*, 224, 382–385.

Zhu, Z., Zhang, J., Yang, Z., Aljaddani, A.H., Cohen, W.B., Qiu, S., Zhou, C. (2020). Continuous monitoring of land disturbance based on Landsat time series. *Remote Sensing of Environment*, 238, 111116.

Zi, Y., Xie, F., Jiang, Z. (2018). A cloud detection method for Landsat 8 images based on PCANet. *Remote Sensing*, 10(6), 877.

5

A Review on Multi-temporal Earthquake Damage Assessment Using Satellite Images

Gülşen TAŞKIN, Esra ERTEN and Enes Oğuzhan ALATAŞ

Istanbul Technical University, Turkey

5.1. Introduction

Earthquakes are one of the most devastating natural disasters, causing serious and severe damage to human life and property. Hence, developing a fast, reliable and automated disaster management system is critical for coordinating emergency response activities and ensuring effective communication among rescue teams following an earthquake. As earthquake damage assessment is a sophisticated and complicated task, involving numerous challenges, multidisciplinary work is needed from a range of scientific expertise, including remote sensing, image processing, computer vision, machine learning, geophysics, seismology, civil engineering and social sciences, each of which specifically focuses on a variety of open problems in damage assessment (Geib and Taubenbock 2013). Among them, remote sensing (RS) has proven to be a very efficient, key and complementary data source that lies at the center of this picture, providing exhaustive information to the related disciplines due to its ability to observe large urban areas from either a

Change Detection and Image Time Series Analysis 2,
coordinated by Abdourrahmane M. ATTO, Francesca BOVOLO and Lorenzo BRUZZONE.
© ISTE Ltd 2021.

spaceborne or airborne platform with a low cost, wide field of view and fast data acquisition capability. Applications for damage assessment with RS typically involve identification of earthquake-induced changes of the land surface, global or building-based damage detection, surface-deformation mapping, co- and post-seismic deformations, earthquake prediction, seismic risk assessment and assessment of seismic hazard and vulnerability (Stramondo *et al.* 1999; Kerle 2016; He *et al.* 2019a, 2019b).

Each application requires a specific type of remote sensing data and faces different challenges. Thermal infrared imagery, synthetic aperture radar (SAR), interferometric SAR (InSAR) and optical and light detection and ranging (LiDAR) are frequently used RS data types in damage assessment. Each RS data source has a different property in terms of its data structure and capability, playing a significant role in the diversity of damage assessment implementations. In this context, the resolution of RS data, including spatial, radiometric, spectral and temporal, has to be taken into account because they are the keys to identifying the extent and level of earthquake damage. Due to such a large volume of diversity in RS data, there is no single way to proceed, and usually the methodologies differ depending on the type of remote sensing data and the user's need.

In the literature, the limitations and potential use of RS in natural hazards have been explored extensively by Tralli *et al.* (2005). Rather than providing a comprehensive treatment of the applications in remote sensing for a specific natural hazard, their paper focused on recognizing the contributions of satellite remote sensing for understanding the underlying phenomena and providing critical information for decision support and the disaster response systems. Gillespie *et al.* (2007) addressed in detail the significant developments in the assessment and prediction of natural hazards associated with the earth, water and fire, as well as the limitations of remote sensing technologies along with future directions of natural hazards. An analysis of exploiting potential options to respond to hazards, including earthquakes, faulting, volcanic activity, landslides, flooding and wildfire, was carried out by Joyce *et al.* (2009). In the context of natural hazards and remote sensing, the benefits and drawbacks of using image processing techniques in information retrieval were extensively discussed and the role of RS as rapid response in disaster management from the perspective of operationalization of damage mapping was explored. Earthquake damage assessment by using remote sensing was comprehensively discussed in the literature from the perspective of earth observation techniques, rapid damage assessment, disaster risk management and methodological challenges. The most notable review studies are listed in Table 5.1, along with their keywords, which most define the corresponding study.

Authors	Title	Journal Name	Keywords
Rubner *et al.* (2001)	*Empirical evaluation of dissimilarity measures for use in urban structural damage detection*	Remote Sensing	change detection, dissimilarity measures, urban structural damage, satellite imagery
Eguchi and Mansouri (2005)	*Use of remote sensing technologies for building damage assessment after the 2003 Bam, Iran, earthquake – Preface to remote sensing papers*	Earthquake Spectra	the 2003 Bam, Iran, earthquake, remote sensing, building damage assessment
Tronin (2006)	*Remote sensing and earthquakes: A review*	Physics and Chemistry of the Earth	remote sensing, earthquake, deformation, temperature, gas
Rezaeian (2010)	*Assessment of earthquake damages by image-based techniques*	Industrial Electronics Conference Proceedings	image based damage assessment, remote sensing, textural features, multi-view arial images, automatic recognition
Voigt *et al.* (2011)	*Rapid damage assessment and situation mapping: Learning from the 2010 Haiti earthquake*	Photogrammetric Engineering and Remote Sensing	damage assessment, earth observation, optical, accuracy, reliability
Dell'Acqua and Gamba (2012)	*Remote sensing and earthquake damage assessment: Experiences, limits, and perspectives*	Proceedings of the IEEE	damage assessment, data fusion, urban areas
Manfré *et al.* (2012)	*An analysis of geospatial technologies for risk and natural disaster management*	ISPRS International Journal of Geo-Information	volunteered geographic information, spatial data infrastructure, remote sensing, disaster management
Dong and Shan (2013)	*A comprehensive review of earthquake-induced building damage detection with remote sensing techniques*	ISPRS Journal of Photogrammetry and Remote Sensing	earthquakes, building damage detection, remote sensing
Geib and Taubenbock (2013)	*Remote sensing contributing to assess earthquake risk: From a literature review towards a roadmap*	Natural Hazards	remote sensing, earthquake, risk, hazard, vulnerability, literature, review, roadmap

Authors	Title	Journal Name	Keywords
Plank (2014)	*Rapid damage assessment by means of multi-temporal SAR – A comprehensive review and outlook to Sentinel-1*	Remote Sensing	disaster, damage assessment, earthquake, tropical storm, SAR, InSAR, coherence, intensity correlation, Sentinel-1, multi-temporal SAR
Huyck *et al.* (2014)	*Remote sensing for disaster response: A rapid, image-based perspective*	Earthquake Hazard, Risk and Disasters (book chapter)	best practices, crowd sourcing, damage assessment, disaster response, remote sensing
Kerle (2016)	*Disasters: Risk assessment, management and post-disaster studies using remote sensing*	Remote Sensing of Water Resources, Disasters, and Urban Studies (book chapter)	hazard and risk assessment, post-disaster response, disaster risk management, earth observation systems
Rahman (2017)	*Applications of active remote sensing technologies for natural disaster damage assessments*	Remote Sensing Techniques and GIS Applications In Earth and Environmental Studies (book chapter)	active remote sensing data for disaster damage assessments, natural disasters
Ghaffarian *et al.* (2018)	*Remote sensing-based proxies for urban disaster risk management and resilience: A review*	Remote Sensing	urban disaster risk management, remote sensing, damage, recovery, vulnerability, resilience, economic, social, proxy, indirect measurement
Barazzetti and Cuca (2020)	*Identification of buildings damaged by natural hazards using very high-resolution satellite images: The case of earthquake in L'Aquila, Italy*	Remote Sensing for Archaeology and Cultural Landscapes: Best Practices and Perspectives Across Europe and the Middle East (book chapter)	L'Aquila, earthquake, Quickbird, high-resolution satellite imagery, remote sensing, historic center

Table 5.1. *Selected previous reviews of earthquake damage assessment by using remote sensing technology*

As inferred from the literature, from the point of view of methodology to detect and monitor the damage from remote sensing images, two approaches exist, namely mono- and multi-temporal approaches (Dong and Shan 2013). The multi-temporal techniques examine the correlations of pixels across the time domain, where sub-groups are determined to represent the level of damage, whereas mono-temporal approaches only use the post-earthquake image (Taşkın *et al.* 2011). Both methodologies have several advantages and disadvantages depending on the purpose of the study, but the multi-temporal approaches are found to be more effective than the mono-temporal approaches in terms of providing an accurate, reliable and rapid damage map (Geib and Taubenbock 2013). As our main focus is on satellite-based earthquake-induced damage identification through pre- and post-event images using supervised learning methodologies, this chapter provides an extensive evaluation of the methodologies used to produce an earthquake-induced change map, especially for urban areas, with an emphasis on their strengths and shortcomings.

5.1.1. *Research methodology and statistics*

This chapter aims to provide a systematic and comprehensive review of satellite-based earthquake damage assessment using multi-temporal remote sensing images. As the research area of earthquakes is quite extensive, we have carefully selected a set of representative keywords to narrow down the scope of our main focus. The keywords are *earthquake, change detection, supervised learning, multi-temporal, damage assessment, remote sensing* and *satellite*. Different combinations of these terms were used to retrieve the relevant studies from *Web of Science*, resulting in 650 papers that formed our database. We manually reviewed each paper to remove ones that were irrelevant to our principal interest, resulting in 276 papers, mostly peer-review articles published between 1993 and 2020. To manage our database, we determined five categories for organizing the papers, which are *types of satellite data, machine learning method used in damage assessment, classification performance, location of the earthquake* and *size of the study area*, on which we conducted a statistical analysis to present the content of our database from a different point of view by providing certain types of graphical visualization. The geographic locations of the earthquakes and the ratio of the studies conducted with SAR, optical and multi-source (SAR, optical, etc.) remote sensing are visualized in Figure 5.1.

The most popular journals from *Web of Science* in which earthquake damage assessment studies based on multi-temporal remote sensing have been published are presented in Figure 5.2. It should be noted that in this figure, only the journals with studies of more than at least five papers were reported. As can be observed from the types of journals, the majority of the papers not only deal with remote sensing applications but also develop new methodologies for damage assessment.

Figure 5.1. *Geographic locations of the earthquakes and the ratio of* Web of Science *publications conducted with SAR, optical and multi-source remote sensing. For a color version of this figure, see www.iste.co.uk/atto/change2.zip*

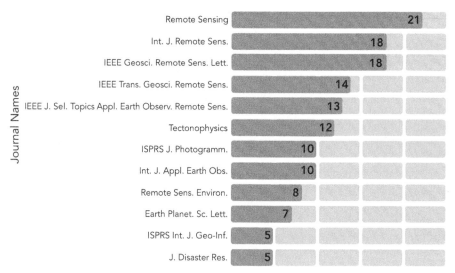

Figure 5.2. *Most popular 12 journals indexed in* Web of Science *in which relevant papers are published. For a color version of this figure, see www.iste.co.uk/atto/change2.zip*

To visualize the content of our database and exploit the research concerns lying in this specific study field, we provide a *word cloud* illustration, which is generated from the titles of the papers involved in this study (Figure 5.3). After eliminating some general and frequently appearing words in the titles, for example, *based on* or *and*, the top 10 words are found to be *earthquake, image, SAR, damage, remote sensing, building, detection, satellite, disaster* and *rapid*.

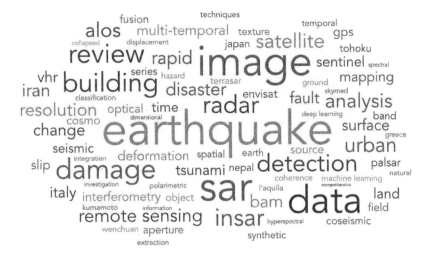

Figure 5.3. *Word cloud generated from the title words of the papers involved in the database used in this study. For a color version of this figure, see www.iste.co.uk/atto/change2.zip*

Compared to optical, SAR appears to be more dominant because of its day and night and all-weather imaging capability, which is a particularly important factor for providing a quick response; thus much more data is available. Another factor affecting such a result is that SAR-based applications are more diverse than optical ones since SAR provides more detailed information than optic sensors for earthquake damage assessment. Moreover, *machine learning* appears, relatively, too small in this visualization because the damage assessment problem poses significant challenges compelling the limits of machine learning methods, which will be extensively discussed in this chapter.

When considering the size of the application area, we classified the papers into four groups, which are *city level (tectonics), city level, medium block level* and *small block level* (building-based). Figure 5.4 shows the distribution of the studies conducted at each group for each earthquake dataset. As seen, most of the studies deal with the assessment of the damage at the *city level*, as *small block-level* studies require higher-resolution satellite images along with more advanced supervised learning methods.

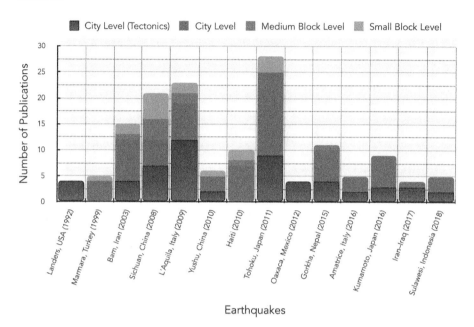

Figure 5.4. *Number of publications with respect to the size of application area for each earthquake dataset. For a color version of this figure, see www.iste.co.uk/atto/change2.zip*

Regardless of which methodology is performed in the analysis, such as building-based or area-based and with SAR or optical, the overall classification accuracy, including the damage class, achieved using supervised learning methods for each earthquake dataset, is shown in Figure 5.5. As can be seen, no study exists in the literature providing an accuracy of more than approximately 95%, and the standard deviation of the accuracies is mostly very large, pointing out the difficulty of earthquake damage assessment with multi-temporal remote sensing image analysis using supervised learning methods.

Figure 5.6 illustrates the distribution of the multi-temporal damage assessment studies using SAR, optical and multi-source remote sensing. It can be easily seen that if available, the optical data is extensively used, e.g. Haiti, Bam, Sichuan, etc. Although many studies are based on multi-spectral optical data, the availability is often limited by weather conditions, specifically over tropical environments such as the Solomon Islands, Peru, Chile and the Bahamas (see Figure 5.1).

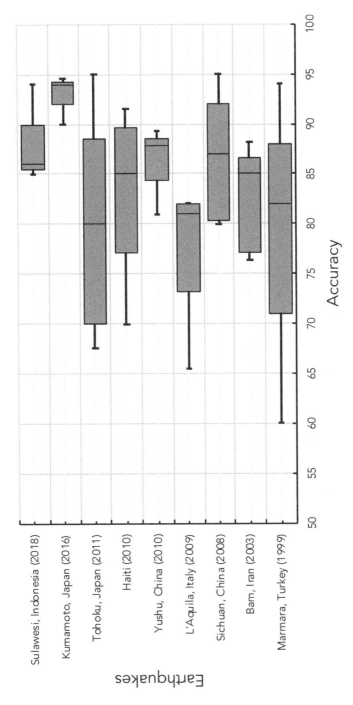

Figure 5.5. *Distribution of overall classification accuracy, including the damage class, achieved using supervised learning methods for each earthquake dataset. For a color version of this figure, see www.iste.co.uk/atto/change2.zip*

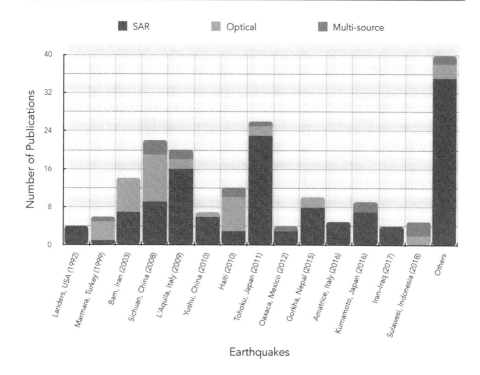

Figure 5.6. *Distribution of the damage assessment studies using SAR, optical and multi-source remote sensing. For a color version of this figure, see www.iste.co.uk/atto/change2.zip*

As it is very clear that implementations of earthquake damage assessment reveal considerable diversity with regard to our literature review, we first developed the main framework, which can be used for earthquake damage assessment applications regardless of RS data type. Later, in order to provide a better understanding of SAR imaging and demonstrate its complementary information about scene monitoring, the studies related to only SAR data are given in a separate section. Although the studies are grouped according to the input data type, earthquake studies with SAR and optical data share the same image mining principles, such as coregistration, statistics, machine learning and computing.

The rest of this chapter is organized as follows. Section 5.2 provides a general framework of satellite-based earthquake damage assessment. In section 5.3, pre-processing of multi-temporal satellite images is discussed, especially in terms of image registration. In section 5.4, the use of multi-source remote sensing image analysis is addressed. In section 5.5, earthquake damage assessment using very high-resolution satellite images is discussed, along with the use of textural features extracted with image processing techniques. Section 5.6 focuses on the multi-temporal image analysis techniques from the machine learning point of view, while section 5.7 presents the studies related to only SAR data for earthquake damage assessment. The use of auxiliary datasets and their advantages in damage assessment are discussed in section 5.8. Qualifying the damage class is reviewed from the earthquake engineering as well as remote sensing image analysis points of view. The final remarks are presented in section 5.10, especially by focusing on challenges faced in satellite-based earthquake damage assessment using multi-temporal image analysis techniques.

Figure 5.7. *Earthquake damage assessment components by using remote sensing. Adapted from Rezaeian (2010). For a color version of this figure, see www.iste.co.uk/atto/change2.zip*

5.2. Satellite-based earthquake damage assessment

Experiences over the past years have showed that multi-temporal approaches include very significant challenges for identification of earthquake-induced changes under different scenarios, which are mainly formed with respect to four significant parameters: resolution, sensor, platform, field of view and monitoring (Figure 5.7). Spatial resolution is a parameter that affects the extent of the damage mapping, which might be damage mapping at either the global or local level, obtained with low- and high-resolution RS data, respectively. After an earthquake, the active and passive types of RS data might be used together or separately, depending on their availability, leading to a single-source or multi-source image analysis. Another parameter is the field of view which induces a discretization of damage levels of the buildings, such as fully collapsed, partially collapsed or intact.

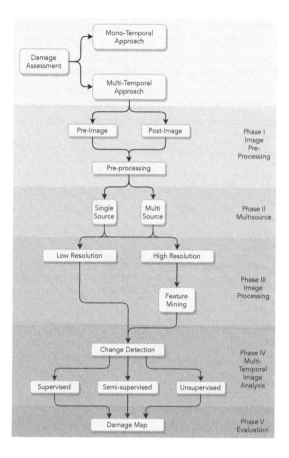

Figure 5.8. *Earthquake damage assessment framework with RS images.*
For a color version of this figure, see www.iste.co.uk/atto/change2.zip

Although data processing techniques involved in damage assessment problems are specifically formed with respect to these scenarios, hence resulting in different types of implementations, the general framework for damage mapping by using multi-temporal approaches can be summarized in Figure 5.8. The earthquake damage assessment framework involves five phases, image pre-processing, multi-source RS image analysis, image processing, multi-temporal analysis and damage map evaluation. In this framework, each phase is considered by maximizing the accuracy and reliability of the corresponding model since a wrong design has a cumulative effect on the performance of the entire change detection procedure. While each phase is partially discussed in the next sections, we will concentrate mostly on *Phase IV*, which includes the use of supervised change detection methods for the analysis of the optical and SAR images in damage assessment problems.

5.3. Pre-processing of satellite images before damage assessment

Change detection methods compare remote sensing images acquired at different times to discover the changes in the land cover, but the images typically have different properties, such as different spatial resolution, type of sensors and the incidence angle. Processing such multimodality in an efficient and reliable way is a challenge. To minimize the negative effects caused by the presence of diversity in the images, the pre-processing step becomes a very important step for providing a reliable change detection model to properly extract the geographical information. The pre-processing step includes image registration, atmospheric and topographic correction, geometric calibration and radiometric calibration. Among them, image registration is considered to be the most challenging due to its strong effect on the detection accuracy, in particular with very high-resolution images (Brunner *et al.* 2010).

Several attempts have been made to alleviate the effects of misregistration on the results of change detection and automate this process for a rapid damage assessment. Bitelli *et al.* (2004) showed the effects of precise coregistration on the performance of the change detection with image rationing using the medium- to very high-resolution (VHR) optical images to assess the earthquake damage at four damage levels in urban areas. Shi and Jiang (2016) proposed an automatic method for registering images with large background variations based on the line segments on the main shape contours, for example, coastal lines, long roads and mountain ridges. Traditional registration methods based on local intensity are limited, as ground control points (GCPs) might not be always available in multiple images due to possible heavy damage and destruction that might cover critical infrastructures and line segments of the land covers to be used for registering the image pairs. As a solution to this, Aicardi *et al.* (2016) introduced a new technique to register multi-temporal high-resolution image blocks without GCPs, specifically designed for UAV images.

As image registration methods, correlation-based approaches are not very efficient for inhomogeneous scenes, but feature-based approaches are more suitable methods because they are image-independent. However, it should be noted that landmarks such as roads, bridges and buildings could be destroyed due to a strong earthquake, affecting the performance of the feature-based approaches. Object-based registration approaches might be an effective alternative to deal with such issues (Ding *et al.* 2010). In this context, Zhang *et al.* (2013) proposed a robust kernel subspace analysis method to capture the common patterns of the variform objects, on which a registration method is developed. Additionally, change detection methods could encounter more challenges when image pairs have different off-nadir angles. This problem was addressed by Barazzetti *et al.* (2015) by proposing a multi-step approach for registering the images with different off-nadir angles via object-based classification based on the shadow of the buildings. They claimed that their approach does not require ancillary data such as spatial database, DEM, or radar images. Many more studies, either directly dealing with image registration or analyzing the effects of misregistration to change detection analysis exist in the literature, and a common outcome inferred from all these studies is that image registration has still been considered to be an open problem in many applications, but especially in damage assessment problems (Radke *et al.* 2005; Prasad *et al.* 2011).

5.4. Multi-source image analysis

The presence of the same source of the satellite images might not be guaranteed shortly after an earthquake; therefore, remote sensing image sources for pre- and post-event are different, either optical or SAR. The optical sensors measure radiometric properties of reflected light in the electromagnetic spectrum, ranging from visual to infrared bands, whereas radar sensors are active sensors, measuring the backscatter of a transmitted signal, typically in a microwave frequency band. Moreover, the SAR images are very advantageous in terms of several factors: all-weather conditions, side-view acquisition capabilities, layover scattering and the backscattering mechanism of multi-polarization, providing very rich information for building damage assessment. From this point of view, the integration of both images is a complementary and very informative process to the damage assessment problem, but brings extra difficulties in terms of effective and efficient data processing and analysis of multimodality in RS data (Mercier *et al.* 2008; Yokoya 2013; Salentinig and Gamba 2015). Since SAR and optical data have different physical and radiometric properties, especially when the two acquisition modalities strongly differ, designing more sophisticated methods is required to fuse these images, especially in the context of change detection analysis, as already mentioned in Bovolo and Bruzzone (2015).

From the change detection perspective, Stramondo *et al.* (2006) inferred that the combination of optical data and some SAR features significantly improves the damage classification, after they compared the capabilities of change detection methods by using different features extracted from both optical and radar data. In the study conducted by Brunner *et al.* (2010), a novel method, effectively using pre-earthquake VHR optical and post-earthquake VHR SAR imagery, was proposed to detect the completely destroyed buildings and also to overcome the requirement of having an image pair that is acquired with same imaging geometry. The idea was based on the simulation of the pre-event SAR image that will be used in change detection analysis, considering the similarity between the simulation and the actual SAR images with normalized mutual information. The building parameters, which are the shape and the size of the buildings, were extracted from pre-event optical image and acquisition parameters of the post-image, respectively, to simulate the pre-event image. The height is determined based on the shadow and sun illumination angle at the time of acquisition of the pre-image. These parameters are then all used together to simulate a pre-SAR image. Even though a satisfactory performance, 90% detection rate, is obtained, their method is limited to being performed in large regions with non-isolated buildings. A similar idea was proposed by Wang and Jin (2012) for change detection and evaluation of building damages utilizing multi-mutual information following an earthquake. For SAR image simulation, the building geometric parameters (height, shape, size, orientation, etc.) were extracted from the pre-earthquake optical image, then multi-mutual information was employed to register post-earthquake real SAR and simulated SAR. The damage grade of the buildings was determined based on the similarity between the real and simulated SAR images. Pan and Tang (2010) demonstrated that a combined use of optical and SAR images or multi-sensor image fusion is a very promising remote sensing technique for post-earthquake damage assessment. Similarly, Kwak *et al.* (2016) fused very high-spatial-resolution multi-temporal optical images and X-band SAR images with a decision-level image fusion method, i.e. morphological transform, to classify urban surfaces in tsunami damage assessment. Tamkuan and Nagai (2017) investigated the fusion of multi-temporal interferometric coherence and optical image data to improve the results of damage classification of the landslides and buildings. Their proposed approach does not require any training data, therefore provides a fast solution to damage assessment problems. Dell'Acqua *et al.* (2011) proposed a new data fusion method to effectively use optical and SAR images and found that optical images are more convenient for distinguishing the damage from the non-damage classes, because the SAR textural features are able to distinguish different classes of damage at the block scale. A combination of interferometric SAR coherence and optical satellite imagery data was addressed in the study conducted by Tamkuan and Nagai (2017), and they concluded that the coherence before the earthquake was found to be useful for separating urban and non-urban areas. Adriano *et al.* (2019) conducted a multi-source data fusion to jointly use SAR, optical remote sensing datasets and their derived features, and explored the contribution of each of these features on the building damage recognition. Their results showed that digital elevation model (DEM)- and SAR-derived features contributed the most in the overall damage classification. As pixel-level image fusion methods do not perform well when a significant spatial resolution between optic and SAR images exist, Jiang *et al.* (2020) proposed a new data fusion method based on superpixel-based belief fusion for building damage assessment. They concluded that their superpixel approach reduces the errors induced by the image-interpolation of pixel-level methods.

The earthquake damage assessment literature clearly demonstrates that the combined use of optical and SAR images improves the quality of the damage map, but it should be noted that multi-temporal image fusion from the perspective of change detection still has challenges that need to be solved. The interested reader can refer to Bovolo and Bruzzone (2015) and Schmitt and Zhu (2016) for more detailed descriptions regarding image fusion.

5.5. Contextual feature mining for damage assessment

Very high-resolution remote sensing images allow the detection of the damage at the building scale, but a high spatial correlation between the pixels leads to a decrease in classification performance (Wang and Li 2019). To overcome this issue, the spatial context should be properly modeled by advanced image processing techniques, resulting in more relevant features to be combined with the spectral features, thereby increasing the separability of the damage class from the other land cover (Taşkın *et al.* 2015; Liao *et al.* 2017). The methods extracting textural patterns, edge densities and structural geometry of buildings are assumed to be potentially the most effective methods for exploiting the contextual information of damage patterns (Cheng and Han 2016; Chen *et al.* 2018b).

5.5.1. *Textural features*

Haralick second-order texture features have proven to be very efficient textural measures derived from the gray-level co-occurrence matrix (GLCM), measuring how often different combinations of gray levels occur in a predefined image neighborhood (Haralick *et al.* 1973). Dell'Acqua *et al.* (2011) extracted the co-occurrence textural features from the SAR image to be used as additional information along with the optical image. Cossu *et al.* (2012) then extended this study to analyze the relationship between textural features and the degree of the damage by using the SAR image with different resolutions. Differently from the conventional implementation of GLCM, Moya *et al.* (2019) extended the concepts of the gray-level co-occurrence matrix texture analysis, which is applied to a single image, to a multi-layered set of images, known as 3DGLCM, concluding that support vector machines (SVM) trained with a 3DGLCM-based approach detect the collapsed buildings more accurately than the classical approach.

Rathje *et al.* (2005) proposed an approach using the textural features to accurately detect building damages and computed five different texture measures, including homogeneity, dissimilarity, contrast, variance and the second moment, based on the gray-level co-occurrence matrix between coregistered pre- and post-event optical images. The predicted damage areas were found to favorably agree with field observations of the damage. The authors pointed out that an abundant number of textural features can be obtained depending on varying several parameters, such as type of input image, size of the sliding window and displacement vector between pixels on which to calculate the co-occurrence, leading to a very large volume of features to process and analyze. Identifying the features that best describe the earthquake damage from other parts of the urban area is therefore of great importance in finding an optimum feature space for a classification task. Based on this motivation, many attempts have been made to find the most descriptive textural features regarding damage patterns. Rathje *et al.* (2005b) used the pairwise feature selection to find the best feature combination for damage assessment in the city of Bam, Iran. Even though the damage map, generated across the entire city with the selected features, was found to be consistent with the field measurements, they specifically mentioned that the selected features might not be robust, and may vary depending on the classification method, type of remote sensing data and the characteristics of the urban structure in a city where the earthquake occurred. Another study made a comparative analysis on the textural features, including energy, correlation, contrast and inverse distance moment, in terms of several change detection methods: image differencing, image rationing, regression analysis and principal component analysis. The results showed that the best performance was achieved with principal component analysis with the feature, the so-called energy (Tomowski *et al.* 2010). A novel method based on image differencing was proposed by Mansouri and Hamednia (2015) using eight Haralick textural features from panchromatic VHR optical satellite images associated with building footprints. The genetic algorithm was performed to select the optimum features, and the textural features, specifically including the mean, dissimilarity and second moment, were found to be the most important features for the damage class. In the study conducted by Sofina and Ehlers (2016), the most reliable textural features to measure the degree of image homogeneity were reported to be the angular second moment, inertia and inverse difference moment for the building change detection. Table 5.9 presents a summary of the representative studies, focusing on the use of the textural features in damage assessment, and highlights the most relevant features that contribute most to the damage class.

According to the results presented in Figure 5.9, the studies performed in the Bam, Iran earthquake dataset usually reported different types of textural features as the most important ones, as was also the case of the Tohoku, Japan dataset. Therefore, we may conclude that even though there is no specific texture-based feature set that defines the best damage pattern independent of the earthquake dataset, certain types of features may be important in the identification of the damage class, such as dissimilarity, mean and contrast.

As alternative textural features, Dumitru *et al.* (2015) computed a set of new texture features – the so-called primitive features – by using Gabor filters with varying scales and orientations, GLCM, nonlinear short-time Fourier transforms and quadrature mirror filters with varying levels of decomposition, and they concluded that the highest accuracy in precision/recall was obtained by Gabor filters. They also pointed out that textural features can be more useful when being used with other auxiliary data sources such as DEMs, GIS, the height and edge density of the buildings. Wang and Li (2015) proposed a method that jointly uses spectral, textural and height information. The variogram texture extracted from LiDAR data and a multivariate variogram texture extracted from pre- and post-earthquake VHR images were used to detect the collapsed buildings. The edges of the buildings can also be used as additional information for separating buildings from the other land cover objects. Huyck *et al.* (2005) introduced an edge dissimilarity algorithm based on Laplacian edge detection and generated the images showing the edges of the buildings, from which neighborhood dissimilarity-based textural images were calculated. The damaged areas were then detected with the per-pixel difference of the dissimilarities and classified by the standard deviation. As the performance of the change detection methods varies with respect to the dataset used, Janalipour and Taleai (2017) proposed an adaptive change detection method by using adaptive network-based fuzzy inference systems, which is suited for integrating the spectral, transformed and textural features. Based on the results obtained, their method seems to be more robust than its other counterparts in detecting building changes following an earthquake.

Study	Dataset	Texture Type	Window Size	Overall Accuracy
Huyck *et al.* 2005	Bam, Iran	Dissimilarity	25 x 25	80.0%
Rathje *et al.* 2005	Bam, Iran	Correlation	6 x 6, 25 x 25	91%
		Entropy	6 x 6, 25 x 25	
		Mean	10 x 10, 25 x 25	
Janalipour *et al.* 2017	Bam, Iran	Homogeneity	3 x 3	90.0%
		Contrast		
		Entropy		
		Variance		
		Dissimilarity		
Liu *et al.* 2019	Bam, Iran	Mean	3 x 3	88%
Wang *et al.* 2015	Haiti	Multivariate	5 x 5	88%
Sofina *et al.* 2016	Tohoku, Japan	Angular Second Moment	Various	84%
		Inertia		
		Inverse Difference Moment		
Moya *et al.* 2019	Tohoku, Japan	Contrast	13 x 13	90.0%
		Dissimilarity		
		Homogeneity		

Figure 5.9. *Representative studies conducted with different texture configurations on several earthquake datasets. The ones colored with red were reported to be the most relevant features for describing the damage pattern. For a color version of this figure, see www.iste.co.uk/atto/change2.zip*

The pixel-based approaches are limited in accurately detecting the building damage even though the textural features are included in the classification, leading to the development of more advanced object-based approaches (Ma *et al.* 2017). Liu and Li (2019) proposed a novel method for extracting the damaged buildings from bi-temporal VHR images by using object-level homogeneity index and object histogram. Once the land cover classes were masked out, collapsed buildings were extracted from bi-temporal images using object histogram and a curve matching method with a multi-reference spectral angle mapper. The results showed that the object histogram approach is capable of quantifying spectral variability within collapsed buildings and provides a useful feature set identifying collapsed buildings from VHR satellite images. Based on the idea that the textural, geometrical and spectral information are complementary to each other when being used together, Vu and Ban (2010) proposed a context-based damage detection approach using all possible types of features. They extracted buildings and debris areas separately from pre- and post-event images using shape, size, spectra and texture information, and they confirmed the effectiveness of the complementary usage of textural, geometrical and spectral information for the classification of the damage at three levels.

5.5.2. *Filter-based methods*

Filtering-based methods are very successful in extracting contextual information from an image by removing redundant spatial details and preserving the geometric characteristics of the objects in the region of interest. Among them, mathematical morphology has been a widely used framework in the field of image processing constructed based on simple mathematical concepts from set theory (Haralick *et al.* 1987). The components of the framework have been used in a wide range of problems such as edge detection, noise reduction, image restoration and segmentation. In a gray-scale image, the pixel intensities represent the relative geometric properties of a surface in a three-dimensional Euclidean space. Morphological operations evaluate these surfaces by ordering pixel intensities to reflect their geometric relations and applying filters to extract the shapes from the ordered pixel intensities. Due to the fact that they are capable of geometric evaluation, they have gained a great deal of interest in this particular research field over recent decades. Pesaresi *et al.* (2007) first used morphological operators to highlight the smallest structures of tsunami-affected areas in the VHR image pairs. In order to emphasize the so-called *white thin* structures on the pre-event image of the Meulaboh region, Indonesia, affected by the 2004 Indian Ocean earthquake and tsunami, the morphological opening transforms were implemented through a small structuring element. A secondary morphological closing–opening operation set was subsequently used to clean the structures, resulting from the prior transforms. Their study showed considerable potential of morphological operations for earthquake damage assessment tasks, as they provide a significant decrease in the number of false alarms.

The use of morphological operations in a sequence allows us to derive geometrical details from an image with the multiple shape forms. The features generated by the sequential implementation with opening and closing operators through reconstruction, considering an increasing size of the structuring element, are called morphological profiles (Pesaresi and Benediktsson 2001). In this context, Parape and Tamura (2011) suggested a method using the differential morphological profiles to extract building footprints from both pre- and post-event images, with the aim of detecting damaged buildings by separately comparing the classified images. More specific structural features might be generated to extract damage information from time series images. For instance, Chen and Hutchinson (2011) proposed a new set of structural features generated using image gradient magnitudes and used this set of features to define multiple statistical distribution-based dissimilarity measures, from which damage information was derived. Chini *et al.* (2015) focused on double-bounced reflections scattered from buildings, identified using morphological profiles with various rotations and the structuring element lengths. Several change detection methods were applied to the extracted profiles, finding out that there may be "*synergy*" between specific features and change detection methods, and their appropriate combination may lead to a better characterization in damage patterns.

Similar to the texture calculations, morphological operations have a variety of parameters that must be set optimally before their implementations. Some of the most sensitive parameters of morphological profiles affecting the performance are the size and shape of the structuring element, which is a moving window used in the transformation, defining the degree of contextual relations in the image analysis. Similarly, Parape and Tamura (2011) proposed an approach to optimize the size and shape of the structuring element for the tasks related to damage detection. They calculated a set of hit-or-miss transformed morphological profiles on segmented pre- and post-event images and then tried to optimize accuracy by selecting the most convenient structuring elements. Their findings clearly showed that optimizing the structuring element significantly improves the quality of the assessment.

The types of geometric properties are likewise essential parameters. Seven different types of geometrical information over segmented pre- and post-earthquake images considering an adaptive network-based fuzzy inference system classification were extracted by Janalipour and Mohammadzadeh (2016). Among them all, the features, including the area, the convexity and the rectangular fitting, were found to be the most effective features for the related classification method. Nonetheless, either because of the large variations in geometrical details existing in different areas and images or because of the underlying structures of the decision method (e.g. classifier), it is challenging to find a general structuring element or a specific type of geometrical information for characterizing the damage patterns. In other words, the optimum features remain substantially specific and differ with regard to the application considered.

5.6. Multi-temporal image analysis for damage assessment

Approaches used to model the temporal variations are typically based on measuring the level of pixel intensity changes between multiple images. Among them, the most commonly used are image differencing, change vector analysis and distance or similarity measures (Reba and Seto 2020). Depending on the availability of the ground reference dataset, change detection (CD) is typically categorized into three methods: unsupervised, semi-supervised and supervised change detection. Unsupervised CD algorithms do not require any training data, but a threshold value needs to be properly set to generate an accurate change map. A variety of studies have been conducted in this regard, but the literature suggests that threshold-based approaches are not very suitable, especially for the high-dimensional datasets and multi-class change detection problems, due to their complexities in finding an optimal solution (Wieland *et al.* 2016). The alternative is to use supervised CD methods, which require an adequate amount of training data to generate an automated learning model, providing the level of changes for the area of interest. However, the availability of the training samples in the multi-temporal domain might be limited in the case of earthquake damage assessment, leading to the use of semi-supervised change detection methods. Semi-supervised methods fuse the advantages of both unsupervised and supervised learning methods by using unlabeled samples in classification and therefore are able to handle the cases when limited training samples are available.

Two common approaches are presented in the literature with respect to the stage of the change detection process in which the classification is performed: stacked vector representation and post-classification comparison. The main idea in stacked vector classification is to stack the feature vectors of the images acquired at the multi-temporal domain and then feed them as input to a supervised learning algorithm. However, it should be noted that a high level of heterogeneity might exist between the pre- and post-event images due to the influence of the season or the time delay between the images, causing an inability to provide a single learning model for the damage assessment problem. As an alternative, post-classification comparisons can be used to reduce such noises as well as the effect of the radiometric differences between the image pairs by considering images as a separate input to a supervised learning method. An independent classification is then conducted, and thematic maps of each image are obtained with the associated learning models to be considered in the change detection analysis. The drawback of this approach is that misclassification errors can propagate through the change detection analysis.

Depending on the ground truth data availability, the classification can be performed in two ways: binary and multi-class. The former has two classes, namely referring to damaged and intact buildings or regions, while the latter has multi-classes such as various land covers. As we know, the classification problem becomes more difficult as the number of land cover classes increases in a classification problem, resulting in high complexity and low performance on the corresponding learning model

(Karpatne *et al.* 2016). Binary change detection is practically more feasible and performs better than multiclass change detection in earthquake damage assessment problems, as reported in Wieland *et al.* (2016). Regardless of whether the change detection is binary or multiclass, the main factor affecting the accuracy of the damage map strongly relies on the quality of the training data as well as the capability of the supervised learning method considered. These two factors should be precisely addressed in accordance with the purpose of the study and the type of remote sensing dataset. In this chapter, we focus on supervised change detection approaches by discussing their challenges from the machine learning point of view.

5.6.1. *Use of machine learning in damage assessment problem*

Thanks to the ability of machine learning (ML) algorithms to process and evaluate the data, supervised change detection provides a fast and automatic damage assessment tool. The ML has been shown to be a very effective approach, providing a predictive model that extracts useful information from data, and is used to model the relationship between the input and output of system behavior (Erten *et al.* 2019). There are two types of application areas: classification and regression, which are categorized with respect to associated types of output. In earthquake damage assessment, the majority of the studies are focused on classification tasks, as the aim is to provide a damage map for the area of interest, indicating the land cover classes: collapsed buildings, roads, open areas, etc. The types of ML methods to be used in damage assessment are defined with regard to the type of RS data, spatial extent, the use of contextual information and the temporal frequency of the satellite images. Once all these factors are resolved, the methodology is transferred to a machine learning problem, in which the classification is performed. Machine learning literature is quite substantial in remote sensing image analysis, but its use is relatively limited in multi-temporal image analysis, particularly in earthquake damage assessment, due to several reasons that will be discussed in detail here. The principle of machine learning, along with its strengths and limitations, will be evaluated from the perspective of change detection and earthquake damage assessment.

As for supervised learning algorithms, support vector machines have mostly been used for a multi-class type of classification in the literature of the damage assessment as it achieves very good classification performance even with a lower number of training samples. In this context, Wieland *et al.* (2016) proposed a very deep analysis to present a learning model with SVM for assessment of the earthquake-induced damage by using change detection in SAR images. The challenges in machine learning, which are sampling approach, location and number of training samples, classification scheme, change feature space and the acquisition dates of the satellite images, were extensively discussed in the context of damage assessment. They concluded that satisfactory performance can be obtained by SVM with an appropriate sampling strategy, i.e. a hundred samples for each class, along with fine parameter tuning and feature selection. The other classification methods, i.e. K-nearest neighbor (KNN), decision tree and fuzzy learning, are also used. An image-based structural damage assessment measure was proposed by Chen and Hutchinson (2011) using bi-temporal structural features based on a correlation-like change detection approach. The proposed statistical measures account for local contextual information and quantify structural damage monotonically. The structural damage was determined by the change in the structural features in bi-temporal images. At the classification stage, the KNN classifier was used due to its simplicity and popularity. The authors concluded that a rapid image-based structural damage assessment using large-sized VHR satellite images can be performed by their proposed method. Janalipour and Mohammadzadeh (2017) proposed a semi-automated fuzzy decision-making system by using Haralick features extracted from bi-temporal optic images. To provide a relation between the extracted features and the extent of the damage to the buildings, Mamdani fuzzy system (MFIS) and genetic algorithms were used, and sensitivity analysis of the classification performance was conducted by setting the parameters of the MFIS. Their proposed method obtained more precise and more accurate results than the four advanced machine learning techniques, including random forests (RF), bagging, boosting and SVM, for building damage detection. Gokon et al. (2015) proposed a new approach based on a decision tree to classify tsunami-induced damage into multiple classes with TerraSAR-X by using statistical relationships between the change ratios in areas with high backscattering and in areas with building damage.

Deep learning has received the most attention from a variety of disciplines, including remote sensing image analysis (Zhu et al. 2017). Although numerous studies have been performed from the perspective of focusing either direct implementation of deep learning or developing new deep architecture in change detection analysis, there are very few studies concerning deep learning in earthquake damage assessment, most of which involve mono-temporal approaches (Bai et al. 2018; Huang et al. 2019; Nex et al. 2019; Song et al. 2020). This is probably due to the fact that collecting the training data in the multi-temporal domain poses several challenges. In the context of change detection, Sublime and Kalinicheva (2019) introduced a new deep learning architecture for detection tsunami-induced areas by using the advantages of the autoencoders for change detection and compared its performance to classical ML methods, showing that their approach is superior to classical methods due to its unsupervised nature, good performance and relative speed of analysis. Even though very good performance is achieved with deep learning methods, their utility for single-sensor and multi-sensor remote sensing data has been very limited, as reported (Dalla Mura et al. 2015). Many more questions concerning deep learning in remote sensing image analysis still remain to be solved (Zhang et al. 2016).

For the evaluation of the performance of the supervised learning method, the overall classification accuracy and kappa coefficients are the most commonly-used metrics. It should be noted that these metrics might be biased, especially when the learning is carried out in an imbalance training set. In such cases, various measures, such as F-measure, are more appropriate to present the performance of the corresponding learning model. Despite proving the performance, the reliability of the damage mapping should be validated based on the ground measurements.

Due to high intra-class variance as well as low inter-class variances of the area of interest, the classification problem becomes difficult in very high-resolution satellite images compared to medium- or low-resolution ones, particularly in terms of the damage class. To increase the separability as well as to improve the performance of the classifier, contextual features are generated by using advanced image processing methods, but this process may cause the curse of a dimensionality problem due to the inclusion of a large number of contextual features into the classification task (Taşkın et al. 2017; Taşkın and Ceylan 2019; Taşkın and Crawford 2019). In such cases, joint use of nonlinear machine learning methods with dimensionality reduction methods might be useful in reducing the effects of the curse of dimensionality. Dimensionality reduction, especially feature selection, plays an important role in damage assessment studies in reducing the abundant number of features generated by using contextual information, and reducing both space and the computational complexity in image analysis (Sun and Du 2019). Many attempts have been made to properly select the contextual features contributing most to the performance of the change detection. Rathje et al. (2005b) conducted a feature selection analysis to determine specific textural features and window sizes that best distinguish earthquake damage. A recursive feature selection method was used by Wieland et al. (2016) to select the most representative features for the SVM classifier. Another work used the feature selection to choose the optimal textural features for distinguishing damaged and intact building image objects (Wei and Yang 2020). As principal component analysis (PCA) is a very efficient method to reduce the noise components in an image, a change detection algorithm based on principal component analysis was proposed by Rejaie and Shinozuka (2004) in order to detect structural change. Similarly, Li et al. (2019) proposed a novel method for multi-temporal SAR images based on PCA to eliminate irrelevant and noisy elements, and correlation change detection was then carried out to detect the changes associated with the building collapse. Unlike these conventional implementations, a PCA-based image fusion was proposed by Ma et al. (2016) for an automatic change detection from optical images.

From the machine learning point of view, the most significant difficulty encountered in earthquake damage assessment is availability, as well as the quality of training samples, which plays an important role in the performance of the classification method. It becomes more difficult for the change detection problems, due to the necessity of having training samples at multiple time domains (Yusuf et al. 2001). Moreover, the form of the variations in the images, such as spatial resolution, inclined angle or type of RS data, acquired before and after the event, makes the selection of training samples even more challenging. In the absence of ground truth data, the technique of visual interpretation between the pre- and post-images is frequently used in selecting the training samples when the images are very high resolution. It should be noted that the training samples should carefully be chosen in such a way that they are the most representative for the class of interest and well distributed across the geographical area, in order to provide a robust, reliable and generalized learning model to distinguish the collapsed buildings and intact buildings.

Another important factor to be taken into account in applying machine learning methods is the imbalanced class distribution, which arises when the number of samples belonging to one class of land covers is considerably smaller than the number of those belonging to another class. The number of training samples for unchanged areas is often lower than damaged pixels, depending on the damage extent caused by the earthquake, as the samples representing the damage class only exist in the post-event image, posing an imbalanced class distribution for a binary classification problem. Additionally, the performance of the post-classification change detection methodology is negatively affected by imbalanced data since the classification errors may propagate across the time domain, resulting in a large number of pseudo-changes, false alarms or inclusion errors.

To counter this, the learning algorithms specifically designed for imbalanced training data show better performance than the conventional learning methods such as SVM, KNN, decision trees and neural networks (Guo et al. 2017). Unlike the other classical learning methods, one-class learning methods require training samples from one class only, which is a target or class of interest. In this context, Wang and Li (2015) proposed a multi-stage collapsed building detection method based on bi-temporal VHR images combined with the post-event airborne LiDAR data to extract the intact buildings and relevant objects, namely pavements, vegetation and shadow. All these land cover types were then masked out to reduce spectral confusion between collapsed buildings and other ground objects. Several types of textures were additionally derived from multiple bands by using the methods multivariate variogram and gray-level co-occurrence matrix texture. All these features were fed to one-class SVM, and a fast and reliable method was proposed for detecting collapsed buildings in an urban area. Their proposed method was applied in Port au Prince, Haiti, but the authors claimed that it can also be applied to other study areas where similar data combinations (i.e. bi-temporal VHR images and post-event LiDAR data) are available. In the study conducted by Li et al. (2009), a method for urban damage detection was proposed by using spatial features, i.e. invariant moments and LISA (local indicator of spatial association) index, and damage detection was obtained by performing the one-class SVM method on the multi-temporal data. The different feature combinations were conducted in the experiments, and the use of spectral information combined with LISA provided the highest classification performance. Another study analyzed the performance of the machine learning algorithms, including random forest, naive Bayes classifier, SVM and KNN, on multi-temporal SAR images along with textural features. They showed that a naive base achieves the highest performance when the number of buildings in the two classes (collapsed and uncollapsed) is balanced whereas SVM and random forest are found to be more effective in the case of an imbalanced dataset. Alternatively, ensemble learning-type learning algorithms have been used to cope with the class imbalance problem. Rather than algorithmic improvements, the data-level approaches are the other techniques dealing with this issue (Galar *et al.* 2012). Different performances on damage assessment may be obtained depending on the capability of the ML methods, which raises a concern about which ML method performs better for damage assessment problems, and thus, ensemble-learning-based classifiers are used to resolve this problem (Brett and Guida 2013). To address this, Adriano *et al.* (2019) proposed using several ensemble learning methods for a rapid damage assessment using SAR and optical images together. For ensemble learning, decision forest-based methods were specifically selected due to their advantages: fast out-of-sample prediction, minimal parameter tuning, capability of handling missing data and its ability to rank feature importance.

Although all the issues described above are inherent in damage assessment, there are some methodology issues that need to be taken care of using more advanced methods that have recently been developed in the literature. In this context, the main problem in supervised change detection is that a large number of high-quality training samples are required for an accurate damage assessment; therefore, they might not be a feasible solution for responding to future disasters due to the absence of such data soon after the disaster. Although this issue can be handled by using semi-supervised learning methods, an imbalanced training dataset still poses a challenge to damage assessment problems. To overcome this issue, the use of advanced learning models, such as multi-instance, multi-label and multi-kernel classification, might be an efficient solution to damage assessment problems (Bucak *et al.* 2014).

5.6.2. *Rapid earthquake damage assessment*

The main advantage of machine learning is to provide an automatic damage assessment model which can be used in the case of an emergency. Rapid damage assessment has been extensively discussed in the literature from both methodological and operational points of view (Wegscheider *et al.* 2013). Gamba *et al.* (2007) proposed a rapid damage assessment tool for urban areas using multi-temporal synthetic aperture radar data. Ancillary data was also used to discard uninteresting parts of the scene and hence to improve the accuracy. The proposed method was enhanced by including spatial features extracted by the Markov random field spatial analysis. They concluded that multi-temporal SAR data may be used for damage assessment by also indicating that VHR data are required for accurate damage mapping. Dell'Acqua *et al.* (2011) introduced a data fusion approach to make use of both SAR and optical data for rapid damage mapping that developed a threshold-based change detection methodology to distinguish the damage and non-damaged areas. They pointed out that finding suitable threshold levels for classification still remains to be solved. Because of this, the classical change detection methods have a low degree of automation. To overcome this issue and to provide a more optimal change detection method that is applicable to high-resolution optical and radar remote-sensing data, Shah-Hosseini *et al.* (2017) proposed an integrated object-level change detection method based on an object-based classifier and support vector data description method. Plank (2014) discussed the limitations of the current SAR satellite missions by also highlighting possible solutions to these limitations with the Sentinel-1 SAR mission for the point of applicability of the damage mapping procedures at an operational level. Niu *et al.* (2018) pointed out a key problem of rapid damage assessment, which is efficient in scheduling multiple earth observation satellites to acquire image data of a large stricken area by coordinating the extent of coverage over the stricken area, timeliness and the spatial resolution. This multiple satellite tasking problem is expressed as a multi-objective optimization method to optimize the parameters, including coverage rate, completion time, average spatial resolution and average slewing angle, for a rapid damage assessment. Voigt *et al.* (2011) discussed possible satellite-based rapid damage mapping strategies for the Haiti earthquake and concluded that the task of rapid damage assessment remains difficult and challenging until more robust and automated methods become available. This outcome is consistent with the nature of the machine learning concept, provided that the dataset to be used in the test phase should come from a similar distribution with the dataset used in the learning phase, resulting in a good performance. This means that an automatic damage assessment model might be applicable when no major differences occur on the damage type of the considered events. Nevertheless, it should be noted that the transferability of the learning model for different earthquake events and different urban areas is a very challenging task when considering the diversity of the scenarios and the complexity of the data in the damage assessment.

The other issue in automatic damage assessment with optical images is the cloud effect, which was addressed in the literature for change detection problems (Gómez-Chova *et al.* 2017). To address this issue, Ma *et al.* (2016) proposed a cloud detection algorithm with temporal simulation based on the result of image fusion and image registration for earthquake damage assessment. The algorithm is able to remove the clouds when the cloud coverage is less than 50% and provides cloudless maps to emergency responders. SAR data is a very useful information source in cloud weather conditions, while the optical images cannot be used when the cloud coverage in the image is more than 80%.

5.7. Understanding damage following an earthquake using satellite-based SAR

For the last three decades, large-scale monitoring of the earthquakes, occurring over blind faults, has been one of the core application fields of SAR remote sensing, which has no limitations regarding weather phenomena or illumination condition. Conventional satellite-based earthquake studies are growing since the beginning of the 1990s as they obviate the necessity for time-consuming *in situ*-based surveys such as leveling and GPS and provide rapid detailed information about the three-dimensional (3D) structure of the monitored target. Earthquake damage assessment with satellite-based SAR have been analyzed and discussed for different earthquake areas (see Figure 5.1) in a variety of studies, which can roughly be categorized under three approaches according to the data type: coherent and incoherent data, depending on whether or not the phase difference is preserved, and their combination (Dong and Shan 2013; Plank 2014; Ge *et al.* 2020). The well-known and powerful coherent data methods, namely interferometric methods, which use the phase difference and its correlation between pre- and post-earthquake SAR images, has been applied to a wide range of earthquakes (see the statistics for *tectonics* and *coherent* classes in Figure 5.10). However, especially considering the outdated satellite-based SAR sensors, the damage assessment with coherent methods has not always been possible due to the requirement of reliable phase information. Instead, incoherent methods, which evaluate the scattering change by amplitude/intensity images due to the earthquake, are not limited to phase stability problems, and hence are intuitive and relatively simple to process. Figure 5.10 shows the number of Science Citation Index (SCI) publications and the SAR satellites annually based on the SAR data type, starting from the 1992 Landers, California earthquake (Massonnet *et al.* 1993) to one of the latest Mw > 6.4 earthquakes, which occurred in Mindanao, Philippines, 2019 (Li *et al.* 2020). After the launch of ERS-1 (European Remote Sensing Satellite-1) in 1991, the first known study in an earthquake was carried out by Massonnet *et al.* (1993) with the interferometry technique. Since then, a large number of articles have been published on this topic, specifically increasing the temporal and spatial resolution of satellites that makes the SAR data indispensable in the studies. Outcomes of the first earthquake studies showed that a long revisit period of satellites was the main drawback for both interferometric and amplitude-based methods. Additionally, missing precise orbit information limited the first studies, specifically on interferometric ones.

Following these first-generation SAR satellites, namely: JERS, ERS-1/2, ENVISAT and RADARSAT-1, different SAR satellites became operational with different frequency, polarization and temporal and spatial resolution (see Table 5.2). With the launch of a new generation of satellites, the required precise orbit has been achieved and the repeated cycle of SAR images decreases with an unprecedented spatial resolution. Figure 5.10, showing an increasing trend in the number of studies annually, indicates how SAR is very active in earthquake studies. Similar to the 1990s, some applications – gathered under the tectonics topic in Figure 5.10 – were aiming to understand and model the fault line. Besides, these new-generation satellite images have also been actively used to validate damage assessment with either coherent or incoherent data. Additionally, they not only improve the information for new earthquakes but also boost the usage of old-generation satellites and provide long-term temporal evaluation of the earthquakes (Costantini *et al.* 2017; Ge *et al.* 2020; Hu *et al.* 2020). However, in reality, such a level of spatial detail in phase and intensity differences between co-seismic images poses new challenges, which will be discussed in the coming sections.

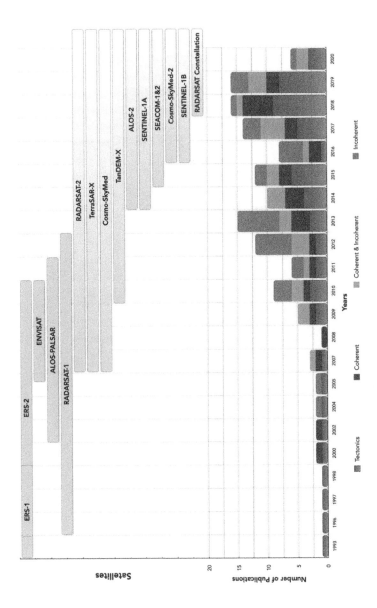

Figure 5.10. *Main SAR satellites used as the source of earthquake studies and the number of SCI publications on this topic on Web of Science. For a color version of this figure, see www.iste.co.uk/atto/change2.zip*

Satellite	Operation	Band	λ [cm]	Polarization	ΔT [day]	Δr [m]	Δa [m]
ERS-1	1991–2000	C	5.66	Polarization	35	25	5
ERS-2	1995–2011	C	5.66	Polarization	35	25	5
JERS-1	1992–1998	L	23.5	Polarization	44	16	7.5
ENVISAT	2002–2012	C	5.62	Polarization	35	25–50	5
ALOS-PALSAR	2006–2011	L	23.6	Polarization	46	9–30	5
RADARSAT-1	1995–2013	C	5.66	Polarization	24	20–30	7.5
RADARSAT-2	2007–	C	5.55	Polarization	24	20–30	7.5
TerraSAR-X	2007–	X	3.11	HH, VV	11	1–3	2.4
TanDEM-X	2010–	X	3.11	HH, VV	11	1–3	2.4
Sentinel-1A	2014–	C	5.55	*VV–VH, HH–HV	12	ΔT	Δa
Sentinel-1B	2016–	C	5.55	*VV–VH, HH–HV	12	ΔT	Δa
ALOS-2	2014–	L	23.8	*HH, HV, VV	14		
COSMO-SkyMed (four satellites)	2007–	X	3.1	*HH, HV, VH, VV	16	3–15	3
COSMO-SkyMed (two satellites)	2016–	X	3.1	*HH, HV, VH, VV	16	Δr	Δa
RADARSAT (three satellites)	2007–	C	5.55	Polarization	12	Δr	Δa

Table 5.2. *Main SAR satellite sensors and their parameters in Stripmap operational mode. Note that the spatial resolution of range (Δr) and azimuth (Δa) direction changes with incidence angle.* * *shows that one polarization can be selected among the options*

When trying to extract information from SAR images, it is essential to understand two properties forming the SAR image. The first is purely related to the system configuration (e.g. the wavelength, temporal and spatial resolution, etc., see Table 5.2), and the second is related to the characteristic of the target/scene (e.g. dielectric constant, geometry, size, location, motion, etc.). Depending on these specific properties, SAR images provide different types of information about unpredictable earthquakes that exhibit complex spatial and temporal dynamics. The focus of the studies is, then, on phases of understanding the tectonics process and rapid response, i.e. building and/or block scale damage assessment, earthquake extension detection and earthquake-induced asset monitoring. A review analysis by Sansosti *et al.* (2014) and Ge *et al.* (2020) reveal that high-resolution SAR data, e.g. TerraSAR-X 1 m resolution, is key to extracting the damage at the building level. Instead, for tectonics and geological studies, medium resolution, e.g. 20 m Sentinel-1, is efficient. Hence the number of studies with coherent data mainly focusing on tectonics has increased by 14% with Sentinel-1 and 10 m ALOS-2 data after 2015. Accordingly, damage grade classification studies have increased with high-resolution TerraSAR-X and CosmoSky-Med.

The current section is an attempt to answer the following question: *what is the state of the art in earthquake applications and how can the current studies by means of temporal SAR imaging be done?* For this, the SAR fundamental parameters and temporal acquisition vector are shortly examined in section 5.7.1. The satellite-based SAR earthquake studies, then, are categorized by whether their input data is coherent (section 5.7.2) or not (section 5.7.3). Section 5.7.5 covers the studies which take into account both data types together. Recommendations and practical limitations for operational applications are summarized in section 5.7.6 with concluding remarks.

5.7.1. *SAR fundamental parameters and acquisition vector*

SAR imaging transmits electromagnetic waves and processes returned waves from a target to produce a high-resolution image of the Earth in Single Look Complex (SLC) format; see Figure 5.11. Once the signal has been processed, it identifies the Earth by means of a target location, target velocity, scattering, phase, etc. Moreover, SAR imaging covers a large spectrum of imaging modes: simple single-channel images to polarimetric SAR (PolSAR) images. PolSAR images yield information about terrain scattering, and they correspond to three-component images obtained with one emission antenna that alternatively emits vertical V and horizontal H polarization. The fully polarimetric images are composed of HH, HV and VV polarizations each in the SLC format. It can be mentioned that, based on the reciprocity theorem, the VH polarized image is not considered in a fully polarimetric image since it is equal to the HV polarization after calibration and symmetrization. Partial polarimetric SAR image collects only two subsets of PolSAR images composed of $HH–VH$ and $HV–VV$ polarizations.

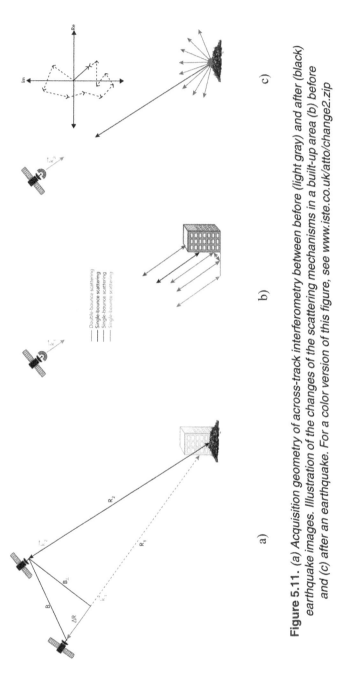

Figure 5.11. *(a) Acquisition geometry of across-track interferometry between before (light gray) and after (black) earthquake images. Illustration of the changes of the scattering mechanisms in a built-up area (b) before and (c) after an earthquake. For a color version of this figure, see www.iste.co.uk/atto/change2.zip*

The SAR image characterizes the scene by amplitude (a) and phase of the backscattered signal (ϕ), producing one complex image for each recording time:

$$k_i = |a_i| \exp(j\phi_i), \quad \phi_i = -\frac{4\pi R_i}{\lambda} + \varphi_{scat_i}, \quad i = 1, 2, \ldots \qquad [5.1]$$

where i refers to the acquisition time of the scene. The observed phase value ϕ_i is the function of the geometric distance R_i (see Figure 5.11), wavelength λ and scattering center φ_{scat_i}. The acquisition vector for an area is then a correlated/uncorrelated process over time depending on the monitored object. In each scenario, the acquisition vector form is the same and characterized by the circular complex process, while its second-order statistic, known as a covariance matrix, is enough for characterizing the whole information of SAR acquisitions.

By combining two SAR acquisitions separated in time with a temporal and spatial baseline, it is possible to characterize the earthquake between the acquisitions. A temporal acquisition vector for each pixel, i.e. $k = [k_1, k_2]^T$, is a complex vector distributed as a multicomponent circular Gaussian that consists of two target vectors $k_1 \sim N(0, \Sigma_{11})$ and $k_2 \sim N(0, \Sigma_{22})$ obtained from temporal multichannel SAR images at times 1 and 2, respectively. Here, the number of elements in one of the target vectors k_i at time i is represented by m, and hence, the temporal target vector k has the dimension of $q = 2 \times m$. For example, $q = 2$ corresponds to interferometric SAR images, whereas $q = 6$ corresponds to polarimetric-interferometric SAR (PolInSAR) images.

It can be remarked that, with single-channel data ($m = 1$), only one copolarized channel $k_i = k_{hh}$ or $k_i = k_{vv}$ is recorded, and the phase carries no useful information for the distributed targets at time i. When multichannel (polarimetric) data are available, for example, $k_i = [k_{hh}, \sqrt{2}k_{hv}, k_{vv}]^T$, phase differences between the channels provide information about the dielectric and geometric properties of the scattering medium in time (Chen and Sato 2013). The covariance matrix Σ_{ii}, which contains sufficient statistics to characterize the acquisition vector k_i, is estimated using a maximum-likelihood method by n-sample (n-look) spatial coherent averaging shown by $\langle . \rangle$:

$$\left\langle k_i k_i^\dagger \right\rangle = \Sigma_{ii} = \begin{bmatrix} \left\langle k_{hh} k_{hh}^\dagger \right\rangle & \left\langle k_{hh} k_{hv}^\dagger \right\rangle & \left\langle k_{hh} k_{vv}^\dagger \right\rangle \\ \left\langle k_{hv} k_{hh}^\dagger \right\rangle & \left\langle k_{hv} k_{hv}^\dagger \right\rangle & \left\langle k_{hv} k_{vv}^\dagger \right\rangle \\ \left\langle k_{vv} k_{hh}^\dagger \right\rangle & \left\langle k_{vv} k_{hv}^\dagger \right\rangle & \left\langle k_{vv} k_{vv}^\dagger \right\rangle \end{bmatrix} \qquad [5.2]$$

where † refers to conjugate transpose. Note that, for $m = 1$, matrix Σ_{ii} reduces to the single polarized intensity scalar a_i. Equation [5.2] defines the scattering mechanism by employing a lexicographic basis. Projecting lexicographic basis scattering matrix onto the Pauli basis coherency matrix, we can easily characterize the target's scattering mechanism. Pauli acquisition elements:

$$k_i = [k_{hh} + k_{vv}, k_{hh} - k_{vv}, 2k_{hv}]^T / \sqrt{2} \tag{5.3}$$

are associated with *surface*, *double-bounce* and *volume* scattering, respectively, and its second-order statistics $\left\langle k_i k_i^\dagger \right\rangle_P$, namely coherency matrix, provides detailed information about the scattering of the target, which forms the basis of incoherent studies.

5.7.2. *Coherent methods for damage assessment*

Phase preserving coherent methods, also called InSAR methods, basically measure the phase difference between two acquisitions acquired in time. Developed within the topographic mapping, InSAR has been mainly used as valuable data for deformation mapping and has been one of the active areas for SAR (see Figure 5.10).

In interferometric multi-channel SAR systems, SAR images are composed of a regular (registered with each other) grid with complex values, which can be decomposed in an amplitude a_i and a phase ϕ_i, $i = 1, 2$ (see equation [5.1]). InSAR uses the phase difference between these two registered SAR images by Hermitian multiplication:

$$I_{int} = \vec{k_1}\vec{k_2}^\dagger = |a_1||a_2| \exp(j(\phi_1 - \phi_2))$$
$$= |a_1||a_2| \exp(j\phi_{int}) \tag{5.4}$$

where ϕ_{int} indicates the interferometric phase. The assumption of having an equal scattering mechanism through temporal acquisitions $\varphi_{scat_1} = \varphi_{scat_2}$ leads to:

$$I_{int} = |a_1||a_2| \exp\left(-\frac{4\pi\Delta R}{\lambda}\right) \tag{5.5}$$

where $\Delta R = R_2 - R_1$ is the range distance between the first and second acquisitions. ϕ_{int} is directly related to the height of the scattering phase center, and its quality is assessed with an absolute value of complex correlation coefficient between images, also called *coherence* γ (Erten 2013):

$$\gamma = \frac{\left\langle k_1 k_2^\dagger \right\rangle}{\sqrt{\langle|k_1|^2\rangle\langle|k_2|^2\rangle}} = |\gamma| \exp(j\phi_{int}), \qquad 0 \leqslant |\gamma| \leqslant 1 \tag{5.6}$$

Once the interferogram is generated by the Hermitian multiplication of the two coregistered phase-preserving focused images (equation [5.5]), the differential InSAR – providing deformation – is obtained by eliminating the topographic phase with external DEM or another interferogram. The result is then a residual, differential interferogram (DInSAR), whose phase depends on the surface displacement (Xia 2010).

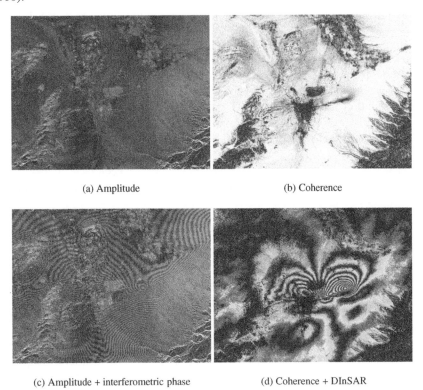

(a) Amplitude   (b) Coherence

(c) Amplitude + interferometric phase   (d) Coherence + DInSAR

Figure 5.12. *(a) ASAR-ENVISAT amplitude image over the city of Bam in the south-eastern part of Iran, which suffered a strong earthquake ($Mv = 6.5$). (b) The coherence ranging from 0 (black) to 1 (white) and (c) the co-seismic interferogram images retrieved from the dataset with a 2 m spatial baseline and 70 day temporal resolution. One cycle corresponds with 2π rad. (d) Line-of-sight displacement map with differential interferogram. One color cycle corresponds with 28 mm displacement in the satellite's line of sight. For a color version of this figure, see www.iste. co.uk/atto/change2.zip*

Specifically, earthquakes are the most remarkable topic where DInSAR plays a role. As an example, Figure 5.12 shows the DInSAR results with real data. The pre-seismic and post-seismic ENVISAT-ASAR images were acquired over the city of Bam in the south-eastern part of Iran, which suffered a strong earthquake ($Mv = 6.5$) in the winter of 2003/2004. Figure 5.12(a) shows the radar amplitude of ENVISAT-ASAR image. Figure 5.12(b) and (c) shows the coherence and the co-seismic interferogram, respectively, generated from the acquisitions at December 3, 2003 (pre-seismic) and January 7, 2004 (post-seismic). Figure 5.12(d) shows a differential interferogram using the external DEM as a reference. Since the Landers earthquake, similar *butterfly* images have been obtained and modeled for earthquakes (Tronin 2010). Measuring millimetric deformation for large areas, DInSAR becomes operational and accepted analysis in tectonics. According to Figure 5.10, ~65% of the studies using DInSAR are published in geodesy and tectonics journals for understanding fault rapture. It can be seen that publications regarding DInSAR for tectonics have grown significantly since 2010 with second-generation SAR systems. Specifically, in the case of the presence of ascending and descending geometry, DInSAR provides displacement information both in vertical and horizontal directions, which is unprecedented information in the lack of dense GPS networks (Dalla Via *et al.* 2012; Fujiwara *et al.* 2017; He *et al.* 2018). A detailed description of tectonic studies with the InSAR technique is beyond the scope of this chapter, and we invite the readers to review the literature for a complete understanding (Weston *et al.* 2012; Atzori 2013; Sansosti *et al.* 2014; He *et al.* 2018; Atzori *et al.* 2019; Xue *et al.* 2020).

In the context of earthquake monitoring, interferometric techniques are not only developed for tectonic studies but also have a huge impact on damage assessment. Specifically, interferometric products, namely coherence data (see equation [5.6]), have been explored for man-made asset damage assessment. As shown in Figure 5.12(b), the coherence image shows the decorrelation (a lower value means higher change and vice versa) of phase information acquired between pre- and post-earthquake images. In the figure, decorrelation appears in the city center due to the severe building damages caused by the earthquake, while normally urban areas are known to show a very high correlation/coherence in time. Moreover, the earthquake's fault line can also be detected in the coherence map (Erten *et al.* 2010).

Fielding *et al.* (2005) conducted the very first coherence study on building damage assessment over the city of Bam after the same earthquake on December 26, 2003, and found a strong relationship between the mean coherence and the damage level of different regions in the city. Although the damage level of the buildings was not reported, the method provided sufficient resolution to reveal destroyed regions left from the strong earthquake. Indeed, in 2018, a similar type of co-seismic coherence data was applied to distinguish five-level building damage ranging from slightly to extremely destroyed in the 2016 Kumamoto earthquakes in Japan. For this study, Natsuaki *et al.* (2018) used 3 m resolution ALOS-2/PALSAR L band data and showed that if the building size is larger than a resolution of coherence pixel and the damage level is larger than level 2 of 5 – classified with the European Macroseismic Scale 1998 (EMS-98) – the co-seismic coherence is able to provide reliable damage-level information. The main weakness of these only coherence-based thresholding methods comes from the fact that coherence values are only reliable when there is a certain amount of correlation (e.g. $\gamma \geqslant 0.45$). Note that, for example, it is not always consistent that $\gamma = 0.2$ associates with more damaged buildings than $\gamma = 0.1$.

Another technique, namely multi-temporal interferometric coherence change detection, consists of at least two pairs of coherence images (i.e. pre- and co-seismic). As first shown by Hoffmann (2007), comparing pre- and co- or post-seismic coherence reduced the loss of coherence due to the earthquake-independent effects, such as misregistration and atmosphere (Plank 2014; Ge *et al.* 2020). For the 2003 Bam earthquake with C-band Envisat data, Hoffmann (2007) defined a coherence-based index:

$$\rho = \frac{\gamma_{pre}}{\gamma_{co}} \qquad [5.7]$$

where γ_{pre} and γ_{co} show the coherence images obtained from pre-seismic and co-seismic interferometric pairs, respectively. And then, the index was classified into four classes according to the damage level. Yonezawa and Takeuchi (2001) and Watanabe *et al.* (2016) used the normalized difference (ND) of equation [5.7] with ERS-1 and ALOS-2, respectively:

$$\rho_{ND} = \frac{\gamma_{pre} - \gamma_{co}}{\gamma_{pre} + \gamma_{co}} \qquad [5.8]$$

Watanabe *et al.* (2016) applied the normalized coherence change detection in every house in Khokana and Sankhu, Japan, affected by the 2015 Gorkha earthquake and obtained lower accuracy (27.1–35.1%) for damaged areas and higher accuracy (97.8–99.2%) for damage-free areas. Sharma *et al.* (2017) used the same index for the rapid detection of earthquake damage visualization (EDV) by using RGB composite imagery (R: forward change equation [5.8], G: backward change equation [5.8], B: no change $(\gamma_{pre} + \gamma_{co})/2$). Most coherence-based methods, however, rely on the availability of co-seismic data, which limits the usability despite its unique information. With an increasing temporal resolution of SAR images, the more recent trend is to develop methods relying on pre- and post-earthquake coherence images (Lu *et al.* 2018; Monterroso *et al.* 2018; Natsuaki *et al.* 2018; Olen and Bookhagen 2018; Ullo *et al.* 2019). These methods made use of the fact that time series of coherence information for each pixel gives a hint about natural cycles of coherence for a given region of interest. After the launch of free available Sentinel-1 and ALOS-2, the pace of growth of the coherence-based earthquake-induced damage assessment has been accelerated due to their high temporal resolution and a longer wavelength, providing high coherence images in time (Monterroso *et al.* 2018). Although coherence can not be guaranteed at a lower wavelength over natural areas even with a high temporal resolution, there are interesting studies with X-band as well, which will be discussed in section 5.7.5 due to the fact that with increasing spatial resolution, coherence-based change analysis coupled with intensity-based change analysis increases the accuracy of damage-level classification (Karimzadeh and Matsuoka 2018). Additionally, Tang *et al.* (2019) used pre- and post-earthquake TanDEM-X (bistatic mission avoiding temporal decorrelations) interferometric pairs to produce DEM in order to understand the change of volume in the earthquake-affected area.

5.7.3. *Incoherent methods for damage assessment*

Compared with coherent interferometric techniques, incoherent SAR intensity-based techniques are not limited by phase stability problems and can reliably be acquired on a regular basis. As they are also less dependent on SAR acquisition (i.e. incidence angle) geometry, intensity-based techniques are appealing for better understanding changes caused by an earthquake. The classical intensity-based change detection algorithms explore the scattering changes in pre- and post-earthquake SAR images. As shown in Figure 5.11(a) and (b), an intact building has a specific backscattering pattern in SAR images: *layover*, *double-bounce* and *shadows*. In contrast to the backscattering of an intact building, one of the collapsed buildings is completely random (see Figure 5.11(c)). Thus, to quantify the changes and relate them with damage level, different parameters have been proposed, such as temporal intensity correlation, ratio and texture. In order to provide an intuitive understanding and the complex scattering mechanisms resulting from pre- and post-SAR, we can refer to the images in the study by Ge *et al.* (2020).

The most traditional change detection methods based on pre- and post- SAR intensity images, then, rely on calculating their intensity difference and correlation coefficient (Lubis and Isezaki 2009). Matsuoka and Yamazaki (2004) investigated the relationship between the intensity correlations and differences derived from pre- and post-ERS earthquake images and the degree of damage over three different earthquake areas: 1999 Kocaeli, Turkey, 2001 Gujarat, India, and 2003 Boumerdes, Algeria, by regression-based analysis. The study underlined the fact that the presence of high-resolution pre-earthquake optic images or existing GIS databases could be necessary for better building damage-level classification, specifically on *foreshortening* areas. Although this intensity-based approach is easy to apply, it suffers from data dependency in the same way as other regression-based methods. Specifically, in low-resolution images, it is not easy to find regression coefficients which are valid for each test site. This is related to the fact that when radar illuminates a surface that is rough on the scale of the radar wavelength, the returned signal consists of waves reflected from many elementary scatters within a resolution cell. Then, as in Figure 5.11(c), the measured reflection is instead represented as a linear combination of the returned signals from the scatters of the different objects. Additionally, the window size used for correlation coefficient analysis causes more of a decrease in spatial resolution than the original one, limiting identification of the damage levels. This is proved by Yamazaki *et al.* (2016), who applied a similar approach to the 2015 Gorkha, Nepal earthquake with TerraSAR-X data. This simple intensity correlation and/or ratio-based method was found to be very successful at large-size collapsed buildings. To tackle this trade-off between the classification accuracy of the damage level and resolution, region-growing and multi-kernel methods were applied. In order to quantify the earthquake-induced displacement, Chae *et al.* (2019) proposed a multi-kernel offset tracking method, which uses the multi-kernel intensity correlation measurement. The method was validated over two earthquake areas: Hector Mine and

Kumamoto with ERS-2 and ALOS-2. It was shown that if offset tracking is the only viable alternative (in the case of absence of an interferometric pair), it can even be used for 3D deformation monitoring studies, specifically with high-resolution SAR images. Lu *et al.* (2021) supported the outcomes of this study and showed that the accuracy of 3D deformation can be further improved by applying multi-kernel offset tracking into high-resolution optical images, together with SAR images. The root-mean-square error values of deformation estimation decreased by 20–50% compared to the one derived with SAR offset tracking only.

Gokon *et al.* (2015) used the ratio and correlation of high-resolution (TerraSAR-X) pre- and post-earthquake intensity images as a feature in a three-class random forest classification: *washed away*, *collapsed* and *slightly damaged*. They applied the classification over Sendai City, which was affected by the 2011 Tohoku earthquake, and in order to ensure the transferability of the method, the classification methodology was applied to the town of Watari as well. Overall accuracy of 67.4% and 58.7% was reached in Sendai City and Watari, respectively. The main limitation of the methodology was related to the geometrical distribution of the buildings. Since the methodology defines the intact buildings using a *double-bounce-layover-shadow* scattering pattern (see Figure 5.11), if the buildings are built close to each other – relative to the resolution of SAR images – layover areas could be superimposed. Marin *et al.* (2015) defined the building damage level based on the same change detection approach of the scattering pattern of the intact building but with multi-scale wavelet representation coupled with fuzzy rules. This multi-scale change detection approach was tested over the 2009 L'Aquila earthquake, Italy, with spotlight (1 m resolution) COSMO-SkyMed images, resulting in only two buildings being misclassified among the 387 buildings labeled. The latest satellite-based SAR imaging systems in spotlight mode (Radarsat-2, COSMO-SkyMed, TerraSAR-X) can provide resolutions of a few centimeters. This capability, coupled with ML techniques, boosts the usage of texture information (see section 5.5). Wu *et al.* (2016) analyzed five types of damaged buildings due to the May 12, 2008 Beichuan earthquake using high-resolution ascending and descending dual-pol TerraSAR-X images. The classification results, in which backscattering and GLCM were used as an input, revealed that the variance of backscattering, the GLCM homogeneity and second moment were found to be the best features for discriminating the different types of damage. Adriano *et al.* (2019) introduced a methodology using curvilinear features between pre- and post-earthquake COSMO-SkyMed images. The results obtained from Port-au-Prince, Haiti, showed that collapsed and seriously damaged buildings can be detected in line with damage estimates made from very high-resolution optical images. However, it was also noted that most of the false alarms were associated with the buildings that do not match backscattering patterns with curvilinear features. To overcome this problem, along with inhomogeneity of scattering in VHR SAR images, Saha *et al.* (2021) proposed unsupervised deep transcoding. The study explores the possibilities of using VHR optic images coupled with a cycle-consistent adversarial network (CycleGAN) for extracting a deep feature from multi-temporal SAR images. The proposed method also used the fuzzy building detection rules, as introduced by Marin *et al.* (2015), to identify the changed/unchanged building samples and improved the results compared to the study by Marin *et al.* (2015) with zero false detection, which previously was two.

The findings of most studies showed the feasibility of single polarization (HH or VV) SAR systems with different frequencies. In 2006, ALOS PALSAR began to provide fully polarimetric L-band data with 46 days of temporal resolution. The studies conducted with full polarimetric data (Dong *et al.* 2011; Watanabe *et al.* 2012; Yamaguchi 2012; Chen and Sato 2013; Park *et al.* 2013) addressed the question of how the incident and received wave change from the pre- and post-earthquake images characterizing the target and its features. The fully polarimetric data allows for the characterization of the scattering model by using the coherency matrix (see equation [5.3]). Chen and Sato (2013) used an odd-bounce scattering model to identify washed-away buildings characterized as double-bounce before the earthquake. In addition to this scattering chance analysis, they used the polarization orientation (PO) angle distribution of post-earthquake images to explore the homogeneity reduction of PO angles to discriminate different damage levels at the city block scale. The stability of the experimental results from the earthquake of March 11, 2011, which occurred beneath the Pacific off the northeastern coast of Japan, underlined the importance of fully polarimetric information. Park *et al.* (2013) applied a change detection technique over the same area by using the expectation–maximization-based thresholding approach to polarimetric features. In the study of tsunami damage analysis following the earthquake of March 1, the identification of tsunami-swept urban areas was improved by 50% compared with the single-polarization SAR approach. A very similar conclusion with a significant reduction of false- and missed-alarm rates was obtained by Sato *et al.* (2012) and Chen and Sato (2013).

Decomposing the coherency matrix including eigenvalue–eigenvector- and model-based decompositions can be seen as the basis of the fully polarimetric studies (Kimura 2008; Dekker 2011; Chang *et al.* 2012; Yamaguchi 2012; Chen and Sato 2013; Park *et al.* 2013). The model-based methods, specifically the four-component scattering model, are based on the fact that the total scattering can be decomposed to four different scattering mechanisms:

$$\left\langle k_i k_i^\dagger \right\rangle_P = f_v \left\langle \Sigma_{vol} \right\rangle + f_d \left\langle \Sigma_{db} \right\rangle + f_s \left\langle \Sigma_{surf} \right\rangle + f_h \left\langle \Sigma_{hel} \right\rangle \qquad [5.9]$$

where Σ and f refer to the physical scattering mechanism and model coefficients for volume (*vol*), double-bounce (*db*), surface (*surf*) and helix (*helix*) scattering (Yamaguchi 2012).

The eigenvalue–eigenvector decomposition of the coherency matrix provides polarimetric features such as entropy, H, anisotropy, A and average scattering angle, α. These polarimetric features characterize the scattering randomness and the second dominant scattering mechanisms, as well as their similarity among the pre- and post-earthquake images used for damage assessment (Rubner *et al.* 2001; Li *et al.* 2012; Yamaguchi 2012; Park *et al.* 2013; Zhai and Huang 2016). In addition to decomposition-based polarimetric features, Chen *et al.* (2018a) investigated polarimetric coherence in the rotation domain along the LOS for urban damage investigation. A pre- and post-earthquake polarimetric coherence-derived damage index was proposed for urban damage-level discrimination and tested over the March 11, 2011, East Japan earthquake area with ALOS PALSAR data. Experimental results underlined that the co-polarization coherence fluctuations can be effectively used if the building damage level is more than 20%.

Although the review study conducted by Park and Jung (2020) also showed that polarimetric features and coherence, coupled with the physical scattering mechanism, provide a significant improvement in the context of damage-level classification compared with the single polarization pre- and post-earthquake SAR images; the availability of fully polarimetric data is limited (see Table 5.2) for very high-resolution SAR images due to its cost compared to the single-polarization case.

5.7.4. *Post-earthquake-only SAR data-based damage assessment*

The requirement for rapid earthquake damage mapping coupled with the recent availability of high-resolution SAR images has boosted damage assessment studies using only post-event SAR data, without any pre-event data. The use of post-earthquake-only SAR data is on the rise due to the lack of pre-earthquake data specifically in undeveloped areas (see section 5.4). Additionally, the lack of fine-resolution spotlight pre-earthquake SAR images has also proved to be a limitation of change-based damage assessment studies in the context of rapid response to operational needs.

As discussed in section 5.7.1, PolSAR data provide important information about the scattering behavior of the monitored areas according to their geometric and dielectric properties. Thus, the first studies using post-event-only SAR data focused on the scattering behavior of earthquake-affected areas (Brunner *et al.* 2010; Li *et al.* 2012; Wang and Jin 2012; Dell'Acqua and Polli 2013; Zhai and Huang 2016). The research by Brunner *et al.* (2010) is one of the first studies to use VHR optical (Quickbird, Worldview) and radar (TerraSAR-X, Cosmo-SkyMed) data for pre- and post-earthquake characterization, respectively. In this study, it is assumed that the building has a rectangular footprint, and they identified it from the pre-earthquake optical images. These buildings were then checked from post-earthquake SAR images using similarity measurements. The feasibility of the method was checked in Yingxiu, China, which was heavily damaged in the Sichuan earthquake of May 12, 2008. In these studies, it is mainly two different types of scattering that play a role in damage assessment: volume and double-bounce scattering mechanisms. The undamaged buildings are characterized by strong double-bounce scattering, and the buildings with damage patterns were characterized by weak volume scattering (see Figure 5.11). Once the scattering mechanisms are defined by polarimetric SAR images, the damage assessment is then conducted by machine learning and/or image processing techniques (see section 5.4). Dell'Acqua et al. (2011) showed that SAR images, specifically their texture information, are more convenient for damage-level identification, while optical images are good at distinguishing damage and non-damage classes. The limited use of space-based post-event SAR data for damage assessment was due to the requirement of high-resolution quad-pol or full polarimetric data, providing the complete scattering behavior of the target. However, the spatial resolution of the current generation of SAR satellites makes the post-event SAR data damage assessments possible. Hence, there has been a remarkable increase in the number of post-earthquake only satellite-based studies. In line with increasing spatial resolution, the recent studies explore texture features with polarimetric information for damage assessment (Bai et al. 2017a, 2017b). The trade-off limitation between polarimetric information versus resolution means some recent studies exploit only texture-based features from SAR images (Timo and Liao 2010; Wu et al. 2016; Bai et al. 2017b, 2018; Ge et al. 2019). Bai et al. (2018) used only TerraSAR-X images from after the 2011 Tohoku earthquake for rapid damage mapping by a deep learning-based framework.

The expanding use of post-earthquake-only SAR data in earthquake response shows that the success of these methods depends on three conditions. First, it is important to have reference data showing the pre-earthquake condition of the scene; it can be pre-earthquake VHR optical imagery (Dell'Acqua et al. 2011; Wang and Jin 2012) and/or cadastral data (Zhai and Huang 2016; Bai et al. 2018). Second, having high-resolution SAR imagery, allowing us to use texture features, is key to rapid damage assessment. Third, access to freely available polarimetric high-resolution SAR imagery will boost the use of post-event earthquake SAR data for operational purposes as Ge et al. (2019) underlines that using only the post-event VHR SAR data achieved similar accuracy to the use of both pre- and post-event data.

5.7.5. *Combination of coherent and incoherent methods for damage assessment*

The potential of coherent (interferometric) data for earthquake studies is explained in section 5.7.2. The studies underlined the DInSAR capability in providing unprecedented line-of-sight (LOS) deformation information in millimeter accuracy and the sensitivity of interferometric coherence to building damage level. Additionally, section 5.7.3 emphasizes the potential of single- and/or multi-polarized intensity images to explore damage conditions using scattering mechanism investigations. When both data types, which provide complementary information to each other, are available, integrated approaches are used in earthquake studies. They can be roughly grouped into two types according to the purpose of the study. The first group includes the generation of three-dimensional deformation maps, mostly for tectonics, while the second group focuses on building damage assessment in disasters.

In the first-group studies, the vertical displacement as a function of LOS is obtained from DInSAR, while the horizontal displacement is obtained either with offset tracking or split-band interferometry methods in the azimuth direction. As in optical images, pixel matching, namely offset tracking between pre- and post-earthquake, can be implemented to estimate 3D deformation. However, since the sensibility of deformation detection is linked to the resolution of the SAR images, not to wavelength as in DInSAR, it is common to apply offset tracking only in the azimuth direction for horizontal displacement. Hashimoto *et al.* (2010) and Yague-Martinez *et al.* (2012) applied offset tracking for ground displacement after the 2008 Wenchuan earthquake and the 2011 Tohoku-Oki earthquake with ALOS-PALSAR and TerraSAR-X data, respectively. A comparison between DInSAR and offset tracking in the range direction showed a good agreement in the presence of high-resolution images like TerraSAR-X, showing a divergence of about 15 cm. From the recent studies (Zhang *et al.* 2016b; He *et al.* 2019b, 2019c), it has been found that offset tracking can be a good alternative in the absence of an interferometric pair for rescue planning after a large-scale earthquake.

Another possible technique for detecting deformation in the azimuth direction is spectral diversity, namely multiple-aperture InSAR (AMI) or split-band interferometry (Jung *et al.* 2013; Liu *et al.* 2014; Zhang *et al.* 2016b; Gomba *et al.* 2017; Liang *et al.* 2017; Polcari *et al.* 2017; Lo *et al.* 2019). Erten *et al.* (2010) first applied this offset-tracking method to quantify 3D displacement after the 2003 Bam earthquake. Although the spectral diversity technique is well suited for deformation monitoring, this technique also requires a coherent SAR dataset as in the case of DInSAR applications. It is less accurate than DInSAR but provides significantly higher accuracy than offset-tracking approaches (Erten *et al.* 2010; He *et al.* 2019c). Although the wide-swath imaging of new generation satellites provides high coherence data due to the high temporal resolution with the cost of azimuth resolution, the spectral diversity method has become a standard routine in tectonic geodesy.

The second-group studies rely on the change analysis of interferometric coherence and intensity together. Their main idea is then defining a mathematical model whose input (temporal coherence and intensity images) and output (building damage level) relationships can be adjusted to be used in disaster response. The integrated use of coherence and intensity images acquired before and after an earthquake for damage-level monitoring was first proposed by Arciniegas *et al.* (2007) in the case of the 2003 Bam earthquake. The results with ENVISAT images showed that even though the accuracy of classification was improved with the integrated method, the accuracy level (50%) was not enough for disaster mitigation. However, they underlined the potential of these integrated approaches for VHR SAR images. Trianni and Gamba (2009) improved the accuracy obtained by Arciniegas *et al.* (2007) with the usage of ancillary information defining urban blocks. The coherence images from ERS acquired before and after the 1999 Kocaeli earthquake, coupled with their intensity, was used as an input in supervised MRF classification and an unsupervised statistical analysis for block-level damage mapping. Both methodologies provide enough information to understand the damage pattern but, as expected, the statistical model was computationally faster than the supervised classification method. Compared with the previous studies, the recent studies by Karimzadeh and Mastuoka (2017); Karimzadeh and Matsuoka (2018) and Hajeb *et al.* (2020) have shown that this type of integrated method has huge potential for building damage-level classification. Karimzadeh and Mastuoka (2017) used temporal coherence and intensity images of dual-polarized Sentinel-1 and ALOS-2 images acquired for the August 24, 2016, Amatrice earthquake. With the usage of linear discriminant functions based on these inputs, a damage proxy map at parcel level was obtained, and accuracies of 84% and 76% were achieved for the Sentinel-1 and ALOS-2, respectively. HH polarization ascending and descending X-band COSMO-SkyMed images acquired over the 2006 Amatrice earthquake were used by Karimzadeh and Matsuoka (2018) in order to estimate damage levels. The study revealed that using ascending and descending geometry together with fuzzy overlay analysis obviates the limitations related to single acquisition geometry, for example, shadows, layover, roof shape, etc. However, the impact of system parameters such as wavelength and spatial and temporal resolutions on the results still has to be investigated. In order to tackle the limitations regarding the trade-off between the type of buildings and spatial resolution, Hajeb *et al.* (2020) used these features and texture information obtained with different window sizes with ALOS-2 data. Then, the damage assessment was performed with supervised classification and overall accuracy of 86% was reached according to the reference VHR optical images. The advantage of such integration consists of facilitating the use of the target's amplitude and phase information together which is changing throughout the image acquisition time.

5.7.6. *Summary*

This section focuses on the general view of the use of SAR images for earthquake studies, including tectonics to damage-level identification. For this purpose, the input image pair is classified as either coherent or incoherent based on whether the pre- and post-earthquake image pair is coherent or incoherent. In the first case, a system is called interferometric, providing a meaningful phase and intensity change information. Contrarily, an incoherent image pair can only provide intensity change information between the image pairs used for earthquake-induced damage analysis. Both types of SAR image pairs are essential to extract information about the damage left by an earthquake. And in both types, system parameters such as the number of the polarimetric bands, wavelength and temporal and spatial resolution play an important role in providing damage information over large areas at a relatively low cost.

First developed in the late 1990s, interferometric imaging – providing superior information on the analysis of scattering center change – has attracted a lot of interest from both tectonics and image processing communities. Measuring the deformation along the LOS direction of the SAR sensor, DInSAR has drawn the attention of a large number of tectonics studies. The interferometric pair also allows the use of intensity changes – incoherent information – between the pre- and post-earthquake images. Their integrated usage has been widely used in seismology for 3D deformation analysis since DInSAR only gives information in a vertical direction. Instead, in the context of image processing for damage-level assessment, an interferometric products, namely coherence – indicating decorrelation between the image pair – has been widely used. The superiority of the coherence comes from the fact that it is more sensitive to minor changes than the intensity-based information, for example, pancake collapse in Figure 5.13, which is not easy to identify with intensity-based approaches. Specifically, the existence of high-resolution interferometric pairs makes building damage level feasible. Although TerraSAR-X and COSMO-Skymed boost the use of coherence on damage-level studies, the availability of a Spotlight mode, which provides a VHR image at the cost of along-track coverage for disaster, is heavily limited due to the fact that it is not a continuous imaging mode. Additionally, favorable coherence data is much more dependent on the system parameters (spatial baseline, wavelength, etc.) and on the earthquake-induced change.

The unique properties of multi-polarization mode SAR images, particularly well suited for exploring the changes in the target's geometry, size, orientation, etc., have also contributed to the promising results. Its sensitivity to physical scattering is the key asset of polarization-based studies. Nevertheless, there are limited full polarimetric data, and the acquired ones have relatively lower resolution (see Table 5.2). However, it has been shown that the coherence-based information can be enhanced if it is integrated with dual-polarization data, which is easier to obtain than full polarimetric data (Watanabe et al. 2016; Sharma et al. 2018). Texture, such as GLCM and Gabor filters, is another important feature for identifying the geometrical characteristics of the target in the presence of high-resolution data. Texture information becomes less important with medium- and lower-resolution data since there is a randomness in the phase and scattering due to the existence of different scatters with different properties inside the resolution cell.

To identify an earthquake-induced damage level at the building scale, it is necessary to use a VHR image. On the contrary, within monitoring in an urban environment at block scale, which is really important for rapid response, the current operational SAR systems (see Table 5.2) coupled with ML techniques provide very useful information, especially with integrated approaches.

5.8. Use of auxiliary data sources

Auxiliary data such as GIS, DEM and light detection and ranging have been frequently utilized as additional data sources for both optical and SAR data to improve performance in terms of both accurateness and real-time response (Yamazaki *et al.* 2017). By combining GIS and remote sensing, Aydoner and Maktav (2009) introduced a methodology to determine land use/land cover after an earthquake with a multicriteria evaluation model which is a decision aid and a mathematical tool allowing particularly for evaluation of land suitability. With similar motivation, Sofina and Ehlers (2016) proposed a semi-automated feature-based damage assessment approach for building-based damage detection. To assess the building integrity, a new feature, so-called detected part of contour, was developed based on the GIS vector data. Since the developed approach was an object-based approach, no spectral information was required. However, buildings completely or partially obscured by the trees cannot be detected as intact buildings, since the detected part of the contour is not able to extract the entire contour of the buildings. Contreras *et al.* (2016) combined the data sources, including multi-temporal remote sensing images, ground observation and GIS, to monitor the recovery of L'Aquila (Italy) after the emergency phase based on a monitoring schedule. Tong *et al.* (2012) used the pre- and post-earthquake IKONOS stereo image pairs to obtain pre- and post-DEMs, the difference of which was used to detect the collapsed buildings, thus providing a three-dimensional damage map compared to a two-dimensional damage map, provided as in the most traditional methods. Even more features, such as height and shadow, are also very useful for accurate detection of the damage. In this context, Wang and Li (2020) used the height features extracted from post-event LiDAR data to extract the building damage with a significant change in spatial variability. Kushiyama and Matsuoka (2019) introduced a method for detecting the collapsed and intact buildings to create a time series of GIS map datasets following the 2016 Kumamoto earthquake.

5.9. Damage grades

Damage maps provide information about pixels or segments whether they belong to damage or the other land cover classes. The intensity of damage to buildings caused by an earthquake, known as damage grades, however, is expressed by more than two classes depending on the severity of the collapse. Earthquake engineers developed several different intensity scales to express the damage grades in different areas of the subjected cities. The European Macroseismic Scale 1998 (EMS-98) is one of the most widely used measures for intensity scales to convey the impact of earthquakes on masonry and reinforced buildings (Grünthal *et al.* 1998) and is assessed at five different levels, including slight damage, moderate damage, substantial to heavy damage, very heavy damage and destruction. The description of each grade is given in Table 5.3.

Satellite-based remote sensing sensors are unable to provide the information to precisely qualify the damage level at five different scales, but mainly at two or three, that are light damage, moderate damage and heavy damage. Although increasing the spatial resolution of RS data, using off-nadir images, extracting textural features and using more complex RS data, such as LiDAR imagery, airborne oblique images and multi-perspective images, allow a better assessment on damage grades, the presence of the collapsed buildings on the post-image plays an important role in the identification of the damage grade. The illustration of the presence of collapsed buildings proposed by Schweier and Markus (2006) is given in Figure 5.13.

Damage level	Class name	Short description
Level 1	Light damage	No visual change in the building roof, but debris is close to the walls.
Level 2	Lightly damaged roof	The walls are standing, and a minor part of the roof is damaged.
Level 3	Damaged roof	Most of the walls are standing, but most of the roof is damaged.
Level 4	Collapsed	The building has collapsed, but the roof is totally or mostly untouched ("pancake" effect).
Level 5	Destroyed	The building is totally destroyed and only debris is visible.

Table 5.3. *Description of the damage grades according to the EMS-98 scale*

As shown in Figure 5.13, certain types of collapsed buildings, including those that come under *heap of debris* and *overturned*, are the easiest (relatively) types to detect from multi-temporal images via change detection methods. The first two types of buildings in the category of *inclined layers* can be partially detected depending on their presence on the multiple images. Moreover, damage assessment via satellite-based images is limited to certain structural types of visible damage, such as the buildings that come under *pancake collapse* and *nonstructural*.

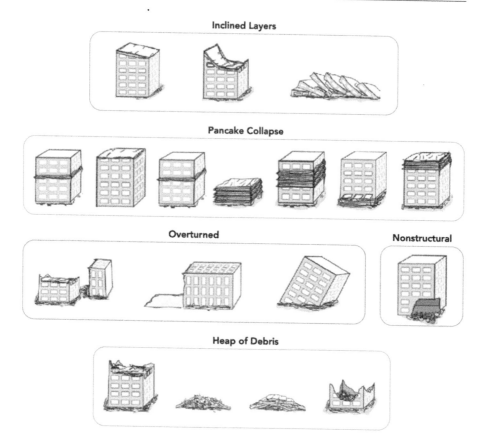

Figure 5.13. *Types of collapsed buildings, categorized by Schweier and Markus (2006)*

In the literature, most researchers focus on understanding the relationship between the damage grades of EMS-98 and the buildings on the remote sensing images (Rezaeian 2010; Dekker 2011; Plank 2014). Using EMS-98, Yamazaki *et al.* (2005) interpreted the building damage using five levels and created a damage map of the Bam earthquake using multi-temporal images. Rastiveis *et al.* (2013) proposed a fuzzy decision-making system that considers the building shape differences between pre- and post-event images and created a five-level damage map. Natsuaki *et al.* (2018) performed an analysis to evaluate the sensitivity as well as the limitations of SAR interferometric coherence for the identification of damage in individual buildings, by taking into account the EMS-98 scale. Their study showed that in addition to the severely damaged (Level 5), interferometric coherence is useful in detecting the moderately damaged (Level 2 or heavier) buildings. Although the images with off-nadir views might be more suitable for more precise damage grading, it should be noted that registration of these images is a much more difficult task compared to those with the nadir view angle (Barazzetti and Cuca 2020). This was pointed out by Barazzetti *et al.* (2015), and a multi-step approach was proposed for automatic change detection through object classification to register the images with an off-nadir view. In the studies conducted by Dell'Acqua *et al.* (2011) and Dell'Acqua *et al.* (2013), a damage index (damaged area ratio) was introduced to convey the damaged buildings in accordance with the EMS-98 grades for each block in the GIS layer, which defines the urban neighborhoods. Each associated block was labeled depending on the value of the damage flag, which is 1 or 0, corresponding to the damage (indicating the damage levels 4 and 5) and non-damage classes. For the 2011 Haiti earthquake, Romaniello *et al.* (2017) conducted a case study to create a damage map with three types of damage levels, including heavy, moderate and light damage. As most researchers have acknowledged, Dell'Acqua and Gamba (2012) showed that low-resolution images are a very good choice for detecting damage at a coarse level but much less accurate for practices at the fine damage level. Unlike the conventional two-dimensional damage change of the collapsed buildings, Tong *et al.* (2012) exploited the use of pre- and post-seismic IKONOS stereo image pairs to obtain 3D geometric changes, particularly the height changes of the buildings, to detect the collapsed buildings, resulting in three-dimensional damage mapping.

Even though more precise damage mapping is possible with the growing developments in remote sensing technology, as well as with development in advanced data processing techniques, binary change detection is more suitable for damage assessment implementations, particularly if supervised learning methods are considered due to the need for multi-temporal training data.

5.10. Conclusion and discussion

Earthquake damage assessment from satellite-based remote sensing images is of great importance in the identification of earthquake-induced damage for rapid and reliable damage mapping and in providing essential information to decision-makers. Despite the promising technological developments regarding high-resolution images, providing a damage map by using satellite data with very high resolutions poses a great challenge. Change detection techniques, supervised, unsupervised and semi-supervised, identify the damage extent and level from the images acquired from pre- and post-earthquake events. In addition to the difficulties encountered in the multi-temporal approaches, the problem of earthquake damage assessment brings extra challenges due to the presence of debris over the other land cover classes, causing distortion in damage maps, especially in the buildings. Moreover, the methodologies developed for the damage assessment might be limited depending on the many challenges, which are summarized as follows:

– The size of geographic regions is an important factor in developing a learning-based damage assessment model in terms of generalization potential of the associated model – the so-called transferability and applicability – since the large areas are more diverse and complex than the small areas.

– The damage identification of the isolated buildings is much simpler than that of the dense buildings, which cause an increase in the complexity of the city, which is the so-called structural density of the city affected by the earthquake. More advanced data processing methods, together with the use of various types of remote sensing data, are required to effectively extract the damage in such areas.

– The performance of the supervised change detection methods is affected by several factors, including sampling technique used for generating training data, the size of the training samples, the classification method and design of feature space, all of which should be carefully designed for accurate damage mapping.

– Supervised change detection methods suffer from the imbalanced training dataset, causing low classification performance on the damage detection. When the earthquake is very destructive, only a few undamaged buildings could be found in the post-earthquake image, resulting in an unbalanced training set, which needs to be taken care of using more advance learning methods.

– Temporal differentiation between the images is an important factor, which may lead to detection of changes not related to earthquakes. The presence of land cover changes (e.g. newly developed areas, changes in road layout) on the satellite images might increase when the time differentiation between the image pairs is large. In such cases, identification and exclusion of such areas from the analysis would help to improve the accuracy of the damage map. Time resolution also affects the process of rapid damage mapping; depending on this, the data type to be used in the analysis might vary as well as the methodology.

– High spatial resolution is very useful, especially for building-based damage detection. The contextual features, extracted with image processing methods by using the neighborhood relations of the pixels, should be combined with spectral features in classification to improve the reliability of the damage map. Furthermore, as the number of features increases, the complexity of the method increases accordingly; therefore, dimensionality reduction methods, including feature extraction and feature selection, should be considered to cope with the so-called curse of dimensionality.

– It is not always possible to identify each damage grade of the structural damage. For example, the pancake type of collapse or heavy structural damage but still standing buildings cannot easily be determined from the optical images. Off-nadir images as well as SAR can be used to identify the damage on such structures.

– The other objects, such as trees or cars, located around the buildings, might be critical factors affecting the performance of the methodology, inducing problems of misclassification in building-scale (local level) damage detection. The auxiliary dataset such as GIS might be helpful to deal with such issues.

– For an accurate change detection, especially at the pixel-based level, image pairs should have the same acquisition parameters and specifically the same viewing configuration. If this is not the case, the rate of false alarms will increase accordingly, resulting in changes that are not necessarily actual changes on the ground.

– The presence of the clouds might cover the areas affected by the earthquake, or bad weather conditions might make the optical sensors unavailable. Although these issues can partially be solved by using more advanced data processing techniques to eliminate the effects of, for example, the clouds, the use of SAR is typically a better solution for this, despite its difficulties in data processing compared to optical images.

– The number of the damage level is associated with the number of classes in the classification. As the number of classes increases, the complexity of the damage assessment problem increases, which affects the performance of the supervised method. Moreover, having training samples corresponding to each class might be difficult especially at the time domain.

– The orientation of the sensors is another parameter affecting the damage assessment process. Off-nadir sensors, known as side-looking sensors, might be more advantageous than nadir-looking ones in terms of providing detailed information, especially relating to wall-type damage of the buildings.

– Image registration plays an important role in providing an accurate damage map. If the image pairs are not correctly registered, change detection suffers significantly, causing a high false alarm rate. This fact becomes more important when dealing with VHR images. Despite this, the use of very high-resolution satellite images combined with textural, structural and geometric features allows a better discretization of the damage levels of the buildings. Even more details on the damage level can be obtained with RS data acquired from side-looking sensors.

– Multi-source image analysis is an important task in the earthquake damage assessment literature because the post-event image, especially the optical image, might not be suitable to process due to several reasons such as cloud coverage or the presence of the post-image source might be different from the pre-event image at the time an earthquake happens. In such cases, the combined use of the images with different sources is mandatory and crucial for accurate and real-time damage mapping.

Technological and scientific developments in the era of remote sensing with the launch of new satellite missions will provide very rich information, enabling us to generate more operational systems for earthquake damage assessment, but posing new challenges. It should be noted that more advanced and sophisticated learning methods will be required to reveal meaningful information and construct accurate and reliable systems.

5.11. References

Adriano, B., Xia, J., Baier, G., Yokoya, N., Koshimura, S. (2019). Multi-source data fusion based on ensemble learning for rapid building damage mapping during the 2018 Sulawesi Earthquake and Tsunami in Palu, Indonesia. *Remote Sensing*, 11(7), 886.

Aicardi, I., Nex, F., Gerke, M., Lingua, A.M. (2016). An image-based approach for the co-registration of multi-temporal UAV image datasets. *Remote Sensing*, 8(9), 1–20.

Arciniegas, G.A., Bijker, W., Kerle, N., Tolpekin, V.A. (2007). Coherence- and amplitude-based analysis of seismogenic damage in Bam, Iran, using ENVISAT ASAR data. *IEEE Transactions on Geoscience and Remote Sensing*, 45(6), 1571–1581.

Atzori, S. (2013). Understanding earthquakes: The key role of radar images. *Nuclear Instruments and Methods in Physics Research, Section A: Accelerators, Spectrometers, Detectors and Associated Equipment*, 720, 178–181.

Atzori, S., Antonioli, A., Tolomei, C., De Novellis, V., De Luca, C., Monterroso, F. (2019). InSAR full-resolution analysis of the 2017–2018 M>6 earthquakes in Mexico. *Remote Sensing of Environment*, 234 (October), 111461.

Aydoner, C. and Maktav, D. (2009). The role of the integration of remote sensing and GIS in land use/land cover analysis after an earthquake. *International Journal of Remote Sensing*, 30(7), 1697–1717.

Bai, Y., Adriano, B., Mas, E., Koshimura, S. (2017a). Building damage assessment in the 2015 Gorkha, Nepal, earthquake using only post-event dual polarization synthetic aperture radar imagery. *Earthquake Spectra*, 33, 185–195.

Bai, Y., Adriano, B., Mas, E., Koshimura, S. (2017b). Machine learning based building damage mapping from the ALOS-2/PALSAR-2 SAR imagery: Case study of 2016 Kumamoto earthquake. *Journal of Disaster Research*, 12, 646–655.

Bai, Y., Gao, C., Singh, S., Koch, M., Adriano, B., Mas, E., Koshimura, S. (2018). A framework of rapid regional tsunami damage recognition from post-event terraSAR-X imagery using deep neural networks. *IEEE Geoscience and Remote Sensing Letters*, 15(1), 43–47.

Barazzetti, L. and Cuca, B. (2020). Identification of buildings damaged by natural hazards using very high-resolution satellite images: The case of earthquake in L'Aquila, Italy. In *Remote Sensing for Archaeology and Cultural Landscapes: Best Practices and Perspectives Across Europe and the Middle East*, Hadjimitsis, D.G., Themistocleous, K., Cuca, B., Agapiou, A., Lysandrou, V., Lasaponara, R., Masini, N., Schreier, G. (eds). Springer Nature, Cham.

Barazzetti, L., Brumana, R., Cuca, B., Previtali, M. (2015). Change detection from very high resolution satellite time series with variable off-nadir angle. *Proceedings of the Third International Conference on Remote Sensing and Geoinformation of the Environment (Rscy2015)*, March 16–19, Cyprus.

Bitelli, G., Camassi, R., Gusella, L., Mognol, A. (2004). Remote sensing imagery for damage assessment of buildings after destructive seismic events. In *Risk Analysis IV*, Brebbia, C. (ed.). WIT Press, Southampton.

Bovolo, F. and Bruzzone, L. (2015). The time variable in data fusion: A change detection perspective. *IEEE Geoscience and Remote Sensing Magazine*, 3(3), 8–26.

Brett, P.T.B. and Guida, R. (2013). Earthquake damage detection in urban areas using curvilinear features. *IEEE Transactions on Geoscience and Remote Sensing*, 51(9), 4877–4884.

Brunner, D., Lemoine, G., Bruzzone, L. (2010). Earthquake damage assessment of buildings using VHR optical and SAR imagery. *IEEE Transactions on Geoscience and Remote Sensing*, 48(5), 2403–2420.

Bucak, S.S., Jin, R., Jain, A.K. (2014). Multiple kernel learning for visual object recognition: A review. *IEEE Transactions on Pattern Analysis and Machine Intelligence*, 36(7), 1354–1369.

Chae, S.H., Lee, W.J., Baek, W.K., Jung, H.S. (2019). An improvement of the performance of SAR offset tracking approach to measure optimal surface displacements. *IEEE Access*, 7, 131627–131637.

Chang, W.Y., Wang, C.T., Chu, C.Y., Kao, J.R. (2012). Mapping geo-hazard by satellite radar interferometry. *Proceedings of the IEEE*, 100(10), 2835–2850.

Chen, Z. and Hutchinson, T.C. (2011). Structural damage detection using bi-temporal optical satellite images. *International Journal of Remote Sensing*, 32(17), 4973–4997.

Chen, S.W. and Sato, M. (2013). Tsunami damage investigation of built-up areas using multitemporal spaceborne full polarimetric SAR images. *IEEE Transactions on Geoscience and Remote Sensing*, 51(4), 1985–1997.

Chen, S.-W., Wang, X.-S., Xiao, S.-P. (2018a). Urban damage level mapping based on co-polarization coherence pattern using multitemporal polarimetric SAR data. *IEEE Journal of Selected Topics in Applied Earth Observations and Remote Sensing*, 11(8), 2657–2667.

Chen, C., Fu, J., Gai, Y., Li, J., Chen, L., Mantravadi, V.S., Tan, A. (2018b). Damaged bridges over water. *IEEE Geoscience and Remote Sensing Magazine*, 69–85.

Cheng, G. and Han, J.W. (2016). A survey on object detection in optical remote sensing images. *ISPRS Journal of Photogrammetry and Remote Sensing*, 117, 11–28.

Chini, M., Anniballe, R., Bignami, C., Pierdicca, N., Mori, S., Stramondo, S. (2015). Identification of building double-bounces feature in very high resolution SAR data for earthquake damage mapping. *Proceedings of the 2015 IEEE International Geoscience and Remote Sensing Symposium (IGARSS)*, Milan, Italy.

Contreras, D., Blaschke, T., Tiede, D., Jilge, M. (2016). Monitoring recovery after earthquakes through the integration of remote sensing, GIS, and ground observations: The case of L'Aquila (Italy). *Cartography and Geographic Information Science*, 43(2), 115–133.

Cossu, R., Dell'Acqua, F., Polli, D.A., Rogolino, G. (2012). SAR-based seismic damage assessment in urban areas: Scaling down resolution, scaling up computational performance. *IEEE Journal of Selected Topics in Applied Earth Observations and Remote Sensing*, 5(4), 1110–1117.

Costantini, M., Ferretti, A., Minati, F., Falco, S., Trillo, F., Colombo, D., Novali, F., Malvarosa, F., Mammone, C., Vecchioli, F., Rucci, A., Fumagalli, A., Allievi, J., Ciminelli, M.G., Costabile, S. (2017). Analysis of surface deformations over the whole Italian territory by interferometric processing of ERS, Envisat and COSMO-SkyMed radar data. *Remote Sensing of Environment*, 202, 250–275.

Dalla Mura, M., Prasad, S., Pacifici, F., Gamba, P., Chanussot, J., Benediktsson, J.A. (2015). Challenges and opportunities of multimodality and data fusion in remote sensing. *Proceedings of the IEEE*, 103(9), 1585–1601.

Dalla Via, G., Crosetto, M., Crippa, B. (2012). Resolving vertical and east-west horizontal motion from differential interferometric synthetic aperture radar: The L'Aquila earthquake. *Journal of Geophysical Research: Solid Earth*, 117(2), 1–14.

Dekker, R.J. (2011). High-resolution radar damage assessment after the earthquake in Haiti on 12 January 2010. *IEEE Journal of Selected Topics in Applied Earth Observations and Remote Sensing*, 4(4), 960–970.

Dell'Acqua, F. and Gamba, P. (2012). Remote sensing and earthquake damage assessment: Experiences, limits, and perspectives. *Proceedings of the IEEE*, 100(10), 2876–2890.

Dell'Acqua, F. and Polli, D.A. (2013). Post-event only VHR radar satellite data for automated damage assessment. *Photogrammetric Engineering & Remote Sensing*, 77(10), 1037–1043.

Dell'Acqua, F., Bignami, C., Chini, M., Stramondo, S., Lisini, G., Polli, D.A. (2011). Earthquake damages rapid mapping by satellite remote sensing data: L'Aquila April 6th, 2009 event. *IEEE Journal of Selected Topics in Applied Earth Observations and Remote Sensing*, 4(4), 935–943.

Dell'Acqua, F., Lanese, I., Polli, D.A. (2013). Integration of EO-based vulnerability estimation into EO-based seismic damage assessment: A case study on L'Aquila, Italy, 2009 earthquake. *Natural Hazards*, 68(1), 165–180.

Ding, M., Tian, Z., Jin, Z., Xu, M., Cao, C. (2010). Registration using robust kernel principal component for object-based change detection, *IEEE Geoscience and Remote Sensing Letters*, 7(4), 761–765.

Dong, L. and Shan, J. (2013). A comprehensive review of earthquake-induced building damage detection with remote sensing techniques. *ISPRS Journal of Photogrammetry and Remote Sensing*, 84, 85–99.

Dong, Y., Li, Q., Dou, A., Wang, X. (2011). Extracting damages caused by the 2008 Ms 8.0 Wenchuan earthquake from SAR remote sensing data. *Journal of Asian Earth Sciences*, 40(4), 907–914.

Dumitru, C.O., Cui, S., Faur, D., Datcu, M. (2015). Data analytics for rapid mapping: Case study of a flooding event in Germany and the Tsunami in Japan using very high resolution SAR images. *IEEE Journal of Selected Topics in Applied Earth Observations and Remote Sensing*, 8(1), 114–129.

Eguchi, R.T. and Mansouri, B. (2005). Use of remote sensing technologies for building damage assessment after the 2003 Bam, Iran, earthquake – Preface to remote sensing papers. *Earthquake Spectra*, 21(1), 207–212.

Erten, E. (2013). Glacier velocity estimation by means of a polarimetric similarity measure. *IEEE Transactions on Geoscience and Remote Sensing*, 51(6), 3319–3327.

Erten, E., Reigber, A., Hellwich, O. (2010). Generation of three-dimensional deformation maps from InSAR data using spectral diversity techniques. *ISPRS Journal of Photogrammetry and Remote Sensing*, 65(4), 388–394.

Erten, E., Taşkın, G., Lopez-Sanchez, J.M. (2019). Selection of PolSAR observables for crop biophysical variable estimation with global sensitivity analysis. *IEEE Geoscience and Remote Sensing Letters*, 16(5), 766–770.

Fielding, E.J., Talebian, M., Rosen, P.A., Nazari, H., Jackson, J.A., Ghorashi, M., Walker, R. (2005). Surface ruptures and building damage of the 2003 Bam, Iran, earthquake mapped by satellite synthetic aperture radar interferometric correlation. *Journal of Geophysical Research: Solid Earth*, 110(3), 1–15.

Fujiwara, S., Morishita, Y., Nakano, T., Kobayashi, T., Yarai, H. (2017). Non-tectonic liquefaction-induced large surface displacements in the Aso Valley, Japan, caused by the 2016 Kumamoto earthquake, revealed by ALOS-2 SAR. *Earth and Planetary Science Letters*, 474, 457–465.

Galar, M., Fernandez, A., Barrenechea, E., Bustince, H., Herrera, F. (2012). A review on ensembles for the class imbalance problem: Bagging-, boosting-, and hybrid-based approaches. *IEEE Transactions on Systems, Man and Cybernetics, Part C – Applications and Reviews*, 42(4), 463–484.

Gamba, P., Member, S., Acqua, F.D., Trianni, G., Member, S. (2007). Rapid damage detection in the Bam area using multitemporal SAR and exploiting ancillary data. *IEEE Transactions on Geoscience and Remote Sensing*, 45(6), 1582–1589.

Ge, P., Gokon, H., Meguro, K. (2019). Building damage assessment using intensity SAR data with different incidence angles and longtime interval. *Journal of Disaster Research*, 14(3), 456–465.

Ge, P., Gokon, H., Meguro, K. (2020). A review on synthetic aperture radar-based building damage assessment in disasters. *Remote Sensing of Environment*, 240(6), 111693.

Geib, C. and Taubenbock, H. (2013). Remote sensing contributing to assess earthquake risk: From a literature review towards a roadmap. *Natural Hazards*, 68(1), 7–48.

Ghaffarian, S., Kerle, N., Filatova, T. (2018). Remote sensing-based proxies for urban disaster risk management and resilience: A review. *Remote Sensing*, 10(11), 1760.

Gillespie, T.W., Chu, J., Frankenberg, E., Thomas, D. (2007). Assessment and prediction of natural hazards from satellite imagery. *Progress in Physical Geography*, 31(5), 459–470.

Gokon, H., Post, J., Stein, E., Martinis, S., Twele, A., Mueck, M., Geiss, C., Koshimura, S., Matsuoka, M. (2015). A method for detecting buildings destroyed by the 2011 Tohoku earthquake and tsunami using multitemporal TerraSAR-X data. *IEEE Geoscience and Remote Sensing Letters*, 12(6), 1277–1281.

Gomba, G., Rodriguez Gonzalez, F., De Zan, F. (2017). Ionospheric phase screen compensation for the Sentinel-1 TOPS and ALOS-2 ScanSAR modes. *IEEE Transactions on Geoscience and Remote Sensing*, 55(1), 223–235.

Gómez-Chova, L., Amorós-López, J., Mateo-García, G., Muñoz-Marí, J., Camps-Valls, G. (2017). Cloud masking and removal in remote sensing image time series. *Journal of Applied Remote Sensing*, 11(1), 015005.

Grünthal, G., MUsson, R., Schwarz, J., Stucchi, M. (1998). *European Macroseismic Scale 1998: EMS-98*. GFZ German Research Centre for Geosciences, Potsdam.

Guo, H.X., Li, Y.J., Shang, J., Gu, M.Y., Huang, Y.Y., Bing, G. (2017). Learning from class-imbalanced data: Review of methods and applications. *Expert Systems with Applications*, 73, 220–239.

Hajeb, M., Karimzadeh, S., Fallahi, A. (2020). Seismic damage assessment in Sarpole-Zahab town (Iran) using synthetic aperture radar (SAR) images and texture analysis. *Natural Hazards*, 103, 347–366.

Haralick, R.M., Shanmugam, K., Dinstein, I. (1973). Textural features for image classification. *IEEE Transactions on Systems, Man, and Cybernetics*, SMC-3(6), 610–621.

Haralick, R.M., Sternberg, S.R., Zhuang, X. (1987). Image analysis using mathematical morphology. *IEEE Transactions on Pattern Analysis and Machine Intelligence*, 9(4), 532–550.

Hashimoto, M., Enomoto, M., Fukushima, Y. (2010). Coseismic deformation from the 2008 Wenchuan, China, earthquake derived from ALOS/PALSAR images. *Tectonophysics*, 491(1), 59–71.

He, P., Ding, K., Xu, C. (2018a). The 2016 Mw 6.7 Aketao earthquake in Muji range, northern Pamir: Rupture on a strike-slip fault constrained by Sentinel-1 radar interferometry and GPS. *International Journal of Applied Earth Observation and Geoinformation*, 73, 99–106.

He, P., Hetland, E.A., Niemi, N.A., Wang, Q., Wen, Y., Ding, K. (2018b). The 2016 Mw 6.5 Nura earthquake in the Trans Alai range, northern Pamir: Possible rupture on a back-thrust fault constrained by Sentinel-1A radar interferometry. *Tectonophysics*, 749, 62–71.

He, P., Wen, Y., Xu, C., Chen, Y. (2019a). High-quality three-dimensional displacement fields from new-generation SAR imagery: Application to the 2017 Ezgeleh, Iran, earthquake. *Journal of Geodesy*, 93(4), 573–591.

He, L., Feng, G., Li, Z., Feng, Z., Gao, H., Wu, X. (2019b). Source parameters and slip distribution of the 2018 Mw 7.5 Palu, Indonesia earthquake estimated from space-based geodesy. *Tectonophysics*, 772, 228216.

He, P., Wen, Y., Xu, C., Chen, Y. (2019c). Complete three-dimensional near-field surface displacements from imaging geodesy techniques applied to the 2016 Kumamoto earthquake. *Remote Sensing of Environment*, 232(9), 111321.

Hoffmann, J. (2007). Mapping damage during the Bam (Iran) earthquake using interferometric coherence. *International Journal of Remote Sensing*, 28(6), 1199–1216.

Hu, B., Li, H., Zhang, X., Fang, L. (2020). Oil and gas mining deformation monitoring and assessments of disaster: Using interferometric synthetic aperture radar technology. *IEEE Geoscience and Remote Sensing Magazine*, 8(2), 108–134.

Huang, H., Sun, G., Zhang, X., Hao, Y., Zhang, A., Ren, J., Ma, H. (2019). Combined multiscale segmentation convolutional neural network for rapid damage mapping from postearthquake very high-resolution images. *Journal of Applied Remote Sensing*, 13(2), 1–14.

Huyck, C.K., Adams, B.J., Cho, S., Chung, H.C., Eguchi, R.T. (2005). Towards rapid citywide damage mapping using neighborhood edge dissimilarities in very high-resolution optical satellite imagery – Application to the 2003 Bam, Iran, earthquake. *Earthquake Spectra*, 21(1), 255–266.

Huyck, C., Verrucci, E., Bevington, J. (2014). Remote sensing for disaster response: A rapid, image-based perspective. In *Earthquake Hazard, Risk and Disasters*, Shroder, J.F. and Wyss, M. (eds). Academic Press, Boston, MA.

Janalipour, M. and Mohammadzadeh, A. (2016). Building damage detection using object-based image analysis and ANFIS from high-resolution image (case study: BAM earthquake, Iran). *IEEE Journal of Selected Topics in Applied Earth Observations and Remote Sensing*, 9(5), 1937–1945.

Janalipour, M. and Mohammadzadeh, A. (2017). A fuzzy-GA based decision making system for detecting damaged buildings from high-spatial resolution optical images. *Remote Sensing*, 9(4), 349.

Janalipour, M. and Taleai, M. (2017). Building change detection after earthquake using multi-criteria decision analysis based on extracted information from high spatial resolution satellite images. *International Journal of Remote Sensing*, 38(1), 82–99.

Jiang, X., He, Y., Li, G., Liu, Y., Zhang, X. (2020). Building damage detection via superpixel-based belief fusion of space-borne SAR and optical images. *IEEE Sensors Journal*, 20(4), 2008–2022.

Joyce, K.E., Belliss, S.E., Samsonov, S.V., McNeill, S.J., Glassey, P.J. (2009). A review of the status of satellite remote sensing and image processing techniques for mapping natural hazards and disasters. *Progress in Physical Geography*, 33(2), 183–207.

Jung, H.S., Lu, Z., Zhang, L. (2013). Feasibility of along-track displacement measurement from Sentinel-1 interferometric wide-swath mode. *IEEE Transactions on Geoscience and Remote Sensing*, 51(1), 573–578.

Karimzadeh, S. and Mastuoka, M. (2017). Building damage assessment using multisensor dual-polarized synthetic aperture radar data for the 2016 M 6.2 Amatrice earthquake, Italy. *Remote Sensing*, 35(5), 429–434.

Karimzadeh, S. and Matsuoka, M. (2018). Building damage characterization for the 2016 Amatrice earthquake using ascending-descending COSMO-SkyMed data and topographic position index. *IEEE Journal of Selected Topics in Applied Earth Observations and Remote Sensing*, 11(8), 2668–2682.

Karpatne, A., Jiang, Z., Vatsavai, R.R., Shekhar, S., Kumar, V. (2016). Monitoring land-cover changes: A machine-learning perspective. *IEEE Geoscience and Remote Sensing Magazine*, 4(2), 8–21.

Kerle, N. (2016). Disasters: Risk assessment, management, and post-disaster studies using remote sensing. In *Remote Sensing of Water Resources, Disasters, and Urban Studies*, Thenkabail, P.S. (ed.). CRC Press, Boca Raton, FL.

Kimura, H. (2008). Radar polarization orientation shifts in built-up areas. *IEEE Geoscience and Remote Sensing Letters*, 5(2), 217–221.

Kushiyama, Y. and Matsuoka, M. (2019). Time series GIS map dataset of demolished buildings in Mashiki town after the 2016 Kumamoto, Japan earthquake. *Remote Sensing*, 11(19), 2190.

Kwak, Y., Yorozuya, A., Iwami, Y. (2016). Disaster risk reduction using image fusion of optical and SAR data before and after tsunami. *Proceedings of the 2016 IEEE Aerospace*, March 5–12, Big Sky, Montana.

Li, P., Xu, H., Liu, S., Guo, J. (2009). Urban building damage detection from very high resolution imagery using one-class SVM and spatial relations. *International Geoscience and Remote Sensing Symposium (IGARSS)*, 5, V–112–V–114.

Li, X., Guo, H., Zhang, L., Chen, X., Liang, L. (2012). A new approach to collapsed building extraction using RADARSAT-2 polarimetric SAR imagery. *IEEE Geoscience and Remote Sensing Letters*, 9(4), 677–681.

Li, Q., Gong, L., Zhang, J. (2019). A correlation change detection method integrating PCA and multi-texture features of SAR image for building damage detection. *European Journal of Remote Sensing*, 52(1), 435–447.

Li, B., Li, Y., Jiang, W., Su, Z., Shen, W. (2020). Conjugate ruptures and seismotectonic implications of the 2019 Mindanao earthquake sequence inferred from Sentinel-1 InSAR data. *International Journal of Applied Earth Observation and Geoinformation*, 90, 102127.

Liang, C., Fielding, E.J., Huang, M.H. (2017). Estimating Azimuth offset with double-difference interferometric phase: The effect of Azimuth FM rate error in focusing. *IEEE Transactions on Geoscience and Remote Sensing*, 55(12), 7018–7031.

Liao, W., Chanussot, J., Dalla Mura, M., Huang, X., Bellens, R., Gautama, S., Philips, W. (2017). Taking optimal advantage of fine spatial resolution: Promoting partial image reconstruction for the morphological analysis of very-high-resolution images. *IEEE Geoscience and Remote Sensing Magazine*, 5(2), 8–28.

Liu, J. and Li, P. (2019). Extraction of earthquake-induced collapsed buildings from bi-temporal VHR images using object-level homogeneity index and histogram. *IEEE Journal of Selected Topics in Applied Earth Observations and Remote Sensing*, 12(8), 2755–2770.

Liu, B., Zhang, J., Luo, Y., Jiang, W., Chen, X., Li, Y. (2014). Error propagation analysis in three-dimensional coseismic displacement inversion, *IEEE Geoscience and Remote Sensing Letters*, 11(11), 1971–1975.

Lo, Y.C., Yue, H., Sun, J., Zhao, L., Li, M. (2019). The 2018 Mw6.4 Hualien earthquake: Dynamic slip partitioning reveals the spatial transition from mountain building to subduction. *Earth and Planetary Science Letters*, 524, 115729.

Lu, C.-H., Ni, C.-F., Chang, C.-P., Yen, J.-Y., Chuang, R. (2018). Coherence difference analysis of Sentinel-1 SAR interferogram to identify earthquake-induced disasters in urban areas. *Remote Sensing*, 10(8), 1318.

Lu, C.-H., Lin, Y.-S., Chuang, R.Y. (2021). Pixel offset fusion of SAR and optical images for 3-D coseismic surface deformation. *IEEE Geoscience and Remote Sensing Letters*, 18(6), 1049–1053.

Lubis, A.M. and Isezaki, N. (2009). Shoreline changes and vertical displacement of the 2 April 2007 Solomon Islands earthquake Mw 8.1 revealed by ALOS PALSAR images. *Physics and Chemistry of the Earth*, 34(6–7), 409–415.

Ma, Y., Chen, F., Liu, J.B., He, Y., Duan, J.B., Li, X.P. (2016). An automatic procedure for early disaster change mapping based on optical remote sensing. *Remote Sensing*, 8(4), 272.

Ma, L., Li, M.C., Ma, X.X., Cheng, L., Du, P.J., Liu, Y.X. (2017). A review of supervised object-based land-cover image classification. *ISPRS Journal of Photogrammetry and Remote Sensing*, 130, 277–293.

Manfré, L.A., Hirata, E., Silva, J.B., Shinohara, E.J., Giannotti, M.A., Larocca, A.P.C., Quintanilha, J.A. (2012). An analysis of geospatial technologies for risk and natural disaster management. *ISPRS International Journal of Geo-Information*, 1(2), 166–185.

Mansouri, B. and Hamednia, Y. (2015). A soft computing method for damage mapping using VHR optical satellite imagery. *IEEE Journal of Selected Topics in Applied Earth Observations and Remote Sensing*, 8(10), 4935–4941.

Marin, C., Bovolo, F., Bruzzone, L. (2015). Building change detection in multitemporal very high resolution SAR images. *IEEE Transactions on Geoscience and Remote Sensing*, 53(5), 2664–2682.

Massonnet, D., Rossi, M., Carmona, C., Adragna, F., Peltzer, G., Feigl, K., Rabaute, T. (1993). The displacement field of the Landers earthquake mapped by radar interferometry. *Nature*, 364(6433). 138–142.

Matsuoka, M. and Yamazaki, F. (2004). Use of satellite SAR intensity imagery for detecting building areas damaged due to earthquakes. *Earthquake Spectra*, 20(3), 975–994.

Mercier, G., Moser, G., Serpico, S.B. (2008). Conditional copulas for change detection in heterogeneous remote sensing images. *IEEE Transactions on Geoscience and Remote Sensing*, 46(5), 1428–1441.

Monterroso, F., De Luca, C., Bonano, M., Lanari, R., Manunta, M., Manzo, M., Zinno, I., Casu, F. (2018). Automatic generation of co-seismic displacement maps by using Sentinel-1 interferometric SAR data. *Procedia Computer Science*, 138, 332–337.

Moya, L., Zakeri, H., Yamazaki, F., Liu, W., Mas, E., Koshimura, S. (2019). 3D gray level co-occurrence matrix and its application to identifying collapsed buildings. *ISPRS Journal of Photogrammetry and Remote Sensing*, 149, 14–28.

Natsuaki, R., Nagai, H., Tomii, N., Tadono, T. (2018). Sensitivity and limitation in damage detection for individual buildings using InSAR coherence: A case study in 2016 Kumamoto earthquakes. *Remote Sensing*, 10(2), 245.

Nex, F., Duarte, D., Tonolo, F.G., Kerle, N. (2019). Structural building damage detection with deep learning: Assessment of a state-of-the-art CNN in operational conditions. *Remote Sensing*, 11(23), 2765.

Niu, X., Tang, H., Wu, L. (2018). Satellite scheduling of large areal tasks for rapid response to natural disaster using a multi-objective genetic algorithm. *International Journal of Disaster Risk Reduction*, 28, 813–825.

Olen, S. and Bookhagen, B. (2018). Mapping damage-affected areas after natural hazard events using Sentinel-1 coherence time series. *Remote Sensing*, 10(8), 1272.

Pan, G. and Tang, D.L. (2010). Damage information derived from multi-sensor data of the Wenchuan earthquake of May 2008. *International Journal of Remote Sensing*, 31(13), 3509–3519.

Parape, C.D. and Tamura, M. (2011). Identifying damaged buildings from high-resolution satellite imagery in hazardous areas using morphological operators. *Proceedings of the 2011 IEEE International Geoscience and Remote Sensing Symposium (IGARSS)*, Vancouver, Canada.

Park, S.E. and Jung, Y.T. (2020). Detection of earthquake-induced building damages using polarimetric SAR data. *Remote Sensing*, 12(1), 137.

Park, S.E., Yamaguchi, Y., Jin Kim, D. (2013). Polarimetric SAR remote sensing of the 2011 Tohoku earthquake using ALOS/PALSAR. *Remote Sensing of Environment*, 132, 212–220.

Pesaresi, M. and Benediktsson, J.A. (2001). A new approach for the morphological segmentation of high-resolution satellite imagery. *IEEE Transactions on Geoscience and Remote Sensing*, 39(2), 309–320.

Pesaresi, M., Gerhardinger, A., Haag, F. (2007). Rapid damage assessment of built-up structures using VHR satellite data in tsunami-affected areas. *International Journal of Remote Sensing*, 28(13–14), 3013–3036.

Plank, S. (2014). Rapid damage assessment by means of multi-temporal SAR: A comprehensive review and outlook to Sentinel-1. *Remote Sensing*, 6, 4870–4906.

Polcari, M., Fernández, J., Albano, M., Bignami, C., Palano, M., Stramondo, S. (2017). An improved data integration algorithm to constrain the 3D displacement field induced by fast deformation phenomena tested on the Napa Valley earthquake. *Computers and Geosciences*, 109, 206–215.

Prasad, S., Bruce, L., Chanussot, J. (2011). *Optical Remote Sensing: Advances in Signal Processing and Exploitation Techniques*, Springer, Berlin, Heidelberg.

Radke, R.J., Andra, S., Al-Kofahi, O., Roysam, B. (2005). Image change detection algorithms: A systematic survey. *IEEE Transactions on Image Processing*, 14(3), 294–307.

Rahman, M.T. (2017). Applications of active remote sensing technologies for natural disaster damage assessments. In *Remote Sensing Techniques and GIS Applications in Earth and Environmental Studies*, Santra, A. and Santra Mitra, S. (eds). IGI Global, Hershey, PA.

Rastiveis, H., Samadzadegan, F., Reinartz, P. (2013). A fuzzy decision making system for building damage map creation using high resolution satellite imagery. *Natural Hazards and Earth System Sciences*, 13(2), 455–472.

Rathje, E.M., Woo, K.S., Crawford, M., Neuenschwander, A. (2005a). Earthquake damage identification using multi-temporal high-resolution optical satellite imagery. *International Geoscience and Remote Sensing Symposium (IGARSS)*, 7, 5045–5048.

Rathje, E.M., Crawford, M., Woo, K., Neuenschwander, A. (2005b). Damage patterns from satellite images of the 2003 Bam, Iran, earthquake. *Earthquake Spectra*, 21, 295–307.

Reba, M. and Seto, K.C. (2020). A systematic review and assessment of algorithms to detect, characterize, and monitor urban land change. *Remote Sensing of Environment*, 242, 111739.

Rejaie, A. and Shinozuka, M. (2004). Reconnaissance of Golcuk 1999 earthquake damage using satellite images. *Journal of Aerospace Engineering*, 17(1), 20–25.

Rezaeian, M. (2010). Assessment of earthquake damages by image-based techniques. PhD Thesis, ETH Zurich Institute of Geodesy and Photogrammetry, Switzerland.

Romaniello, V., Piscini, A., Bignami, C., Anniballe, R., Stramondo, S. (2017). Earthquake damage mapping by using remotely sensed data: The Haiti case study. *Journal of Applied Remote Sensing*, 11(1), 016042.

Rubner, Y., Puzicha, J., Tomasi, C., Buhmann, J.M. (2001). Empirical evaluation of dissimilarity measures for use in urban structural damage detection. *Remote Sensing*, 11(4), 2347–2350.

Saha, S., Member, G.S., Bovolo, F., Member, S., Bruzzone, L. (2021). Building change detection in VHR SAR images via unsupervised deep transcoding. *IEEE Transactions on Geoscience and Remote Sensing*, 59(3), 917–1929.

Salentinig, A. and Gamba, P. (2015). Combining SAR-based and Multispectral-based extractions to map urban areas at multiple spatial resolutions. *IEEE Geoscience and Remote Sensing Magazine*, 3(3), 100–112.

Sansosti, E., Berardino, P., Bonano, M., Calò, F., Castaldo, R., Casu, F., Manunta, M., Manzo, M., Pepe, A., Pepe, S., Solaro, G., Tizzani, P., Zeni, G., Lanari, R. (2014). How second generation SAR systems are impacting the analysis of ground deformation. *International Journal of Applied Earth Observation and Geoinformation*, 28(1), 1–11.

Sato, M., Chen, S., Satake, M. (2012). Polarimetric sar analysis of tsunami damage following the March 11, 2011 East Japan earthquake. *Proceedings of the IEEE*, 100(10), 2861–2875.

Schmitt, M. and Zhu, X.X. (2016). Data fusion and remote sensing: An ever-growing relationship. *IEEE Geoscience and Remote Sensing Magazine*, 4(4), 6–23.

Schweier, C. and Markus, M. (2006). Classification of collapsed buildings for fast damage and loss assessment. *Bulletin of Earthquake Engineering*, 4(2), 177–192.

Shah-Hosseini, R., Safari, A., Homayouni, S. (2017). Natural hazard damage detection based on object-level support vector data description of optical and SAR Earth observations. *International Journal of Remote Sensing*, 38(11), 3356–3374.

Sharma, R.C., Tateishi, R., Hara, K., Nguyen, H.T., Gharechelou, S., Nguyen, L.V. (2017). Earthquake damage visualization (EDV) technique for the rapid detection of earthquake-induced damages using SAR data. *Sensors (Switzerland)*, 17(2), 235.

Sharma, K., Saraf, A.K., Das, J., Baral, S.S., Borgohain, S., Singh, G. (2018). Mapping and change detection study of Nepal-2015 earthquake induced Landslides. *Journal of the Indian Society of Remote Sensing*, 46(4), 605–615.

Shi, X. and Jiang, J. (2016). Automatic registration method for optical remote sensing images with large background variations using line segments. *Remote Sensing*, 8(5), 426.

Sofina, N. and Ehlers, M. (2016). Building change detection using high resolution remotely sensed data and GIS. *IEEE Journal of Selected Topics in Applied Earth Observations and Remote Sensing*, 9(8), 3430–3438.

Song, D., Tan, X., Wang, B., Zhang, L., Shan, X., Cui, J. (2020). Integration of super-pixel segmentation and deep-learning methods for evaluating earthquake-damaged buildings using single-phase remote sensing imagery. *International Journal of Remote Sensing*, 41(3), 1040–1066.

Stramondo, S., Tesauro, M., Briole, P., Sansosti, E., Salvi, S., Lanari, R., Anzidei, M., Baldi, P., Fornaro, G., Avallone, A., Buongiorno, M.F., Franceschetti, G., Boschi, E. (1999). The September 26, 1997 Colfiorito, Italy, earthquakes: Modeled coseismic surface displacement from SAR interferometry and GPS. *Geophysical Research Letters*, 26(7), 883–886.

Stramondo, S., Bignami, C., Chini, M., Pierdicca, N., Tertulliani, A. (2006). Satellite radar and optical remote sensing for earthquake damage detection: Results from different case studies. *International Journal of Remote Sensing*, 27(20), 4433–4447.

Sublime, J. and Kalinicheva, E. (2019). Automatic post-disaster damage mapping using deep-learning techniques for change detection: Case study of the Tohoku tsunami. *Remote Sensing*, 11(9), 1123.

Sun, W. and Du, Q. (2019). Hyperspectral band selection: A review. *IEEE Geoscience and Remote Sensing Magazine*, 7(2), 118–139.

Tamkuan, N. and Nagai, M. (2017). Fusion of multi-temporal interferometric coherence and optical image data for the 2016 Kumamoto earthquake damage assessment. *ISPRS International Journal of Geo-Information*, 6(7), 188.

Tang, C., Tanyas, H., van Westen, C.J., Tang, C., Fan, X., Jetten, V.G. (2019). Analysing post-earthquake mass movement volume dynamics with multi-source DEMs. *Engineering Geology*, 248, 89–101.

Taşkın, G. and Ceylan, O. (2019). An adaptive affinity matrix optimization for locality preserving projection via heuristic methods for hyperspectral image analysis. *IEEE Journal of Selected Topics in Applied Earth Observations and Remote Sensing*, 12(12), 4690–4697.

Taşkın, G. and Crawford, M.M. (2019). An out-of-sample extension to manifold learning via meta-modelling. *IEEE Transactions on Image Processing*, 28(10), 1–1.

Taşkın, G., Musaoglu, N., Ersoy, O. (2011). Damage assessment of 2010 Haiti earthquake with post-earthquake satellite image by support vector selection and adaptation. *Photogrammetric Engineering and Remote Sensing*, 10, 1025–1035.

Taşkın, G., Ersoy, O., Kamasak, M. (2015). Earthquake-induced damage classification from postearthquake satellite image using spectral and spatial features with support vector selection and adaptation. *Journal of Applied Remote Sensing*, 9(1), 096017.

Taşkın, G., Hüseyin, K., Bruzzone, L. (2017). Feature selection based on high dimensional model representation for hyperspectral images. *IEEE Transactions on Image Processing*, 26(6), 2918–2928.

Timo, B. and Liao, M. (2010). Building-damage detection using post-seismic high-resolution SAR satellite data. *International Journal of Remote Sensing*, 31(13), 3369–3391.

Tomowski, D., Klonus, S., Ehlers, M., Michel, U., Reinartz, P. (2010). Change visualization through a texture-based analysis approach for disaster applications. *ISPRS Proceedings*, pp. 1–6.

Tong, X., Hong, Z., Liu, S., Zhang, X., Xie, H., Li, Z., Yang, S., Wang, W., Bao, F. (2012). Building-damage detection using pre- and post-seismic high-resolution satellite stereo imagery: A case study of the May 2008 Wenchuan earthquake. *ISPRS Journal of Photogrammetry and Remote Sensing*, 68(1), 13–27.

Tralli, D.M., Blom, R.G., Zlotnicki, V., Donnellan, A., Evans, D.L. (2005). Satellite remote sensing of earthquake, volcano, flood, landslide and coastal inundation hazards. *ISPRS Journal of Photogrammetry and Remote Sensing*, 59(4), 185–198.

Trianni, G. and Gamba, P. (2009). Fast damage mapping in case of earthquakes using multitemporal SAR data. *Journal of Real-Time Image Processing*, 4(3), 195–203.

Tronin, A.A. (2006). Remote sensing and earthquakes: A review. *Physics and Chemistry of the Earth, Parts A/B/C*, 31(4), 138–142.

Tronin, A.A. (2010). Satellite remote sensing in seismology: A review. *Remote Sensing*, 2(1), 124–150.

Ullo, S.L., Addabbo, P., Martire, D.D., Sica, S., Fiscante, N., Cicala, L., Angelino, C.V. (2019). Application of DInSAR technique to high coherence Sentinel-1 images for dam monitoring and result validation through in situ measurements. *IEEE Journal of Selected Topics in Applied Earth Observations and Remote Sensing*, 12(3), 875–890.

Voigt, S., Schneiderhan, T., Twele, A., Gaehler, M., Stein, E., Mehl, H. (2011). Rapid damage assessment and situation mapping: Learning from the 2010 Haiti earthquake. *Photogrammetric Engineering and Remote Sensing*, 77(9), 923–931.

Vu, T.T. and Ban, Y. (2010). Context-based mapping of damaged buildings from high-resolution optical satellite images. *International Journal of Remote Sensing*, 31(13), 3411–3425.

Wang, T.L. and Jin, Y.Q. (2012). Postearthquake building damage assessment using multi-mutual information from pre-event optical image and postevent SAR image. *IEEE Geoscience and Remote Sensing Letters*, 9(3), 452–456.

Wang, X. and Li, P. (2015). Extraction of earthquake-induced collapsed buildings using very high-resolution imagery and airborne LiDAR data. *International Journal of Remote Sensing*, 36(8), 2163–2183.

Wang, Y. and Li, M. (2019). Urban impervious surface detection from remote sensing images: A review of the methods and challenges. *IEEE Geoscience and Remote Sensing Magazine*, 7(3), 64–93.

Wang, X. and Li, P. (2020). Extraction of urban building damage using spectral, height and corner information from VHR satellite images and airborne LiDAR data. *ISPRS Journal of Photogrammetry and Remote Sensing*, 159(November 2019), 322–336.

Watanabe, M., Motohka, T., Miyagi, Y., Yonezawa, C., Shimada, M. (2012). Analysis of urban areas affected by the 2011 off the Pacific coast of Tohoku earthquake and tsunami with L-Band SAR full-polarimetric mode. *IEEE Geoscience and Remote Sensing Letters*, 9(3), 472–476.

Watanabe, M., Thapa, R.B., Ohsumi, T., Fujiwara, H., Yonezawa, C., Tomii, N., Suzuki, S. (2016). Detection of damaged urban areas using interferometric SAR coherence change with PALSAR-2. *Earth, Planets and Space*, 68(1).

Wegscheider, S., Schneiderhan, T., Mager, A., Zwenzner, H., Post, J., Strunz, G. (2013). Rapid mapping in support of emergency response after earthquake events. *Natural Hazards*, 68(1), 181–195.

Wei, D. and Yang, W. (2020). Detecting damaged buildings using a texture feature contribution index from post-earthquake remote sensing images. *Remote Sensing Letters*, 11(2), 127–136.

Weston, J., Ferreira, A.M., Funning, G.J. (2012). Systematic comparisons of earthquake source models determined using InSAR and seismic data. *Tectonophysics*, 532–535, 61–81.

Wieland, M., Liu, W., Yamazaki, F. (2016). Learning change from synthetic aperture radar images: Performance evaluation of a support vector machine to detect earthquake and tsunami-induced changes. *Remote Sensing*, 8(10), 792.

Wu, F., Gong, L., Wang, C., Zhang, H., Zhang, B., Xie, L. (2016). Signature analysis of building damage with Terra SAR-X new staring SpotLight mode data. *IEEE Geoscience and Remote Sensing Letters*, 13(11), 1696–1700.

Xia, Y. (2010). *Sciences of Geodesy I: Advances and Future Directions*, Springer-Verlag, Berlin, Heidelberg.

Xue, F., Lv, X., Dou, F., Yun, Y. (2020). A review of time series interferometric SAR techniques: A tutorial for surface deformation analysis, *IEEE Geoscience and Remote Sensing Magazine*, 8(1), 22–42.

Yague-Martinez, N., Eineder, M., Cong, X.Y., Minet, C. (2012). Ground displacement measurement by terraSAR-X image correlation: The 2011 Tohoku-Oki earthquake. *IEEE Geoscience and Remote Sensing Letters*, 9(4), 539–543.

Yamaguchi, Y. (2012). Disaster monitoring by fully polarimetric SAR data acquired with ALOS-PALSAR. *Proceedings of the IEEE*, 100(10), 2851–2860.

Yamazaki, F., Yano, Y., Matsuoka, M. (2005). Visual damage interpretation of buildings in Bam city using quickbird images following the 2003 Bam, Iran, earthquake. *Earthquake Spectra*, 21(S1), 329–336.

Yamazaki, F., Bahri, R., Liu, W., Sasagawa, T. (2016). Damage extraction of buildings in the 2015 Gorkha, Nepal earthquake from high-resolution SAR data. *Land Surface and Cryosphere Remote Sensing III*, 9877.

Yamazaki, F., Moya, L., Liu, W. (2017). Use of multitemporal LiDAR data to extract changes due to the 2016 Kumamoto earthquake. In *Remote Sensing Technologies and Applications in Urban Environments II*, Erbertseder, T., Chrysoulakis, N., Zhang, Y., Heldens, W. (eds). SPIE, Bellingham, WA.

Yokoya, N. (2013). Hyperspectral and multispectral data fusion mission. *IEEE Geoscience and Remote Sensing Magazine*, 4086–4089.

Yonezawa, C. and Takeuchi, S. (2001). Decorrelation of SAR data by urban damages caused by the 1995 Hyogoken-Nanbu earthquake. *International Journal of Remote Sensing*, 22(8), 1585–1600.

Yusuf, Y., Matsuoka, M., Yamazaki, F. (2001). Damage assessment after 2001 Gujarat earthquake using Landsat-7 satellite images. *Journal of the Indian Society of Remote Sensing*, 29(1–2), 17–22.

Zhai, W. and Huang, C. (2016). Fast building damage mapping using a single post-earthquake PolSAR image: A case study of the 2010 Yushu earthquake. *Earth Planets and Space*, 68(1), 1–12.

Zhang, Z., Tian, Z., Ding, M., Basu, A. (2013). Improved robust kernel subspace for object-based registration and change detection. *IEEE Geoscience and Remote Sensing Letters*, 10(4), 791–795.

Zhang, L., Xia, G.S., Wu, T., Lin, L., Tai, X.C. (2016a). Deep learning for remote sensing data. *IEEE Geoscience and Remote Sensing Magazine*, 4(2), 22–40.

Zhang, B., Ding, X., Zhu, W., Wang, C., Zhang, L., Liu, Z. (2016b). Mitigating ionospheric artifacts in coseismic interferogram based on offset field derived from ALOS-PALSAR data. *IEEE Journal of Selected Topics in Applied Earth Observations and Remote Sensing*, 9(7), 3050–3059.

Zhu, X.X., Tuia, D., Mou, L., Xia, G., Zhang, L., Xu, F., Fraundorfer, F. (2017). Deep learning in remote sensing: A comprehensive review and list of resources. *IEEE Geoscience and Remote Sensing Magazine*, 5(4), 8–36.

6

Multiclass Multilabel Change of State Transfer Learning from Image Time Series

Abdourrahmane M. ATTO, Héla HADHRI,
Flavien VERNIER and Emmanuel TROUVÉ

University Savoie Mont Blanc, Annecy, France

6.1. Introduction

During the past decade, automated and remotely controlled imaging systems have allowed the acquisition of image time series describing the dynamics of huge semi-rigid Earth surface features such as glaciers, ice sheets, volcanoes, etc. In the same decade, deep learning algorithms were designed in a wide range of frameworks to solve classification issues for small objects encountered in everyday life. In this chapter, we will consider transferring some of the most relevant among the above frameworks for a specific spatio-temporal change of state analysis. We will consider as a case study image time series observations associated with the Argentière glacier. Glaciers pertain to the Earth's surface cryosphere features which can contribute to assessing climate variation, not only at a local scale, but also at a global scale. Glacier shrinkage for instance is recognized as a high-confident climate indicator, and glaciers are now labeled as an "Essential Climate Variable" (Bojinski *et al.* 2014). The analysis of the evolution of glaciers over time is necessary to better understand their dynamics in terms of geomorphology, deformation and displacements.

Change Detection and Image Time Series Analysis 2,
coordinated by Abdourrahmane M. ATTO, Francesca BOVOLO and Lorenzo BRUZZONE.
© ISTE Ltd 2021.

Figure 6.1. *Argentière glacier: arrows reported on the glacier indicate its displacement direction. For a color version of this figure, see www.iste.co.uk/atto/change2.zip*

Optical proximal[1] imaging is a favorite acquisition system for fine observation of spatio-temporal variations by using time-lapse. Nevertheless, it suffers from a great dependence on the acquisition conditions and therefore requires favorable conditions or special pre-processing to allow the derivation of geophysical measures. For instance, in the Argentière glacier case study, the limitations observed can be summarized in terms of two types of occultation for:

– the scene: presence of fresh or melted snow, clouds on the area of interest, variable shadowing effects caused by differential scene illumination or the local climate variability;

– the camera: presence of humidity or water droplets on the camera lens, different movements due to wind or thermal variability.

---

1. Proximal: this term must be understood in the relative sense because, to observe entirely a large object by using a single camera, the latter must be placed far enough away: a few hundred meters in observation of objects on the Earth's surface.

Pre-processing to analyze observability conditions and glacier states is therefore a necessary task (Hadhri *et al.* 2019) that conditions the derivation of precise physical measures such as the velocity or acceleration of a glacier. The chapter focuses on this pre-processing step and proposes an evaluation benchmark for selecting the best relevant deep convolutional neural network (CNN) in terms of generalization property with respect to a transfer learning dedicated to glacier surface change of state analysis.

The chapter is organized as follows. Section 6.2 presents a coarse- to fine-grained change of state dataset associated with the Argentière glacier observed by several ground-based cameras during the period 2016–2020. This dataset is made up of images with descriptible semantics in the sense of identifiable geophysical and perceptual properties over the observed glacier area. Section 6.3 presents a library of deep learning networks and compares their main characteristics. Section 6.4 is associated with coarse- and fine-grained evaluation of this deep learning library for change of state analysis, including sensitivity to training hyperparameters. The fine-grained decision issue will be formulated in terms of interacting disturbances (class refinements). This will allow us to effectively evaluate the capability of deep learning frameworks to capture the low- to high-level coarse- to fine-grained semantics of visual change of states.

6.2. Coarse- to fine-grained change of state dataset

We consider three experiments in the following.

Experiment#1 is a binary decision problem: its goal is to determine if a given glacier image $\mathcal{I}_k = \mathcal{I}(t_k)$ is sufficiently *vivid* (textured, sharp and interference-free, except at the image edges). The output classes corresponding to this experiment are called, respectively:

– State#1-Vivid; see examples given in Figure 6.2; and

– State#2-Interference; see for instance Figures 6.3, 6.4, 6.5 and 6.6.

The vivid State#1 corresponds to glacier image acquisition in excellent visibility conditions. State#2 corresponds to any type of undesirable interference impacting the visibility of the surface of interest (glacier and its surrounding areas). These interferences include disturbances due to condensation, different shadowing effects or the presence of snow on the surface of interest. The dataset corresponding to Experiment#1 is described in Table 6.1.

Note that Experiment#1 is designed as a monolabel classification issue since the output label cannot be a mixture between states.

Figure 6.2. *State#1-Vivid examples of the Argentière glacier. For a color version of this figure, see www.iste.co.uk/atto/change2.zip*

Figure 6.3. *State#2-Interference[Condensation] examples of the Argentière glacier. For a color version of this figure, see www.iste.co.uk/atto/change2.zip*

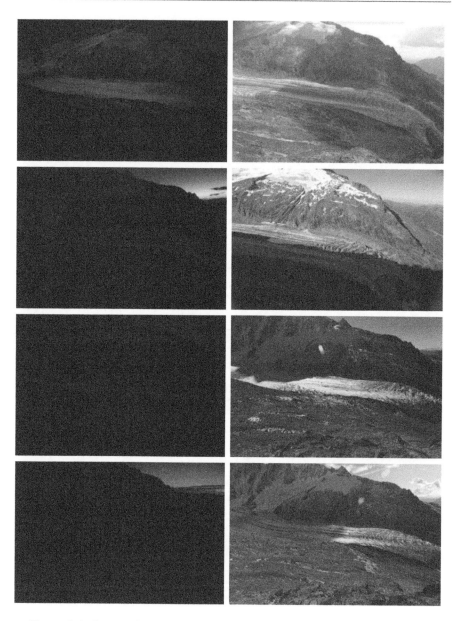

Figure 6.4. *State#3-Interference[Shadow] examples of the Argentière glacier. For a color version of this figure, see www.iste.co.uk/atto/change2.zip*

Figure 6.5. *State#4-Interference[Snow] examples of the Argentière glacier. For a color version of this figure, see www.iste.co.uk/atto/change2.zip*

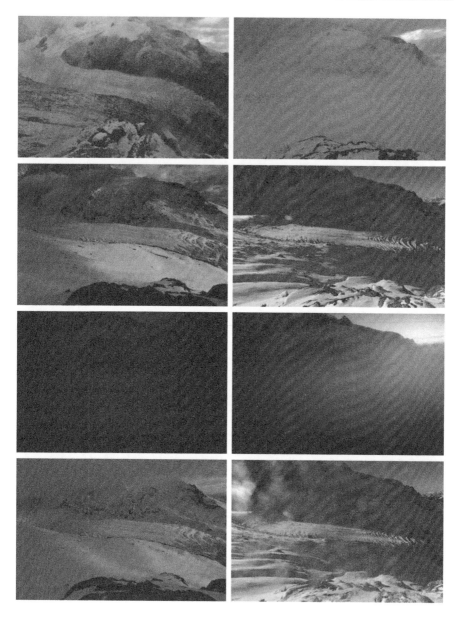

Figure 6.6. *Examples of multiple interferences corresponding to: State#5-Interference [Condensation-&-Snow] (row 1), State#6-Interference[Snow-&-Shadow] (row 2), State#7-Interference[Condensation-&-Shadow] (row 3) and State#8-Interference [Condensation-&-Snow-&-Shadow] (row 4) over the observed Argentière glacier surface. For a color version of this figure, see www.iste.co.uk/atto/change2.zip*

Experiment#1: Monolabel-Binary		
Change classes	Vivid	Interference
Number of samples	405	1898

Table 6.1. *Experiment#1: monolabel-binary change assumption from a vivid to an interfered observation state (presence of a disturbance)*

Experiment#2 addresses identifying the different types of elementary interferences affecting the glacier state. In addition to the vivid class, the elementary classes of interest are associated with observability interference caused by condensation, shadow effects and snow deposits: these phenomena can hide the rare geometric features detectable on the glacier and its rocky surrounding areas, the latter being useful in third-party applications for fixed-point matching in multiview and 3D reconstruction. The classes for Experiment#2 include, in addition to the State#1-Vivid, possible state switches with respect to the following "disturbed" classes:

– State#2-Interference[Condensation];

– State#3-Interference[Shadow]; and

– State#4-Interference[Snow].

The interfering condensation disturbances are generally due to mist, fog, water droplets on the camera lens or camera acquisitions in cloudy conditions (see Figure 6.3 for instance). Condensation can make fully or partly invisible the surfaces of interest. The interfering shadowing effects can be due to the sun's position (partially up/down) or possible nocturnal acquisitions (see Figure 6.4). The interfering snow-type disturbances are deposits of fresh snow or the presence of melted snow on the surfaces of interest (see Figure 6.5). Fresh and melted snow can blur the glacier surface texture, making inconsistent, glacier velocity/acceleration measures (absence of reliable reference points on the glacier surface) in third-party applications.

Experiment#2 is also a monolabel classification issue, but it is multiclass (more than two output classes), in contrast with the binary Experiment#1. The dataset corresponding to Experiment#2 is described in Table 6.2.

Experiment#2: MonoLabel-MultiClass				
Change classes	Vivid	Interference (three classes)		
		Condensation	Shadow	Snow
Number of samples	405	460	335	448

Table 6.2. *Experiment#2: monolabel-multiclass change assumption from a vivid state to one among three possible interfered states*

Experiment#3 explores a multiclass and multilabel change classification issue, where the multilabeling consists of taking interactions of the elementary interferences encountered in Experiment#2 into account. In addition to states #1-to-#4 used in Experiment#2, we have to integrate the following classes:

– State#5-Interference[Condensation-&-Snow];

– State#6-Interference[Snow-&-Shadow];

– State#7-Interference[Condensation-&-Shadow]; and

– State#8-Interference[Condensation-&-Snow-&-Shadow].

Examples of joint interfering disturbances associated with condensation-&-snow, snow-&-shadow, condensation-&-shadow and condensation-&-snow-&-shadow are given in Figure 6.6. The dataset corresponding to Experiment#3 is described in Table 6.3.

Experiment#3: Multilabel-MultiClass			
Classes	Vivid	Interference (seven subclasses)		
Samples	405	Condensation 460	Shadow 335	Snow 448
Classes Samples		Condensation-&-Snow 265	Snow-&-Shadow 307	Condensation-&-Shadow 46
Class Samples		Condensation-&-Snow-&-Shadow 37		

Table 6.3. *Experiment#3: multilabel-multiclass change of state analysis associated with a vivid state and seven possible interference states*

6.3. Deep transfer learning models for change of state classification

6.3.1. *Deep learning model library*

The library of CNNs that will be used as a case study to learn about classifiers of state changes are a variety of pre-trained networks that have shown high performance on the Imagenet (Russakovsky *et al.* 2015) classification challenges. These CNNs are: AlexNet (Yoon *et al.* 2015; Krizhevsky *et al.* 2012), DarkNet53 (Redmon and Farhadi 2018), DenseNet201 (Huang *et al.* 2017), EfficientNetB0 (Tan and Le 2020), GoogleNet (Szegedy *et al.* 2015), Inception-ResNet-V2 (Szegedy *et al.* 2016), MobileNetV2 (Sandler *et al.* 2018), NasNetLarge and NasNetMobile (Zoph *et al.* 2018), ResNet101 (He *et al.* 2016), SqueezeNet (Iandola *et al.* 2016), VGG19 (Simonyan and Zisserman 2014) and Xception (Chollet 2017). A description of these CNNs is summarized in Table 6.4, with respect to some main characteristics developed below in sections 6.3.2 (graph structures) and 6.3.3 (learnable parameters).

Name	Spatial input size	#micro-layers	#macro-layers	#meta-layers	meta-layer intricacy	#total-learnables (millions)	busy-micro-layer name	busy-micro-layer position	#learnables at busy-layer (millions)
NasNetLarge	[331, 331]	1243	-	1	7	88.9	fc^1	1241	4.0
NasNetMobile	[224, 224]	913	-	1	7	5.3	fc^2	911	1.1
InceptionResNetV2	[299, 299]	824	164	43	4	55.9	conv_7b	818	3.2
DenseNet201	[224, 224]	708	201	98	2	20.1	fc1000	706	1.9
ResNet101	[224, 224]	347	101	33	2	44.7	$conv^1$	315	2.4
EfficientNetB0	[224, 224]	290	82	31	2	5.3	fc^3	288	1.3
DarkNet53	[256, 256]	184	53	23	2	41.6	conv44	150	4.7
Xception	[299, 299]	170	71	12	2	22.9	$conv^2$	164	3.1
MobileNetV2	[224, 224]	154	53	10	2	3.5	fc^5	152	1.3
GoogleNet	[224, 224]	144	22	9	4	7	fc^4	142	1.0
SqueezeNet	[227, 227]	68	18	8	2	1.2	conv10	64	0.5
VGG19	[224, 224]	47	19	0	-	143.7	fc6	39	102.8
AlexNet	[227, 227]	25	8	0	-	61	fc6	17	37.8

Table 6.4. Library of CNNs considered about transfer learning. Specific labels: $fc^{1,2}$: "predictions"; fc^3: "efficientnet-b0|model|head|dense|MatMul"; fc^4: "loss3-classifier"; fc^5: "Logits"; $conv^1$: "res5a_branch2b"; $conv^2$: "block14_sepconv2_point-wise". NasNetLarge and NasNetMobile have intricate node splits and recombination strategies so that the concept of a macro-layer can lead to multiple definitions

6.3.2. *Graph structures for the CNN library*

We recall that a graph $\mathcal{G}$ is given by:

– an at most countable set of elements called nodes or vertices (objects having each, a finite set ports, for interconnection); and

– a set of elements called edges (links or lines for interconnection).

Any graph of the CNNs pertaining to the library described above is directed (edges are oriented) and acyclic (no loop from a node to this node by passing through other nodes). Some structures from these CNNs are simple (only one sequence of nodes composing $\mathcal{G}$), whereas other structures are very intricate (several node subdivisions yielding different sequences of nodes operating in parallel and called branches).

Macro-layer. A node of $\mathcal{G}$ is called a *layer* in *deep learning* graphs. This terminology, used for the sake of shortening deep graph description, is somewhat confusing because the layer under consideration performs several operations: we will call such a node a *macro-layer* from now on.

Micro-layers: a look inside the macro-layer. A *micro-layer* is defined as a homogeneous sequence of operators with the same nature and included in a macro-layer. A series of convolution filters pertaining to a macro-layer is an example of a micro-layer. The activation functions of this macro-layer define another micro-layer. Note that a macro-layer is assumed to encapsulate a micro-layer *of different nature*: in general, a series of linear operators followed by one or several nonlinear functions operating on the outputs of the linear operators. In recent CNNs, a macro-layer can contain up to seven different micro-layers (including convolution, pooling, batch normalization, regularization and activation function).

Meta-layer/meta-node: encapsulating groups of concurrent and strongly connected macro-layers. We define a *meta-layer* as a subgraph that satisfies the following constraints: (i) the subgraph is neither empty nor reduced to a single sequence of nodes; and (ii) the subgraph begins with the subdivision of a given node (root of subgraph) and ends with a single terminal node performing the fusion of the different branches, yielded by the subdivision of the above root node. The AlexNet graph, for instance, is composed of a single sequence of macro-layers (nodes): it admits no meta-layer. In contrast, the Xception graph is composed of 12 meta-layers, in addition to some standard sequence of macro-layers. An illustration of the differences between micro-, macro- and meta-layers is given for the Xception graph in Table 6.5.

The *meta-layer intricacy* for $\mathcal{G}$ is defined as the number of splits associated with the meta-layer node of $\mathcal{G}$ having a maximal subdivision. After viewing Table 6.4, we note that NasNetLarge and NasNetMobile are really huge: they are each composed of a single meta-layer with intricacy level 7 and encapsulating thousands of micro-layers (several local fusions, but no intermediate global fusion). Such network graphs are unusual, and we are curious to observe the true generalization performance of these networks on change of state analysis...

Meta-layer	Macro-layer	Micro-layer	Operators	
			Input layer	
-	-	0	0	
	1	1	Convolution-1	
		2	Normalization-1	
		3	Activation-1	
	2	4	Convolution-2	
		5	Normalization-2	
		6	Activation-2	
1	4 and 3	8 and 7	Convolution-4-xy	Convolution-3
		10 and 9	Convolution-4-z	Normalization-3
		11	Normalization-4-xyz	
		12	Activation-4-xyz	
		13	Convolution-5-xy	
		14	Convolution-5-z	
	5	15	Normalization-5-xyz	
		16	Pooling	
			Fusion (addition)	
...	...	...	...	

Table 6.5. *Example of micro-layer, macro-layer and meta-layer numbering associated with the Xception graph. Notations xy, z and xyz are, respectively, associated with spatial, channel and joint spatio-channel variables*

6.3.3. *Dimensionalities of the learnables for the CNN library*

We will consider hereafter two additional complexity criteria to describe the test CNNs. The first criterion is the standard total number of *learnable*[2] parameters (see Table 6.4). The second criterion relates to the complexity of the feature space associated with CNN decomposition. It is worth noting that the test CNNs share a common characteristic when decomposing an image: an expansion associated with more and more neuro-convolutional operators (in series and/or in parallel), before gradually descending to the classification layer whose number of outputs corresponds to the number of classes.

We define the *busy-micro-layer* as the micro-layer having the largest number of learnable parameters. This layer is a good representative of the dimensionality of a CNN representation space. The total number of learnable parameters for the busy-micro-layers of the different test CNNs are reported in Table 6.4. We can note from Table 6.4, that for all the test CNNs, the busy-micro-layer is either a convolution[3] layer or a fully[4] (densely) connected layer located very deep in the CNN graph. For example, InceptionResNetV2 alternates neuro-convolutional decompositions in series and concurrent nodes, until reaching a convolutional busy-micro-layer having more than 3 million learnable parameters. This is not very surprising because earlier image decomposition spaces such as wavelets are constructed in terms of pyramidal graphs and the larger the decomposition level, the larger the refinements of the feature space.

---

2. A learnable parameter is a standard *variable* of the CNN loss function: starting from a random number, this variable is updated during training by using a gradient descent algorithm with respect to the cost function.

3. The main parameters of a convolutional layer in deep learning networks are:

  – number of convolution filters;

  – spatial size (common) of a convolution filter for the layer under consideration;

  – number of convolution channels;

  – stride (translation factor of the convolution filter over the input during the convolution operation);

  – bias (determined by the number of convolution operators);

  – expansion factor (dilatation operation of the convolution filter);

  – zero-padding (extension of image support before convolution by adding rows and columns composed of zeros).

4. The main parameters of a fully-connected layer in deep learning networks are:

  – number of weights associated with the matrix multiplication representing this layer;

  – number of bias terms (number of rows of this matrix, determined by the desired number of outputs).

We will see later how such a design can impact the generalization performance with respect to change of state issues.

The question now asked is: which of the combinations of characteristics summarized in Table 6.4 will be the most robust in terms of transfer to a classification problem of state changes *on the basis of observations from the same dynamic geophysical phenomenon*? The answer is the subject of the next section. Before developing this answer, we provide additional learnable information for the *last fully-connected layer* (LFCL, placed just upstream of the categorical probability layer) for the CNN library under consideration: Table 6.6 provides the total learnables in the LFCLs for these CNNs.

CNN	NasNetLarge	NasNetMobile	InceptionResNetV2	DenseNet201
#learnables	4,033,000	1,057,000	1,537,000	1,921,000
Names	ResNet101	EfficientNetB0	DarkNet53	Xception
#learnables	2,049,000	1,281,000	1,025,000	2,049,000
CNN	MobileNetV2	GoogleNet	SqueezeNet	VGG19
#learnables	1,281,000	1,025,000	513,000	4,097,000
CNN	AlexNet			
#learnables	4,097,000			

Table 6.6. *Total learnable parameters of the LFCL per test CNN in the Imagenet learning framework*

A comparison between the learnables of the busy-micro-layers (Table 6.4) and the LFCL (Table 6.6) shows that the re-trainable fully connected layers that will be used later in transfer learning are such that:

– InceptionResNetV2's LFCL has half as many learnables as its busy-micro-layer;

– ResNet101's LFCL has slightly less learnables than its busy-micro-layer;

– DarkNet53's LFCL has 4 times less learnables than its busy-micro-layer;

– Xception's LFCL has 1/3 less learnables than its busy-micro-layer;

– VGG19's LFCL has 25 times less learnables than its busy-micro-layer; and

– AlexNet's LFCL has 9 times less learnables than its busy-micro-layer.

Other CNNs that are present in Table 6.4 but whose LFCL are not listed in the items given just above are such that their LFCLs correspond exactly to their busy-micro-layers.

6.4. Change of state analysis

In this section, we study state changes by using the dataset described in section 6.2 and the CNN library described in section 6.3.2.

6.4.1. *Transfer learning adaptations for the change of state classification issues*

Consider, for the sake of illustration, the Xception network. It is worth emphasizing that without modifying the terminal nodes of the graph of this network, we cannot efficiently train the Xception network with respect to the three changes of state experiments considered in the chapter: the change of state datasets have numbers of output classes that are different from the number 1000 of output classes given in Imagenet. Thus, it is necessary to modify the terminal nodes (output layers) in order to comply with the size of the new classification issues. In practice, for building output activations that will correspond to the number of classes 2, 4 and 8, respectively, for Experiments #1, #2 and #3 of section 6.2, it suffices to clone Xception three times and replace the (original) LFCL of the clones by new LFCLs yielding, respectively, three output vectors with respective sizes 2, 4 and 8.

The same remark holds true for any of the other test CNNs. Denote Q_o the number of LFCL learnable parameters for a given original test network. The formula for deriving the total number Q of the new clone network LFCL learnable parameters is:

$$Q = \frac{\mathcal{N}(Q_o - \mathcal{N}_o)}{\mathcal{N}_o} + \mathcal{N} = \frac{\mathcal{N}Q_o}{\mathcal{N}_o} \qquad [6.1]$$

where $\mathcal{N}$ and $\mathcal{N}_o$ are, respectively, the numbers of output classes for the new and original experiments, with $\mathcal{N}_o = 1000$ and $\mathcal{N} \in \{2, 4, 8\}$ for Experiments #1, #2 and #3. Table 6.7 provides the total learnables for the new LFCLs of the test networks by using this formula.

CNN	NasNetLarge	NasNetMobile	InceptionResNetV2	DenseNet201
#learnables / $\mathcal{N}$	4033	1057	1537	1921
CNN	ResNet101	EfficientNetB0	DarkNet53	Xception
#learnables / $\mathcal{N}$	2049	1281	1025	2049
CNN	MobileNetV2	GoogleNet	SqueezeNet	VGG19
#learnables / $\mathcal{N}$	1281	1025	513	4097
CNN	AlexNet			
#learnables / $\mathcal{N}$	4097			

Table 6.7. *Total learnable parameters of the LFCL per CNN test in the transfer learning framework associated with change of state classification, where $\mathcal{N} = 2, 4, 8$, respectively, for change of state Experiments #1, #2 and #3*

Consider the new Xception network obtained by replacing the original Xception LFCL with a new LFCL having $2049 \times \mathcal{N}$ learnable parameters (see Table 6.7). Assume that we want to retrain this new network on a given change of state issue by re-initializing all the learned parameters loaded from the original Xception network. The terminology used in this case is known as *training from scratch* and this, whatever the network. This training turns out to be extremely time-consuming, not only because of the delicacy of gradually descending towards an optimum associated with millions of variables, but also because the dataset of state changes is disproportionate (some classes contain much less data than others and above all, not enough data to hope to obtain satisfactory solutions when starting from "nothing but noise" and wanting to learn a huge number of parameters).

We will thus consider that a significant part of the parameters issued from the original network should be forced to be *non-learnable*, a strategy called *transfer learning*. More specifically, we will consider all the loaded parameters from the original network to be non-learnable, except the new LFCL attached to this network. In this respect, change of state learning will concern only the weights and bias of the modified LFCLs for any test CNN.

6.4.2. *Experimental results*

The experimental tests performed involve testing the sensitivity of the learners with respect to *training hyperparameters* that are the learn rates for weights and biases for the LFCLs associated with the test networks. We will not only provide a maximum of accuracy, but also a tensor of statistics related to the performance distribution for fixed mini-batch size and number of training epochs. Denote X the top 50% accuracies obtained by a CNN when learning rates are sampled in $)0, 1($ respectively, for weight and bias learnables. The *performance tensor* proposed for comparing test CNNs is (for a color version of this equation, see www.iste.co.uk/atto/change2.zip):

$$\mathfrak{P}(X) = \left[\text{Min}(X), \begin{pmatrix} \text{Mean}(X) \\ \text{Median}(X) \end{pmatrix}, \text{Max}(X) \right] \qquad [6.2]$$

The three features of this tensor: $\text{Min}(X)$, $\begin{pmatrix} \text{Mean}(X) \\ \text{Median}(X) \end{pmatrix}$ and $\text{Max}(X)$, are ordered in the norm sense. Regarding the central feature: $\begin{pmatrix} \text{Mean}(X) \\ \text{Median}(X) \end{pmatrix}$, $\text{Mean}(X) \gg \text{Median}(X)$ means a heavy tailed accuracy distribution: very few learning hyperparameters have led to some very large accuracy values in X, whereas a large amount of accuracies pertaining to X are rather small. Such episodic large accuracies can be assimilated to a lack of robustness for the corresponding learner when $\text{Min}(X)$ is not sufficiently large.

The datasets proposed in Experiments #1, #2 and #3 (see section 6.2) are divided into three sets for *training* (data labels are seen by the network at every iteration), *validation* (data and labels are partially seen by the network every now and then) and *testing* (data and labels are never seen by the system during its successive training iterations and epochs). We will provide performance only for the validation and test datasets. Tables 6.8, 6.9 and 6.10 provide $\mathfrak{P}(X)$ for the library of CNNs described in section 6.3, when considering change of state Experiments #1, #2 and #3. This table also provides the mean $M_{\mathfrak{P}(X)}$ of the performance tensor $\mathfrak{P}(X)$ as an additional information measure. This mean is defined by:

$$M_{\mathfrak{P}(X)} = \frac{1}{4} \left(\text{Min}(X) + \text{Mean}(X) + \text{Median}(X) + \text{Max}(X) \right) \qquad [6.3]$$

In cases where X shows a uniform performance distribution for instance, $M_{\mathfrak{P}(X)} = \text{Mean}(X) = \text{Median}(X) = (\text{Min}(X) + \text{Max}(X))/2$. We bring out three main behaviors depending on $\mathfrak{P}$:

– **robust deep learner**: $\text{Min}(X)$ is expected to be sufficiently large: the network is stable and performant for different hyperparameter settings;

– **laborious deep learner**: $\text{Max}(X)$ is large, but $\text{Min}(X)$ is small and $\text{Mean}(X) \gg \text{Median}(X)$;

– **ineffective deep learner**: $\text{Max}(X) \ll 80\%$. Despite the good accuracy of the network on the original challenge (ImageNet), its weights located downstream of the LFCL do not straightforwardly allow discriminating change of states. It is worth noting here that the changes of states considered in the chapter imply seeing the same object in different classes and this can be confusing for a machine that has originally learned to discriminate only different objects (case of ImageNet challenge).

From Tables 6.8, 6.9 and 6.10, we derive the following ranking:

[Top networks]: **NasNetMobile** and **Xception** (see the red values given in the tables) are the best relevant networks for change of state classification in the tested library. They comply with the robustness criterion highlighted above with respect to the different experiments.

[Second networks]: **EfficientNetB0**, **InceptionResNetV2**, NasNetLarge (see the blue values given in the tables).

[Relatively efficient networks]: MobileNetV2, DenseNet201, ResNet101, GoogleNet and DarkNet53 show performance up to expectations for the binary classification issue.

[Less effective networks]: AlexNet, SqueezeNet and VGG19 are misled[5] by change of state events.

---

5. A weighted cross entropy, used to take class imbalance into account, can probably solve the issue encountered by AlexNet, SqueezeNet and VGG19 which affect almost all the data into a single class in several experiments. But this is out of scope for the global comparison performed by in the chapter.

	Validation		Test	
Measure \ CNN	$\mathfrak{P}$	$M_{\mathfrak{P}}$	$\mathfrak{P}$	$M_{\mathfrak{P}}$
NasNetLarge	$\left[89.13, \begin{pmatrix} 91.58 \\ 91.21 \end{pmatrix}, 95.65\right]$	**91.89**	$\left[90.67, \begin{pmatrix} 92.23 \\ 91.87 \end{pmatrix}, 95.01\right]$	**92.44**
NasNetMobile	$\left[91.30, \begin{pmatrix} 94.35 \\ 94.57 \end{pmatrix}, 98.37\right]$	**94.65**	$\left[93.06, \begin{pmatrix} 94.09 \\ 94.14 \end{pmatrix}, 96.53\right]$	**94.45**
InceptionResNetV2	$\left[89.67, \begin{pmatrix} 92.39 \\ 92.30 \end{pmatrix}, 96.20\right]$	**92.64**	$\left[92.19, \begin{pmatrix} 93.44 \\ 93.28 \end{pmatrix}, 95.23\right]$	**93.53**
DenseNet201	$\left[82.43, \begin{pmatrix} 87.44 \\ 87.86 \end{pmatrix}, 94.38\right]$	**88.03**	$\left[82.86, \begin{pmatrix} 88.30 \\ 88.29 \end{pmatrix}, 96.96\right]$	**89.10**
ResNet101	$\left[90.04, \begin{pmatrix} 91.82 \\ 91.21 \end{pmatrix}, 95.65\right]$	**92.18**	$\left[91.76, \begin{pmatrix} 93.38 \\ 93.28 \end{pmatrix}, 96.10\right]$	**93.63**
EfficientNetB0	$\left[91.49, \begin{pmatrix} 93.73 \\ 93.84 \end{pmatrix}, 96.56\right]$	**93.90**	$\left[92.84, \begin{pmatrix} 94.07 \\ 93.93 \end{pmatrix}, 95.23\right]$	**94.02**
DarkNet53	$\left[82.43, \begin{pmatrix} 82.43 \\ 82.43 \end{pmatrix}, 82.43\right]$	**82.43**	$\left[82.43, \begin{pmatrix} 82.63 \\ 82.43 \end{pmatrix}, 84.60\right]$	**83.02**
Xception	$\left[90.04, \begin{pmatrix} 92.20 \\ 91.58 \end{pmatrix}, 95.83\right]$	**92.41**	$\left[93.49, \begin{pmatrix} 94.18 \\ 94.14 \end{pmatrix}, 95.23\right]$	**94.26**
MobileNetV2	$\left[89.31, \begin{pmatrix} 92.68 \\ 92.21 \end{pmatrix}, 97.46\right]$	**92.92**	$\left[91.97, \begin{pmatrix} 93.15 \\ 93.06 \end{pmatrix}, 94.36\right]$	**93.14**
GoogleNet	$\left[82.43, \begin{pmatrix} 89.16 \\ 88.41 \end{pmatrix}, 97.46\right]$	**89.36**	$\left[82.43, \begin{pmatrix} 88.74 \\ 90.02 \end{pmatrix}, 93.49\right]$	**88.67**
SqueezeNet	$\left[17.57, \begin{pmatrix} 22.98 \\ 17.57 \end{pmatrix}, 82.43\right]$	**35.14**	$\left[17.57, \begin{pmatrix} 22.98 \\ 17.57 \end{pmatrix}, 82.43\right]$	**35.14**
VGG19	$\left[17.57, \begin{pmatrix} 22.98 \\ 17.57 \end{pmatrix}, 82.43\right]$	**35.14**	$\left[17.57, \begin{pmatrix} 22.98 \\ 17.57 \end{pmatrix}, 82.43\right]$	**35.14**
AlexNet	$\left[17.57, \begin{pmatrix} 39.19 \\ 17.57 \end{pmatrix}, 82.43\right]$	**39.19**	$\left[17.57, \begin{pmatrix} 27.48 \\ 17.57 \end{pmatrix}, 82.43\right]$	**37.48**

Table 6.8. *Performance tensor* $\mathfrak{P}$ *and its mean* $M_{\mathfrak{P}}$ *for binary change of state Experiment#1 associated with the dataset presented in Table 6.1. For a color version of this table, see www.iste.co.uk/atto/change2.zip*

Note, from Table 6.4, that NasNetLarge is too huge, encompasses a huge memory load and a very long training time, without being more performant than NasNetMobile and Xception. Thus, for increasing performance in a fusion-of-decision-based strategy, we will recommend using the networks NasNetMobile, Xception, EfficientNetB0 and InceptionResNetV2.

Now, if we must point out a single top network, then Xception is the better solution: Xception has (i) a slightly higher average tensor performance than NasNetMobile (see

Tables 6.8, 6.9 and 6.10); (ii) a simpler graph breadthwise (meta-layer intricacy is 2 for Xception and 7 for NasNetMobile); (iii) a simpler graph lengthways (5 times less micro-layers); and (iv) more LFCL learnables than NasNetMobile (see Table 6.4). The latter property is especially outstanding for transfer learning. Thus, Xception can be recommended from a pedagogical point of view for teaching, for example. Indeed, the intricate nature of NasNetMobile or NasNetLarge is not mandatory to obtain high performance and generalization capabilities.

Measure CNN	Validation $\mathfrak{P}$	$M_{\mathfrak{P}}$	Test $\mathfrak{P}$	$M_{\mathfrak{P}}$
NasNetLarge	$\left[80.96, \binom{85.74}{84.01}, 92.64\right]$	**85.84**	$\left[82.73, \binom{87.55}{85.91}, 96.67\right]$	**88.21**
NasNetMobile	$\left[81.98, \binom{87.90}{86.68}, 96.45\right]$	**88.25**	$\left[84.24, \binom{90.33}{90.30}, 94.24\right]$	**89.78**
InceptionResNetV2	$\left[75.13, \binom{83.78}{83.38}, 92.39\right]$	**83.67**	$\left[79.39, \binom{86.89}{88.94}, 92.42\right]$	**86.91**
DenseNet201	$\left[53.05, \binom{64.28}{61.80}, 86.04\right]$	**66.29**	$\left[51.82, \binom{65.68}{60.30}, 85.76\right]$	**65.89**
ResNet101	$\left[37.31, \binom{53.70}{42.89}, 94.16\right]$	**57.02**	$\left[35.15, \binom{52.40}{41.21}, 93.33\right]$	**55.52**
EfficientNetB0	$\left[86.29, \binom{88.81}{88.71}, 91.12\right]$	**88.73**	$\left[90.00, \binom{91.62}{91.82}, 93.94\right]$	**91.84**
DarkNet53	$\left[34.01, \binom{40.31}{39.21}, 52.54\right]$	**41.52**	$\left[34.85, \binom{38.61}{36.52}, 53.03\right]$	**40.75**
Xception	$\left[81.22, \binom{88.32}{89.09}, 93.91\right]$	**88.13**	$\left[88.18, \binom{92.35}{93.03}, 94.24\right]$	**91.95**
MobileNetV2	$\left[60.15, \binom{79.04}{82.23}, 89.34\right]$	**77.69**	$\left[63.03, \binom{78.74}{78.79}, 94.24\right]$	**78.70**
GoogleNet	$\left[27.16, \binom{58.59}{60.66}, 94.42\right]$	**60.21**	$\left[22.73, \binom{57.20}{58.64}, 91.21\right]$	**57.44**
SqueezeNet	$\left[24.62, \binom{24.62}{24.62}, 24.62\right]$	**24.62**	$\left[24.55, \binom{24.55}{24.55}, 24.55\right]$	**24.55**
VGG19	$\left[24.62, \binom{25.47}{24.62}, 27.16\right]$	**25.47**	$\left[20.30, \binom{24.04}{24.55}, 27.27\right]$	**24.04**
AlexNet	$\left[27.16, \binom{27.54}{27.54}, 27.92\right]$	**27.54**	$\left[27.27, \binom{27.58}{27.58}, 27.88\right]$	**27.58**

Table 6.9. *Performance tensor $\mathfrak{P}$ and its mean $M_{\mathfrak{P}}$ for multiclass-monolabel change of state Experiment#2 associated with the dataset presented in Table 6.2. For a color version of this table, see www.iste.co.uk/atto/change2.zip*

Measure\ CNN	Validation		Test	
	$\mathfrak{P}$	$M_{\mathfrak{P}}$	$\mathfrak{P}$	$M_{\mathfrak{P}}$
NasNetLarge	$\left[51.09, \binom{58.64}{58.79}, 67.75\right]$	**59.07**	$\left[56.96, \binom{64.55}{64.24}, 73.70\right]$	**64.86**
NasNetMobile	$\left[61.05, \binom{68.25}{68.30}, 76.27\right]$	**68.47**	$\left[60.87, \binom{70.38}{70.11}, 78.48\right]$	**69.96**
InceptionResNetV2	$\left[50.54, \binom{65.32}{66.85}, 80.07\right]$	**65.70**	$\left[53.91, \binom{68.57}{68.59}, 78.91\right]$	**67.50**
DenseNet201	$\left[29.53, \binom{36.31}{35.42}, 52.17\right]$	**38.36**	$\left[30.43, \binom{37.43}{33.04}, 56.96\right]$	**39.47**
ResNet101	$\left[25.91, \binom{34.18}{28.80}, 49.46\right]$	**34.59**	$\left[25.00, \binom{34.28}{28.80}, 51.09\right]$	**34.79**
EfficientNetB0	$\left[62.50, \binom{68.15}{68.48}, 75.54\right]$	**68.67**	$\left[70.00, \binom{73.39}{72.83}, 77.17\right]$	**73.35**
DarkNet53	$\left[23.37, \binom{28.61}{26.81}, 37.68\right]$	**29.12**	$\left[24.35, \binom{28.77}{25.76}, 42.39\right]$	**30.32**
Xception	$\left[60.14, \binom{67.62}{68.57}, 73.01\right]$	**67.33**	$\left[67.61, \binom{76.36}{77.07}, 80.87\right]$	**75.48**
MobileNetV2	$\left[26.81, \binom{49.46}{48.28}, 78.44\right]$	**50.75**	$\left[26.74, \binom{49.60}{52.07}, 73.91\right]$	**50.58**
GoogleNet	$\left[26.27, \binom{53.50}{60.69}, 68.84\right]$	**52.32**	$\left[25.22, \binom{53.70}{60.00}, 68.48\right]$	**51.85**
SqueezeNet	$\left[17.57, \binom{18.49}{17.57}, 28.62\right]$	**20.57**	$\left[17.61, \binom{18.26}{17.61}, 25.43\right]$	**19.73**
VGG19	$\left[17.57, \binom{18.88}{19.38}, 19.93\right]$	**18.94**	$\left[11.52, \binom{16.87}{19.57}, 20.00\right]$	**16.99**
AlexNet	$\left[19.93, \binom{19.93}{19.93}, 19.93\right]$	**19.93**	$\left[20.00, \binom{20.00}{20.00}, 20.00\right]$	**20.00**

Table 6.10. *Performance tensor $\mathfrak{P}$ and its mean $M_{\mathfrak{P}}$ for multiclass-multilabel change of state Experiment#3 associated with the dataset presented in Table 6.3. For a color version of this table, see www.iste.co.uk/atto/change2.zip*

6.5. Conclusion

We conclude this chapter by emphasizing that the ranking derived in the above experimental section must be understood with respect to (i) a straightforward training and (ii) robustness with respect to different experiments (binary and multiclass, monolabel and multilabel, coarse-grained to fine-grained state of change analysis). It is worth highlighting that: *it is probably easy[6] to "martingale" deep learning*

---

6. When assuming the availability of powerful computing resources.

hyperparameters to obtain a performant configuration[7] for any CNN from the library considered. However, such a procedure is counterintuitive and questionable in terms of artificial intelligence. Therefore, we have based the above comparison, not only with respect to a maximum of accuracy, but by using a performance tensor operating on several hyperparameters.

6.6. Acknowledgments

The authors would like to acknowledge the support from the Centre National d'Etudes Spatiales (CNES) through the access to the computing and storage facilities of the PEPS platform and through the funding of the APR SHARE project.

6.7. References

Bojinski, S., Verstraete, M., Peterson, T.C., Richter, C., Simmons, A., Zemp, M. (2014). The concept of essential climate variables in support of climate research, applications, and policy. *Bulletin of the American Meteorological Society*, 95(9), 1431–1443.

Chollet, F. (2017). Xception: Deep learning with depthwise separable convolutions. *2017 IEEE Conference on Computer Vision and Pattern Recognition (CVPR)*, 1800–1807.

Hadhri, H., Vernier, F., Atto, A.M., Trouvé, E. (2019). Time-lapse optical flow regularization for geophysical complex phenomena monitoring. *ISPRS Journal of Photogrammetry and Remote Sensing*, 150, 135–156 [Online]. Available at: http://www.sciencedirect.com/science/article/pii/S0924271619300401.

He, K., Zhang, X., Ren, S., Sun, J. (2016). Deep residual learning for image recognition. *Proceedings of the IEEE Conference on Computer Vision and Pattern Recognition (CVPR)*.

Huang, G., Liu, Z., van der Maaten, L., Weinberger, K.Q. (2017). Densely connected convolutional networks. *Proceedings of the IEEE Conference on Computer Vision and Pattern Recognition (CVPR)*.

Iandola, F.N., Han, S., Moskewicz, M.W., Ashraf, K., Dally, W.J., Keutzer, K. (2016). Squeezenet: Alexnet-level accuracy with 50x fewer parameters and <0.5mb model size, Research report. arXiv: 1602.07360.

---

7. For AlexNet, SqueezeNet and VGG19, most of the hyperparameter settings have led to inefficient learning (see for instance the min and median performance values given in Tables 6.8, 6.9 and 6.10), however, a few hyperparameter configurations have led to somewhat satisfactory results in the binary case of Table 6.8.

Krizhevsky, A., Sutskever, I., Hinton, G.E. (2012). Imagenet classification with deep convolutional neural networks. In *Advances in Neural Information Processing Systems 25*, Pereira, F., Burges, C.J.C., Bottou, L., Weinberger, K.Q. (eds). Curran Associates, Inc., Red Hook, NY.

Redmon, J. and Farhadi, A. (2018). YOLOv3: An incremental improvement. Research report. arXiv: 1804.02767.

Russakovsky, O., Deng, J., Su, H., Krause, J., Satheesh, S., Ma, S., Huang, Z., Karpathy, A., Khosla, A., Bernstein, M., *et al.* (2015). Imagenet large scale visual recognition challenge. *Int. J. Comput. Vision*, 115(3), 211–252.

Sandler, M., Howard, A., Zhu, M., Zhmoginov, A., Chen, L.-C. (2018). Mobilenetv2: Inverted residuals and linear bottlenecks. *Proceedings of the IEEE Conference on Computer Vision and Pattern Recognition (CVPR)*.

Simonyan, K. and Zisserman, A. (2014). Very deep convolutional networks for large-scale image recognition. *CoRR*, abs/1409.1556.

Szegedy, C., Sermanet, P., Reed, S., Anguelov, D., Erhan, D., Vanhoucke, V., Rabinovich, A. (2015). Going deeper with convolutions. *2015 IEEE Conference on Computer Vision and Pattern Recognition (CVPR)*, 1–9.

Szegedy, C., Ioffe, S., Vanhoucke, V., Alemi, A.A. (2016). Inception-v4, inception-resnet and the impact of residual connections on learning. *ICLR 2016 Workshop* [Online]. Available at: https://arxiv.org/abs/1602.07261.

Tan, M. and Le, Q.V. (2020). Efficientnet: Rethinking model scaling for convolutional neural networks. Research report, arXiv: 1905.11946.

Yoon, Y.-G., Dai, P., Wohlwend, J., Chang, J.-B., Marblestone, A.H., Boyden, E.S. (2015). Bvlc AlexNet model [Online]. Available at: https://github.com/BVLC/caffe/tree/master/models/bvlc_alexnet.

Zoph, B., Vasudevan, V., Shlens, J., Le, Q.V. (2018). Learning transferable architectures for scalable image recognition. *Proceedings of the IEEE Conference on Computer Vision and Pattern Recognition (CVPR)*.

List of Authors

Enes Oğuzhan ALATAŞ
Istanbul Technical University
Turkey

Abdourrahmane M. ATTO
University Savoie Mont Blanc
Annecy
France

Francesca BOVOLO
Fondazione Bruno Kessler
Trento
Italy

Lorenzo BRUZZONE
University of Trento
Italy

Mihai DATCU
German Aerospace Center
Oberpfaffenhofen
Germany

Corneliu Octavian DUMITRU
German Aerospace Center
Oberpfaffenhofen
Germany

Esra ERTEN
Istanbul Technical University
Turkey

Héla HADHRI
University Savoie Mont Blanc
Annecy
France

Ihsen HEDHLI
Institute Intelligence and Data
Université Laval
Quebec City
Canada

Dino IENCO
UMR TETIS Laboratory
INRAE
University of Montpellier
France

Jukka MIETTINEN
VTT Technical Research Centre
of Finland Ltd
Espoo
Finland

Matthieu MOLINIER
VTT Technical Research Centre
of Finland Ltd
Espoo
Finland

Gabriele MOSER
University of Genoa
Italy

Charlotte PELLETIER
IRISA Laboratory UMR 6074
Université Bretagne Sud
Lorient
France

Shi QIU
University of Connecticut
Mansfield
USA

Sebastiano B. SERPICO
University of Genoa
Italy

Gülşen TAŞKIN
Istanbul Technical University
Turkey

Emmanuel TROUVÉ
University Savoie Mont Blanc
Annecy
France

Silvia VALERO
CESBIO Laboratory UMR 5126
University of Toulouse
France

Flavien VERNIER
University Savoie Mont Blanc
Annecy
France

Josiane ZERUBIA
INRIA
Université Cote d'Azur
Nice
France

Zhe ZHU
University of Connecticut
Mansfield
USA

Index

Summary of Volume 1

Preface
Abdourrahmane M. ATTO, Francesca BOVOLO and Lorenzo BRUZZONE

List of Notations

Chapter 1. Unsupervised Change Detection in Multitemporal Remote Sensing Images
Sicong LIU, Francesca BOVOLO, Lorenzo BRUZZONE, Qian DU and Xiaohua TONG

Chapter 9. Statistical Difference Models for Change Detection in Multispectral Images

Massimo ZANETTI, Francesca BOVOLO and Lorenzo BRUZZONE

Printed and bound by CPI Group (UK) Ltd, Croydon, CR0 4YY